Entrancing Relationships

Entrancing Relationships

Exploring the Hypnotic Framework of Addictive Relationships

Don J. Feeney, Jr.

PRAEGER

Westport, Connecticut
London

Library of Congress Cataloging-in-Publication Data

Feeney, Don J., 1948–
    Entrancing relationships : exploring the hypnotic framework of
addictive relationships / Don J. Feeney, Jr.
        p.   cm.
    Includes bibliographical references and index.
    ISBN 0–275–96415–9 (alk. paper)
    1. Relationship addiction.   2. Hypnotism.   I. Title.
    RC552.R44F44   1999
    616.86—dc21   98–47747

British Library Cataloguing in Publication Data is available.

Library of Congress Catalog Card Number: 98–47747
ISBN: 0–275–96415–9

First published in 1999

Praeger Publishers, 88 Post Road West, Westport, CT 06881
An imprint of Greenwood Publishing Group, Inc.
www.praeger.com

Printed in the United States of America

The paper used in this book complies with the
Permanent Paper Standard issued by the National
Information Standards Organization (Z39.48–1984).

10 9 8 7 6 5 4 3 2 1

Dedicated to my daughter Kelly,
who persists as a beamer and beacon
of enlightenment.

CONTENTS

ACKNOWLEDGMENTS

Inspiration for this kind of work has emerged from both clinical practice and enriched family relationships. I am grateful to the many clients who, through personal challenge and recovery in their own lives, have contributed invaluable perspectives in completion of this work. Warmth and heartfelt gratitude is deeply conveyed to my family, especially my daughter Kelly, who initially assisted in the distillation of ideas and preparation for this work. I am extremely thankful for the enduring, literary assistance of my editor, Nita Romer, who has been steadfast at my side with professional critique and guidance throughout the project. I want to extend my profound respect and value for the magnanimous, creative achievements of Milton H. Erickson, M.D., the founder of modern day hypnosis upon whose tenets serve as a part of the foundation to this work. I also wish to thank the numerous Ericksonion trainers with whom I have studied for sharpening my understandings and expertise, supportive of my work. Finally, I want to express my sincere gratitude to Susan Dziedzic for her tenacity and persistence throughout the countless hours of arduous manuscript revisions and its final production.

INTRODUCTION

There are many forces in the universe: gravity, electromagnetic, and nuclear just to name a few. Yet, in the course of human (and maybe not so human) events, there is none stronger or more powerful than the passion one lover feels for another. When grown men and women of wealth and power enter into chaotic encounters and risk everything for the love of another, we need to ask poignantly, "What's really going on here?" "What's the driving force?"

Dysfunctional relationships are at the core of practically every mental health issue, life stress, and job impairment in this country. Sixty-five percent of all new marriages end in divorce and one-third of all babies are born out of wedlock (Martin and Bumpass, 1989). Bars are filling (as are churches) with new singles everyday. For the first time in modern history, single people outnumber married people (60 percent of the adult population is single). The paradox is that there are more marriages and divorces than ever before in modern times. Successfully married people are in the minority.

U.S. Senator William Proxmire once said that love should not be researched, as it was the one quality that should be held sacred from analysis. Yet myths and illusions of love create untold misery. We need to realize that loving involves more than hormones. It involves more than romantic illusions, fantasies, and erotic escapism from everyday reality.

Loving involves the healthy totality and alignment of spirit-mind-body, psychobiological synergy. The mind, the soul, the emotions, the senses, and body chemistry all are systems which need to be aligned and readied in launching that relationship into orbit. When we enter into a relationship, we do not even begin to understand the forces with which we are playing. The enormous amount of suffering needlessly encountered by naïve (and not so naïve) partners entering into potentially dangerous liaisons is almost pitiful.

Loving relationships exert and elicit tremendously powerful and many times unknown forces deep within and between partners. These forces are felt and sensed but rarely accessed in a conscious and enlightened frame. The energizing field forces (erotic pull of entrancement) of loving invoke a matching and resonance of rapport between partners' minds, emotions, senses, and chemistry. These field forces of rapport have a name: entrancement.

Entrancement is an alignment of matching energies and expectations at one of the deepest levels of human experience, which constitute attraction, resonance, and union between thematically (thinking and believing) similar and congruent partners at many levels of their life experiences (images, feelings, characters, fantasies, chemistry, etc.). Entrancement involves suspension of critical faculties (meaning we lose our mind and surrender ourselves to some strange, new girl or guy, then lose sleep because we cannot stop thinking about them). It also involves selective attention (she or he is the only one for me in the entire world of billions of people). These and many other facets suggest that the power of entrancement is hypnotic in origin. Romantic addictive relationships can be comprehended in such a hypnotic framework.

Thus, the essential premise of this book is that romantic, addictive enmeshment is the result of what is experienced as irresistible pulls from hypnotic entrancement. Entrancement involves a coming together or fusion of idealized images superimposed upon physical attributes of one partner by another. Each partner brings to the relationship ideals or images of his or her perfect mate. Partners merge their ideal images of love and beauty with the size, shape, and contour of their mates.

Such fusion unleashes incredible forces far beyond each partner's conscious comprehension. The scope of this book is to inspire and guide the reader's heart, mind, and soul on a journey into and through the inner and outer storms. Through this turbulent journey, the hidden self is revealed as an anchor of sensory motifs.

CHAPTER 1

HYPNOSIS: QUALITIES AND DYNAMICS OF TRANCE

Hypnosis presents a wonderful metaphor and framework for understanding the addictive quality in romantic relationships. In hypnosis
there is a powerful fixation, absorption, and induction of a trancelike
phenomenon. It requires people to become suspended of conscious,
critical faculties as they become more and more absorbed into their personal experiences. It has a very powerful, sensory concentrated nature.
The qualities of the hypnotic experience parallel addictive relationships.
However, to fully understand this parallel, it is essential to fully grasp
the essence of the hypnotic experience.

HYPNOTIC QUALITIES

In understanding the rationale and position of using hypnosis as a
framework or structure for understanding addiction, it is important to
realize that addictive relationships have the qualities and elements of a
regressive sense of loss of control, which diffuses the sense of self.
What this means is that partners feel hopeless and helpless as they in-
tertwine in an intense, angry, isolated, and unrewarding pursuit of their
hypnotic, childlike fantasies. Each person experiences mutual disap-
pointment, frustration, and aggravation with his or her partner.

Hypnosis has a unique parallel to that type of paradigm or framework in the sense that hypnosis involves getting the individual's permis-
sion, piquing his or her interest, and a narrowing of attention. It involves a turning inward and, at times, regressing back or forward in
time. It involves a quality of selective concentration where the individ-

ual or couple becomes intensely absorbed, focused, and fixated to the extent of the loss of an outer sense of a generalized reality orientation.

Partners perceive qualities in each other that seem charismatic. Such qualities may be physical features (body shape) and/or personality traits (enthusiasm, extroversion), which merge together in ways that fixate (narrowing of attention) partners on their perfect fantasy (selective concentration). Inner, compulsive feelings (turning inward) to possess each other emerge. Partners lose track of time and daily agendas (loss of generalized orientation). Such an encounter could be construed as a form of hypnotically induced hallucination. Hypnotized subjects can positively hallucinate or see images of their fantasies in front of them that aren't there. It can be said that partners are in a mild trance, hallucinating their idealized fantasy onto one another. Partners are quite oblivious to the real character within due to entrancement.

The romantic perceptual alterations and changes seem to match those hypnotic phenomena. They illustrate in part what can happen when partners become addicted and absorbed in one another to the extent that they are losing themselves in the relationship. Such an experience can be called a lost-self-in-relationship romance. Depicting romantic relationships in such a framework sets the stage to appreciate and value what hypnotic qualities are and how they operate.

The definition of hypnosis can be stated as a special state of consciousness wherein selective capacities are emphasized while others fade into the background. Nine out of ten people can be hypnotized. Arnold Ludwig (1966) coined the term "altered state of consciousness" (ASC). He utilized the following definition:

Any mental state(s), induced by various physiological, psychological or pharmacological maneuvers or agents, which can be recognized subjectively by the individual himself (or by an objective observer of the individual) as representing sufficient deviation in subjective experience or psychological functioning from certain general norms for that individual during alert, waking consciousness (p. 167).

He is suggesting that such altered states be defined in terms of an individual's subjective experience and altered psychological function. These states result from changes in sensory experiences (sights, images, smells, unique sounds, tastes, feelings, etc.). Changes in altered states can also result from various physical activities (a runner's high), focused vigilance (intensely looking out for danger or a special loved one), and physiological alterations (alcohol- and/or drug-induced). Hypnotic states are altered states that create changes in how individuals perceive themselves and their way of dealing with outer surroundings. The absorption and engrossment in what and how the individual is perceiving and experiencing are greatly increased compared to the awakened individual. For example, hypnotized individuals can be intensely absorbed in dreams, hallucinations of people who aren't really there, or numbed to painful dental procedures. Their sense of time is greatly distorted, as a five-minute childhood memory can subjectively be perceived to last all day. Individuals in these states are quite resistant to outside interruptions and distractions. A special feature of hypnotic states is that it takes energy and applied attention to induce, alter and change states. This is an important dynamic principle of hypnosis and has significant implications for future change work in romantic couples.

Another important feature of hypnosis is that it generates two types of attentional absorption, both resistant to outside interruptions and distraction. The first type is called selective attention, which is usually good for problem-solving on a specific skill level (dealing with educational concerns, weight loss, and smoking cessation programs, etc.). The other type of attention is called expansive and allows a full range of stimulation and associations to be received through a stream of consciousness (witness the rush of sensations and attentional flow of riding a motorcycle at high speeds).

It appears that selective attention will increase the intensity of the specific experience at hand (staring at a moving watch can intensify the impact and sensation of movement on the observer as well as any suggestions given about people, places, or things). Expansive attention will allow increases of receptivity to a stream of consciousness of feelings and memories (hearing a favorite song can open an individual to a vast range of memories, feelings, and nostalgia). Hypnotic states can be induced through application of these various types of attention and focus. The implication of various forms of attention on romantic relationships can be considered quite significant.

Relaxation and hypnosis are usually associated with one another, as creating a relaxed and tranquil mind occurs through a relaxed and tranquil body. Yet hypnosis can occur in states of physical arousal and alertness. For example, when a car's headlights shine into the eyes of a deer standing by the side of the road, it will freeze in an alert and aroused position. It is in an altered state, yet hardly relaxed. Hypnosis can occur in both relaxed hypoarousal and tense, vigilant hyperarousal.

Hypnosis also alters our General Reality Orientation (GRO) (Tart, 1969). When we are driving on the highway, it is our GRO that prevents us from crossing over the white line separating lanes, even when our minds are on something else. In hypnosis, the stable internal frame of reference created by the GRO is diminished. Hypnotized individuals may have some awareness of outside sounds and sensations, like people talking or cars going by, but they are less acutely aware or responsive to their presence. They are less distracted and more focused.

In deep hypnosis where individuals have completely relinquished their GRO, the higher cognitive functions of analysis and interpretation of here-and-now sensations are reduced. Such a reduction occurs when an individual is so attracted and absorbed by something (a great-looking car, job, house, etc.) and/or someone (a well-shaped physique) that the individual unconsciously lowers his or her rational guard and impulse fantasies are entertained. At this point, sensory hallucinations and distortions may occur (there may be analgesic experiences where the pain of a toothache may be numbed).

Hypnosis involves dissociation where tranced individuals may have memories and perform acts without realizing that they are actually doing them (take the case of automatic writing where hypnotized subjects will unconsciously write out ideas and feelings but have no recognition that they are doing it or what they wrote).

Hypnosis also creates what is known as trance logic (Brown and Fromm, 1986). This refers to the ability of hypnotized individuals to put together perceptions partially based upon their real-world experience mixed and intertwined with those that are based on fantasy and imagination. The resultant perspective is that such a fusion of reality and fantasy creates hallucinations and distorted thinking patterns among hypnotized individuals. Because they are in an altered state, there is extreme tolerance for contradictions and ambiguity. An example of this is the hypnotized individual believing he sees a close friend whom he hallucinates to be his mother or father. There may be distorted logic of thought. If that close friend smiles or frowns, then the individual will think that the hallucinated parent is either loving or rejecting.

A further quality of hypnotized individuals is perceived involuntarism. Here, hypnotized individuals seem to be passively observing themselves act in ways that have no purpose. They feel as if things are happening by other forces. The case of hypnotized individuals unable to open their eyes as a result of hypnotic suggestion creates the effect that automatic eye closure is involuntary and beyond conscious control. Yet, paradoxically, the hypnotized individual is utilizing a strategic trance logic to achieve the goal of hypnotic eye closure by splitting his awareness. That is, as he consciously attends to the watch moving in front of him, he is distracted from awareness of how his eye concentration causes fatigue, closure, and inner associations. When this perceived involuntarism occurs during an absorbed state of a stream of consciousness, there can be vivid imagery, memories, and changes of body images ("I felt like an airplane and decided to fly; my nose became the shape of a bird's beak"). Trance increases the quality and sense of realism of imaginary experiences and illusions. Because hypnotized individuals reason and think with a sensory, trance logic (the feeling of being like an airplane must mean that I am one and can now act like one), they are especially prone to feeling involuntarily controlled by inner and outer stimuli and sensations.

A key aspect of hypnosis is the special nature of the hypnotic relationship (Brown and Fromm, 1986). The increased availability of inner feelings, associations, images, and memories in hypnotized individuals begins to filter and shape the relationship with the hypnotist. There is a strong intensity and intimacy that emerges between the hypnotist and the individual hypnotized. The vivid internal imagery and other highly personal sensations create a regressive affect. There is an infantilism where the individual experiences gratification of infantile wishes (attention, centeredness, and parental-like guidance). In addition, the fading of the GRO that results from a restriction of input from the outside world and a narrowing of range communication (the hypnotist is the only one the individual is able to contact) all creates a dependent, parent-childlike relationship with the hypnotist. It is not unlike the special relationship of a mother-child bond. The effects of such a special intense bond create powerful transference effects (transferring or shifting perceptions and images from past significant parental figures to the here-and-now person of the hypnotist). The skillful hypnotist can utilize such a regressive intensity for meaningful therapeutic change. The hypnotist realizes that his or her impact on the individual can be so intense as to seem almost magical.

Hypnosis involves expectation, motivation, and suggestibility (Barber, 1984). While hypnotized individuals need to be motivated and expecting of what they believe is hypnotic role playing (being a good subject and acting the part), this doesn't account for hypnosis as an altered state. Hypnotized individuals indeed experience shifts and changes in consciousness states that involve nonsequential events (that do not follow the logic of cause-and-effect time regarding the sequence of past, present, and future) with real alterations in perceptions of self and reality.

SIGNS OF HYPNOTIC TRANCE

The signs of trance involve such concepts as depth of trance or responsiveness to suggestion. For example, arm catalepsy (when the hypnotized individual discovers his or her arm rigid) indicates a depth of trance and responsiveness to hypnotic suggestion. Many times there are no behavioral signs of trance, only that the individual subjectively feels deeply hypnotized and intensely absorbed. Yet this same individual may not behaviorally respond. Accurate assessment involves gaining information from both behavioral and subjective experiences of trance depth. The degree of hypnotizability or susceptibility involves behavioral measures of response (can the individual demonstrate arm catalepsy). The issue of how hypnotizable an individual is varies depending on such factors as what is expected, what is motivating, the individual's attitude, anxiety levels, mood, and rapport with the hypnotist. These factors not withstanding, hypnotizability tends to vary in the general population. Many studies suggest that up to 98 percent of all individuals have some capacity for being hypnotized (Brown and Fromm, 1986).

Hypnotized individuals usually experience and/or demonstrate some or all of the following signs: ideomotor phenomena (alterations in physical movements caused by thinking and imagining such as arm catalepsy), cognitive and sensory effects (easier access to the inner world of dreams, imagery, emotions, memories, and amnesia and age regression to early childhood experiences) (Brown and Fromm, 1986).

Further signs of trance experience involve the persistent effects of posthypnotic suggestions and amnesia. Here, hypnotized individuals will be given suggestions to act or think a certain way after being awakened from the trance. They will also be given suggestions for amnesia or forgetting that such suggestions for posthypnotic behavior were ever given. For example, individuals may be given the suggestion that their understanding of conflicts and problems will become more and more clear over time after they awaken and leave the room.

Special cognitive abilities occur in trance as hypnotized individuals are capable of changing the meaning and value of words, fantasies, thoughts, and beliefs about experience (new insights and understandings discovered). There can be perceptual changes in reality, illusions, hallucinations, and delusions created (factual reality can merge with fantasies creating hallucinations as in a real flower fantasized to be smiling; alterations in self-concept and self-esteem inflated or amplified by imaging self as successfully performing in school or work). Listed below are ten criteria of signs of trance:

1. Relaxation/drowsiness
2. Responsive to suggestions
3. Absorption/involuntary experiencing
4. General reality orientation fading
5. Vivid imagery/hallucination
6. Selective or expansive attention
7. Unconscious involvement
8. Access to inner sensing
9. Age regression
10. Time distortion
11. Amnesia and hyperamnesia
12. Parallel awareness
13. State-dependent learning, memory, and behavior beyond waking consciousness

STAGES OF HYPNOSIS

There are four basic states of hypnosis (Hadley and Staudacher, 1985): (1) pretalk or preparation about what hypnosis is; (2) the induction of the trance itself; (3) deepening the trance, utilizing imagery and dream work, and planting suggestions for posthypnotic reawakening; and (4) reawakening and ratifying that trance has occurred.

Pretalk is primarily designed to educate and prepare the subject for what hypnosis is. Motivation for and anticipation of the process, safety, and clear goals are built into this educating state. Subjects are taught that all hypnosis is controlled by the individual being hypnotized. This empowers them to feel that they retain ultimate authority and safety for their experience.

In the induction phase, there can be several types of style. There can be permissive ("You [the subject] can go into trance whenever you're ready") or commanding ("You will now go into trance"). Inductions usually involve mind-body relaxation, narrowing of focused attention, reduced awareness of external environment and everyday concerns, greater internal awareness of sensations, and a trance state. Inductions also utilize fixation of attention. They may take a slow, time-consuming directive: "Get into a comfortable position, focus attention on a very narrow point such as a spot on the wall, candle, or moving pendulum." As the subject concentrates, he or she may be given suggestions for eye closure and relaxation. The entire induction could take seconds or up to fifty minutes.

Rapid inductions can produce trance experience in what seems like the twinkle of an eye. You might see this in stage hypnosis, where the hypnotist gives short, rapid commands like "Close your eyes, raise your arm over your head, and when your hand feels a tingling sensation at its highest point you will be in trance."

Indirect induction using analogies or metaphors is more useful for those less suggestible and/or resistant subjects. For example, using images of floating like a leaf in the wind, telling stories about children in a schoolyard enjoying a relaxed, letting-go experience will induce trance in more resistant subjects. When subjects don't know (distracted by casual, vague, informal language patterns) what suggestions for relaxation they are receiving, they have a more difficult time resisting them. Essential components of induction involve fixation and orientation to trance as well as the detached, letting-go experience of dissociation (it's not me making it happen, trance seems to occur by itself).

The deepening and dream-work component of trance, which is the third stage in hypnosis, involves many levels. It is designed to establish a mental learning set for change, metaphors, and structured interventions; and a deep, unconscious search for resolution. For simplification purposes, we will present three general levels of deepening in trance work: light, moderate, and deep. Light trance involves body relaxation, slow breathing, absorption into self, and directing attention internally to some real or imagined task such as seeing yourself vacationing in the Bahamas.

At the level of moderate trance there is a loss of awareness of surroundings, eye-closure, increase in awareness of internal functions such as breathing, imagery, and more literal interpretation of language. Such is the case when the hypnotized subject is asked a double-binding question (which presupposes trance) if he or she could find their eyes closing slowly or quickly. The response is affirmative (everyone has the ability to close their eyes and hypnotic subjects act out these abilities under the misdirected illusion that it is the hypnotist's suggestion that makes these so-called involuntary actions and abilities happen). With eye closure, subjects also begin to actively imagine themselves in some altered, fantasized state.

Deep trance is an even further reduction of external activity awareness and energy. There may be numbness or limb stiffness, more narrowing of attention, sensory illusions, and sensitizing of creativity. One no longer just imagines one's self floating down some relaxing stream. At this level, the internal experience is one of actually doing it. Such an internal experience can be defined as an altered state of intense absorption.

The deepest level of trance is called "sleep" but this is not actual sleep (where the body and mind begin to shut down). At this level, subjects can experience suspension of voluntary movement and activity. Subjects also experience a significant decrease and/or absence of conscious, rational processing and thinking as these shift to unconscious primary (nonanalytical) processing and complete absorption of suggestions and information. It is at this level that subjects are fully participating in their dreamlike activities. Subjects perceive that they are actually living in their dreams, whatever they may be.

Suggestibility isn't always contingent on the depth of trance level. Usually, being in trance allows the subject to feel a variety of sensations, images, and time distortions (warmth, cold, negative or positive hallucinations, speeding or slowing time where fifty minutes seems like fifty hours, etc.) It is common to experience a sort of unrealness or oddness about self and reality while in trance. Some people report floating outside or next to their body. Some even sense they have drifted back and forth along their line of time from the past to the future. Others may not experience any of this as each person is unique in having his or her own perceptions. All respond in accordance to their own preconceived notions and expectations of what is to happen while they are in trance. Trance can also involve a hypervigilance (hypermnesia) where subjects experience vivid, detailed memory recall of significant emotional events, past and/or present.

The last component of trance is reawakening and ratifying that the subject has reemerged from the trance, has experienced some evidence of being in trance, and that, indeed, something unusual has happened (arm rigidity or catalepsy) beyond his or her control. There may have been posthypnotic suggestions planted such that when the subject hears a word or is in some stressful situation, the suggestion for dealing with it in some healthy, relaxed way is acted out. The subject then realizes that suggestions were implanted during trance that are still affecting him or her in some way. Posthypnotic suggestions for amnesia can be installed where subjects are instructed to selectively forget to remember what occurred in trance to facilitate learning and change.

The stages of pretalk, trance induction, deepening, and reemergence correspondingly encourage the subject to become oriented to inner fantasies and sensations, release conscious control and go through the entrance to their inner fantasy world, deepen them, and then resurface to reality with suggestions for change. Trance may involve fantasized, idealized images which capture the attention. These induce a trance-like fixation paralleling the romantic stage of idealization which ultimately deteriorates (regresses deeper into entrancement) into the stage of disillusionment. In addictive relationships, the deeper the entranced state the more deteriorated partners can treat each other.

Pretalk is a necessary stage in the induction of hypnosis. Pretalk introduces the person to hypnosis describing and educating him or her as to what it is. Many suggestions about motivation and imagination may be planted and embedded at this time. As the person becomes more and more exposed to the progressive, inductive effects of hypnotic phenomena, fixation and absorption into his or her internal sensory experiences begin to occur.

The hypnotist induces fixation in subjects to allow imaging and motivating sensory experiences that become more and more internalized. They become more absorbing as the person becomes preoccupied with internal self-talk and visualization. The hypnotist may initiate focus on body sensations of relaxation, breathing, and muscle tension. The subject's attention is directed inward toward personal, sensory experiences as a way of inducing internalized imaging and absorption.

For example, the hypnotist may say, "As you become aware of your breathing, you can notice sensations of relaxation spreading throughout your body and mind. And, as relaxation spreads, you may imagine a relaxing scene or memory." The subject, without realizing it, (unconsciously) begins to think, feel, and imagine inside him- or herself what the hypnotist is saying and suggesting, which is what causes trance. All of these physical and mental stimuli merge together and induce the subject to go deeper and deeper inside into trance fixation and concentration. As the hypnotic induction progresses, the subject enters into a hypnotic dream. The hypnotist uses this dream for treatment purposes. The hypnotist will accomplish fading of reality orientation by having the subject intensely watch a point on the wall. This creates fatigue, fading of outside reality, and drifting of thoughts and images such as when we are bored. In boredom, the mind begins to wander as rational connections blur, giving way to sensory trance logic where almost anything can be made to appear real (as in virtual reality).

The hypnotist may utilize this and have the subject attend to the space between two fingers held close together. The subject is asked to imagine rubber bands wrapped around them, pulling the fingers together. The fingers now seem to close by themselves. The subject observes his or her fingers moving by themselves (by misdirecting attention to the fingers, the subject ignores how his or her imagination is directing the action), experiences floating sensations, shifting attention, and other internal experiences emerging on their own. Involuntarism is now present. This is a sign of trance depth and a clue of how hypnosis disconnects the subject's present experience from the larger, whole picture of reality.

Critical to this hypnotic process is the concept of fractionation and recycling. As subjects are moved in, out, and back into trance again and again (fractionation) and recycled through the stages of trance, the depth and speed of going into trance increases. What this means is that the more subjects go through trance inductions and deepenings, the more profoundly absorbed and adept they become in their "tranceability." They demonstrate their "tranceportability" of movement in and out of state (trance). The implications of this dynamic for entranced relationships will become powerfully apparent. For now, it is important to remember that each recycling through these hypnotic components serves to deepen trance levels as if one were peeling the layers of an onion. At the onion's core is space, which is where subjects first feel some loss of their everyday self, yet find a new self with fascinating abilities.

The hypnotic characteristics and dimensions in the induction and deepening process are listed below. These will assist in comparing later the characteristics of hypnotic phenomena to the dynamics of entrancing, addictive relationships.

SUMMARY OF HYPNOTIC STAGES

I. *PreTalk*: To educate, motivate, and prepare for trance induction.

II. *Induction*: Permissive and/or authoritarian approaches involving attention fixation, absorbing, sensory experiences, stories, jokes, puns, relaxation and imagery rapid or prolonged procedures. Designed to fixate, orient, and facilitate dissociation in initial trance.

III. *Deepening*: Degree of depth varies from light, moderate, or deep inner absorption and loss of awareness of surrounding environment; dream work

occurs at this stage as well as literal interpretation of ideas, absorbing images that appear real, time distortion, and unconscious age regression.
Posthypnotic suggestions are embedded and inserted at this stage. Deepening involves establishing a mental learning set for deep unconscious
change, metaphors, and structured intervention, and for deep, unconscious
search for resolution.

IV. *Reawakening and Ratifying*: Evidence of trance experience. Effects of
posthypnotic suggestion are experienced and/or acted out.

Hypnosis may be induced and manifest in quite natural and indirect
ways. Milton Erickson (1976), known as the father of modern-day hypnosis, employed naturalistic, indirect methods. He utilized everything in
the individual's physical senses, mental images, associations, emotions,
beliefs, memories, and experiences to induce and deepen therapeutic,
healing trances for his patients.

Erickson demonstrated that indirect, conversational dialogues, stories, metaphors, and/or confusing, unexpected surprises could induce
trances. Such unexpected surprises might occur when the subject
reaches out to shake hands, or the hypnotist drops to his or her knees and
straightens his or her socks and shocks the subject into trance. In addition, by simply having a dialogue with an individual, Erickson could
induce trance without using any informal procedures. He would hypnotize an individual by describing how that person could pick a spot on the
wall and notice how his or her eyes might get tired and remain open only
as long as they needed to before they closed. The individual might describe how he or she felt, indicating some nervousness. Erickson would
reframe and incorporate that feeling of nervousness by saying how that
feeling was really the excitement and anticipation of going into trance.
Sometimes Erickson would tell stories of various events and situations
to indirectly induce trance to assist the individual in having therapeutic
learning experiences. He might tell the story of how he spent the night
in a noisy, hot, congested factory and learned how to utilize selective
attention, tuning out some stimulating events over others to allow him to
sleep. He was always demonstrating many abilities that individuals
didn't realize they had until they experienced trance.

Erickson demonstrated that individuals were capable of split or parallel awareness. This is where a hypnotized individual can both experience involuntary trance behavior like arm catalepsy or visual hallucinations while being aware as an observer that this is happening at the same
time. He was quite focused on how the mind and body could operate in
many different capacities. For example, he might suggest to hypnotized

individuals that their mind could awaken but their body could remain asleep. Such a suggestion allowed the individual freedom of mental imagery and changes while his or her sensory body was quieted in "sleep" from anxious interruption. He might ask if he could "borrow" an individual's hand or arm where it would move in an involuntary way (hang in the air). The hypnotized individual would experience that the hand or arm was moving by itself without the person making it move. This separation of mind from body is called involuntary dissociation.

Erickson demonstrated that hypnotized individuals could narrow their focus of attention, become so absorbed in their experience that they would be able to separate and disconnect part of their body or any other piece of experience (split off fragments of an idea or fantasy), while ignoring the larger whole or picture. Erickson realized that hypnosis could develop and evolve into deep trances by gaining rapport and matching to the individual's experience. He would use truisms (statements of factual truth) about the individual to create rapport and induce trance. He might say that a person can breathe in and out at one's own pace. He might suggest that one's eyelids will blink at some point or that some of one's thoughts and images have been very pleasant. All these are truisms in that it is true that living people breathe, will blink their eyes, and usually will have had some pleasant thoughts and images in their lives.

Erickson developed rapport by relating and identifying such obvious experiences. In time, he would anticipate what the individual might say, feel, or do (that one's eyes will close after intense staring or will feel relaxed as one breathes easy) in the future, which strengthens and deepens close feelings of rapport, oneness, and trance. While volumes have been written about Erickson's hypnotic work, it is sufficient for our present purposes to illustrate how intense, hypnotic experiences could occur in quite natural, informal ways. Erickson illustrates how natural, informal communications can affect such outcomes.

Erickson would get an individual's attention by using shock and confusion in his conversational way of inducing trance. He once worked with a young child who was embarrassed that she had freckles. He first said to her that she was a thief. She was quite upset by this. It confused and distracted her from thinking about her freckles. While in this receptive state, Erickson told her an elaborate story of how she sneaked into the kitchen, tipped over the cinnamon jar, and it spilled all over her face. This suggested reframe of the spots on her face as sprinkles of cinnamon gave her a laugh. With this new frame of reference, she could find humor associated with her freckles and avoid feeling embarrassed. Erickson would embed and intersperse suggestions in his conversational inductions. He might say that, "I don't know when you will go into trance" or "I wonder how long it will be before you will feel relaxation spreading throughout your body" or "Some people like you can, when they feel comfortable, go into a trance." Notice that the underlined portion of the previous sentences embed and intersperse (strategically placed suggestions spread out over the conversation) subtle suggestions for trance without the individual consciously recognizing them.

This is another example of split awareness, where the conscious mind hears the verbal words and the unconscious mind responds to the embedded and interspersed suggestions by going into trance. A telltale sign of the split awareness of trance is when subjects observe themselves acting "involuntarily" yet thinking or knowing that at any time they could break out of this induced state but choosing not to do so. The lack of motivation to exercise choice is a sign of trance and prevents them from exiting the trance. This lack of motivation to exercise choice will be of powerful importance in understanding and dealing with entrancement.

Before closing, there is one more important point to establish, which is the concept of utilization in hypnosis. This refers to pacing and incorporating in the hypnotized individual's trance induction whatever is going on in their current experience. For example, as an individual begins to relax and go into a light trance, his or her head may drop or tilt. The skilled hypnotist utilizes that current movement by saying, ". . . and as you relax and your head drops, this means you can go even deeper into trance." Such utilization of current experience serves to deepen trance as more and more of an individual's acts, feelings, thoughts, and images are incorporated and made a part of such an entrancing experience. Essentially, everything happening or about to happen to that individual going through trance induction now becomes an important contribution and intensification of an ever-deepening hypnotic experience. Intense rapport and one-to-one connections are now possible.

Rapport can be enhanced by utilizing various experiences of the individual. For example, creating the illusion of choice can have powerful, inductive affects. The hypnotist could say that the individual can go into trance now or some time in the future. While there is the appearance of illusion that the individual has a choice about trance, the message presupposes that, at some point, the individual will go into trance. It's only a matter of time. In this way, more and more of the individual's reality becomes reframed and subsumed under the guise of trance induction and deepening. Other hypnotic illusions of choice are, "Your eyes can close slowly or quickly. You may feel relaxation more or less in various parts of your body. You can imagine memories that may be pleasant or not pleasant." These illusions of choice and incorporations fixate and absorb the individual more and more into trance.

To emerge from the trance, all the hypnotist has to do is break with the trance rapport. For example, if the hypnotized individual is told, while sitting in a relaxed and focused state, that he is standing and feeling tension in his left toe. As this is an abrupt shift and an inaccurate description of the sensory experience of the hypnotized individual, he or she will begin to lose a fixated absorption and start to come out of trance. The traditional approach of having the individual awaken as they count upward from one to five achieves the same outcome but in a smoother transition. The point here is that the degree of accurately matching the individual's sensory and mental current experience will affect rapport and therefore whether he or she will go into or out of trance. The more plausible the statements of the hypnotist are in providing a fitting frame or reframe of what the individual is going through, the deeper and longer the trance will be.

Hypnotic rapport serves to break the individual's hold on his or her own personal worldview by interrupting self-focused absorption with distraction and fixation. The individual to be hypnotized comes out of the everyday focus and absorption and reenters into the absorption and entrancing fixation of the hypnotist's induction. Well-established rapport allows the hypnotist to anticipate and determine what the individual will experience next (dreams, arm rising, etc.). The individual may release preoccupations with daily schedules and worries about bills to pay and instead shift attention to the voice of the hypnotist and references to mental and physical relaxation and imagery.

Hypnotic rapport can clearly alter and release conscious states in the individual's general reality orientation (focused rapport can lead hypnotized individuals into the surprising and confusing experience of not being able to open their eyes). Once the individual's hold on his or her reality view of the world is loosened and ultimately broken, all the hypnotic phenomena previously discussed can now occur. Such a loosening and release creates a temporary state of uncertainty, confusion, and an inner search to reestablish meaning. Susceptibility to suggestions in trance increases with such a release of reality. In addition, critical faculties of judgment, reality testing, and mature problem solving are reduced and eventually eliminated in deep trance. Regression to earlier levels of childlike functioning occurs in terms of preoccupation with sensory experiences, time distortion, and overexaggeration of childhood events. In this state of dependent learning, objects like parents can appear to be ten feet tall.

Hypnotic trances have been found to occur naturally in the course of an individual's daily experience. For example, driving a car, reading a book, or simply staring out a window all involve an absorbed, inner attentiveness with the mind wondering, at times unconsciously, onto imagery and mental associations. Also, trances have been discovered in pathological conditions where individuals disconnect from reality in terms of amnesia or imagery (traumatized individuals suffering from early childhood sexual and/or physical abuse). Here, individuals have learned to self-induce their own self-hypnotic procedure (under conditions of severe pain and duress they may focus on an object in their room such as a rocking horse and induce and deepen a dream trance surrounding this object).

It is worth noting that individuals can access trance quickly simply by recalling times, places, and events of previous trance experiences. For example, in retelling a story of trauma or triumph that involves an entrancing experience, this will recall the trance induction in and of itself. This points to the very quick induction that hypnotists can use with individuals going into trance. A simple procedure, therefore, is have them recall times when they were previously in a trance and this will induce hypnotic states. Individuals who are retelling stories over and over again of entrancing experiences are reinducing and deepening altered states of consciousness in the process. Imagine the intense, programming effect on an individual's relationship if he or she continues to retell, relive, and recreate hypnotically induced, altered states of entrancement with each new partner. The point here is that trances occur in both normal and abnormal life conditions.

CHAPTER 2

HYPNOTIC FRAMEWORK OF ROMANTIC ADDICTIVE RELATIONSHIPS

The main premise advanced in this chapter is that romantic relationships intimately parallel hypnotic relationships. Because partners in couples do not realize the presence and power of hypnotic dynamics, they are vulnerable to addictive fixations in their relationships. The main premise suggests that romantic relationships involve, if not require, hypnotic dynamics and forces to sustain them.

ENTRANCEMENT PRINCIPLE OF SUBMERGENCE

A key feature to entrancement is that the more partners act on their fantasy ideal, the more intense and powerful it becomes. Entranced couples may find themselves with partners they really don't like or value. Partners can date each other for years, disliking numerous aspects of one another (talkative, superficial, rude). Yet they are too frightened to say anything or to leave for fear of being alone. Such tolerance for what is unacceptable intensifies entrancement and submergence.

Partners really don't know the inner dynamics that actually keep them together. Enduring unacceptable, abusive experiences is indicative of entranced "love." The harder partners struggle for control and resolution in the relationship, the less they actually have. Such intense struggles propel them deeper into entrancement with their fantasy ideal. Entranced couples can be entrenched in conflicting positions involving negativity, fear, loss, terrorizing abandonment, or smothering engulfment. Partners in such positions believe they are fighting for their fantasy ideal. The reality is that acting on these negative motives only intensifies them and serves to deepen entrancement. The paradoxical consequence is that such intensification of negative feelings makes their fantasy ideal even more elusive than before.

The effects of hypnotic dynamics in romantic relationships are called entrancement. These hypnotic dynamics are what contribute to such paradoxical consequences that result from the perceptual distortion effects of entrancement. Entrancement is defined as a way romantic partners engage and relate, where suggestive imagery and sensory stimuli merge to form a fusion or bond. For example, when a man holds an ideal image in his head of a charismatic, tall, slender, blue-eyed blonde and a woman of that description walks past his visual field, it could be said that a mild state of entrancement has been induced (if the man is in conversation, there may be a silent moment, eye-fixation, and a brief head turn attending to the person in question). There is a matching of inner fantasy and outer reality such that the boundaries blur between the two. This type of experience fits the description of perceptual changes in reality occurring under hypnosis presented in the previous chapter. The inner imaginary fantasies and external world of reality (what is real about the other person) collapse and merge together in romantic relationships. This merger or fusion of fantasy and factual reality is called entrancement.

It may be helpful to understand that there are essentially two kinds of entrancement. The first is what was just described and is referred to as a sensory-based trance. The focus is on appearance, personality, language style, and other sensory stimuli. This type of entrancement occurs in the beginning stages of romantic relationships. Healthy couples evolve out of this level of sensory entrancement to what is termed character entrancement which is distinguished by a depth focus. By depth focus is meant being able to perceive the inner nature or character of a person's real self. For example, a husband beholds the evolved image of his wife's uniqueness as a human being and long-term partner. As she walks past him, he reflects and meditates on her inner beauty and special qualities that make her the unique character she really is and the one he really loves.

It is important to note that evolving from one level of entrancement to another requires time, maturity, and progressive, successful stage development. Partners progressively learn to love and respect the inner character of each other by moving from external to internal perceptions of each other's true nature. However, romantic relationships of necessity need to progress through various stages of growth.

At the initial stage of romantic contact, an absorbing, fixating allure may be essential to getting the relationship off the ground. Such an absorbing, fixating allure involves entrancement. Entrancement in a romantic encounter is similar to the initial ignition of a rocket about to launch. There is a need for a fiery, energetic thrust to get the vehicle off the ground.

Entranced relationships become addictive when they are unable to progress successfully from one stage to the next. They experience difficulty in releasing one section or stage of their relationship growth for the next one that would assist them in continuing their journey. It is important to note that most couples are not aware, or are only vaguely aware, of the extent to which hypnotic entrancements operate in their relationships. When couples do not evolve in their entrancement, they experience chronic problems (conflicts, verbal and/or physical abuse, and other struggles). It is at this level of restrictive relating that they experience the perverse twist of addictive bonds. Without learning to master, understand, and gain a perspective on hypnotic entrancement, couples risk the nightmarish perversion into addictive bonding.

The concept of addicted relationships refers to the capacity of two or more individuals who begin to engage in a type of relating and communicating that has a perverse give-and-take quality. For example, partners constantly criticize and harass one another for needing time alone or feel pressured to behave in artificially perfect ways. One partner may demand constant attention from the other through hand-holding and eye contact and humiliate the other for acting silly in public.

There is usually an obsessive quality of dwelling on and living through the other partner. Partners feel compelled to spend all their time together and feel abandoned and lonely when apart. There may also be a kind of rigid role playing where one partner always tries to be happy-go-lucky, while the other assumes a depressive, almost morbid sadness.

The focus on the relationship, while it may have had admirable and well-intentioned beginnings, leads to qualities of obsessiveness, loss of control, frustrations, anger, and rage. There are usually various forms of abuse and fixation hallucination. Addictive relationships foster a fantasy ideal or illusion around which the addiction is organized. This is in contrast to the evolved character entrancement, which emphasizes how each partner can enjoy and enhance a sense of self, character, and integrity with the relationship. Mature relationships organize themselves on the contributions of each partner's unique character. As such, partners in healthy bonds are in the relationship but do not experience the source of their lives as coming primarily from their relationship. While their relationship is primarily important to both, it is not essential for their lives to continue.

Just the opposite is true for entranced relationships restrictive in their evolution. Partners feel they will die (perhaps literally) if the other one leaves them. In severely addictive relationships, this may be more of a reality than a metaphor, as in the case of one partner preferring to kill the other to prevent the loss. Notice the paradoxical perversity in the entranced logic of loss (to kill the lover to keep him or her). This is where sensory entrancement has perversely twisted itself into addictive bonding. Figures 2.1, 2.2, and 2.3 depict the positive and negative cor-relations concerning absorption, entrancement, and boundary confusion. Notice that as absorption and sensory entrancement increase, so does the degree of boundary confusion (Figure 2.1). This indicates a progressive loss of reality-testing and problem-solving ability. When observing the relationship between boundary confusion and character entrancement, there is an opposite negative correlation (Figure 2.2). As character trance increases, boundary confusion and its concomitant reality distor-tions decrease (Figure 2.3).

Figure 2.1
Absorption and Entrancement

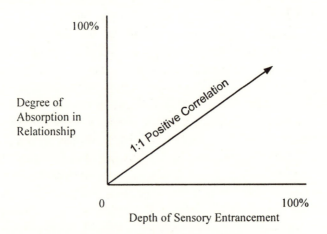

Degree of absorption as related to progressive depth of entrancement.

Figure 2.2
Boundaries and Sensory Entrancement

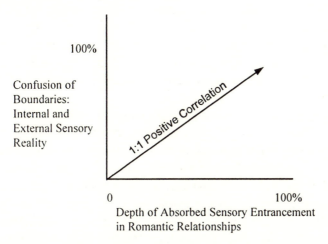

Degree of inner and outer boundary confusion in reality frames as related to depth of
Absorbed Sensory Entrancement in Romantic Relationships.

Figure 2.3
Boundaries and Character Entrancement

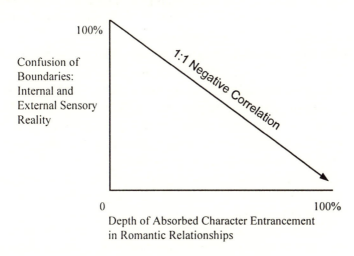

Degree of inner and outer boundary confusion in reality frames as related to depth of
Absorbed Character Entrancement in Romantic Relationships.

Addictive partners adhere to fantasized, rigid, close-ended ideals of what their romantic vision of the encounter should and must be. In order to "truly" fulfill and satiate their highly sensitized, emotional need requirements, they lose sight of enhancing their individuality as part of the relationship. This prevents a sense of partnership and oneness where they could learn to be themselves in a relationship. They learn to abuse each other's self in attempting to have this wonderful (so-called) idealistic fixation.

Healthy relationships have a balancing system where each partner's identity and genuine sense of self remain intact. Where they have discovered mutuality and grown together in a common ground of shared experience, partners release only a select sense of self in becoming one together. For example, one married couple of thirty years had very unique characters yet worked quite well together. The husband was in his early fifties, a former marine and successful in sales with a dry sense of humor, somewhat self-contained, and disciplined in character. The wife, in her later forties, had successfully raised with her husband their three daughters and was quite energetic, bubbly, and sociable and worked as a secretary. Both valued high standards of living and invested much time and energy in the home and family. Recently, they cleaned their four-bedroom home's carpets, working like a swat team together, and they got the job done in almost no time at all. They each have their own character and style, yet share common values and commitments, mutually releasing distinct realms of their identities to be one with each other.

An entrancing couple, by contrast, tends to thrive on emotional and problem overwhelm. The entrancing couple magnifies and overly complicates daily problem-solving tasks of communication, trust, and shared task responsibilities. Such couples become polarized with tasks and achievements. They may become either highly ineffective in task completion or obsessed with all-encompassing successes that dominate their relationship lives. Remember that in hypnotic trances, individuals can regress to a childlike level of sensory preoccupation and overmagnification of how severe events really are. In this regressed state, they lack mature adult cognitive resources.

Such magnification and cognitive distortion from hypnotic entrancement can be seen in the way couples overgeneralize their problems. This is where one failure in attempting to solve a problem or resolve conflicts in the ideal relationship is overgeneralized into all-or-nothing thinking. Couples may think regressively that one failure means all is lost. Catastrophizing (prediction that conflicts and problems could mean the end of a relationship) and awfulizing (how terrible such problems are to go through) distortions further confuse and complicate the way entrancing couples solve problems.

Such distortions in thinking, created by entrancement, can lead to taboos in how couples will relate in order to defend against such fantasized disasters. Partners communicate double messages to each other. One partner may assert how beautiful the relationship is while, at the same time, critiquing and ridiculing the other's way of dressing and acting in public. Protests from the other partner are met with a quick subject change, establishing the taboo against expressions that might cast a shadow of a doubt on their ideal and beautiful bond. Such taboos restrict partners' ability to resolve negative communication and maturely evolve the intimacy in their relationship.

Entrancing relationships are regressed states of hypnosis where partners symbolically represent childlike images and demanding ways of being treated in highly individualistic and self-serving ways. If partners are not treated in such specialized, perfect ways, they experience rejection and loss of idealized love. Such is the power of regressed, entranced bonds on here-and-now realities. Partners will not feel this rejection from friends and colleagues as they have reestablished mature, adult perspectives being out of entrancement. The instant partners encounter their entranced relationship, severe and painful feelings are released as regression from entrancement has set in. Partners can always be hurt more by the one in which they are in love (or entranced).

In addictive relationships, partners are fixated in their merged positions. This fixation creates a feeling of being out of control, unrewarded, unfulfilled, unrequited (which creates miserable experiences for each person). Partners don't feel free in such a relationship and therefore feel a pressure to try and "break free" but fail to do so. Partners may insist that their relationship has an essential fantasy, ideal or hallucination, which is a hypnotic absorption they believe must materialize to fulfill their needy emotional lives. They believe that being with one another in some mysterious, special, magical way holds the key to their personal fulfillment.

Partners experience such magical moments when anticipating that being with one another will soothe all their worries and frustrations of the day. Partners believe that the magic (entrancement) of the other's presence lifts them out of the mundane, ordinary routine of daily living. This is a classic example of losing hold of one's creative capacity to create one's own reality. It is not unlike the magic of a mother's kiss upon a bruised knee of her child who has fallen. The belief in her healing power to make it better with a kiss is very real. Such magical powers ascribed to the fantasy ideal are actually hypnotic suggestions empowered by each partner's self-induced belief.

Recall in the previous chapter that a hypnotized individual appears to behave involuntarily (arm rigidity). Yet, if the hypnotic induction suggests a kind of imagining and associating that has a goal-directed purpose (of creating arm rigidity) this will be the outcome. Since critical faculties of judgment are suspended, this allows the hypnotized individual to function at a regressed level of immaturity, preoccupied with sensory gratification without conscious censorship or interference.

Such imaginary, associative, goal-directed strategy and regressed immaturity with a suspension of critical faculties operates in entrancing relationships. Entranced couples appear to act in involuntary, rigid ways, yet the imagery and strategy of their idealism creates a goal-directed outcome. In this case, it is a fixated, rigid way of treating each other so as to maintain the fantasized idealism of the relationship. It's a kind of "arm rigidity" of a fixated mind-set. This can lead to apparent, involuntary actions and reactions from each partner. Conflicts can ensue with both being surprised at how they are acting. They are not aware of an unconscious strategy and goal-fixated behavior.

One partner may feel more in control and confident than the other (known as being one-up [Delis and Philips, 1990]). The other partner may feel more vulnerable to losing the relationship. One partner may perceive the other as having more control, feel vulnerable, and attempt to secure the other's commitment in more reassuring ways. Various strategies involve moving closer, trying to please, or acting distant and detached seeking to enlist attention and interest. Such maneuvering may trigger escalations of equal and opposite reactivity. Quite frequently, entranced couples misperceive and miscalculate the posture of their partners. Each tends to over- or underestimate the other's degree of commitment.

The resulting instability serves only to intensify their preoccupation and their entrancement with one another. The struggle for who is more in control of the relationship, of who will be more independent and less needy to the other's involvement, threatens to erode intimacy and trust. Such a struggle is based on the false illusion that one partner could actually control and make the other partner love him or her. Yet they may both be "out of their control comfort zones," as such struggles and conflicts are actually the involuntary dynamics of entrancement.

The control issues of the maneuvering "one-up" partner (flirtatious and exhibitionist acts seeking to draw the attention of the "one-down" victimized partner) actually mirror their hypnotic dance. These pursuit-withdrawal tactics are designed to maintain the fixated, hypnotic set-point.

If one feels bored and needs stimulation to reenergize and reorganize the fantasy ideal, the flirtateousness of the woman (it could also happen with the man) in front of her boyfriend can provoke renewed interest and energy. If the man comes across as the passive, one-down needy partner, the woman's flirtatious provocation can incite him to riotous, active interest, bringing him out of his passive, dormant state. The two may have conflicting words about it, which creates painful involvement. This is a way of deepening the entrancement (drawing them closer into the trap of the hypnotic pull). There may then be brief moments of euphoric pleasure (they end up having sex all night to soothe the pain, reigniting the fantasy, and again strengthening the hypnotic pull of enmeshed fantasy). This pain-pleasure alternation maintains a balanced point of set levels of intimacy. Yet such alternating pain-pleasure cycles actually serve to deepen entrancement.

HYPNOTIC SET-POINTS IN FANTASY

Such couples as just described tend to seek adventure, risk, uncertainty, and the excitement of the unknown. This serves to activate the sympathetic nervous system. Anything that activates the nervous system becomes energy available to be used in a variety of contexts. According to what is known as the "Jukebox Theory" (Barbach, 1995), when you place a quarter in the jukebox (excite the nervous system with charged emotions like fear, anger, jealousy, love, compassion, etc.) the music that plays depends on which button is pushed (the situation and context determine which triggers will be selected to elicit certain outcomes). If the context is an erotic one, sexual activity may result. Such excitation is only self-serving for temporary distractions and rarely results in any genuine increase of intimacy. The point at which intimacy is consistently interrupted is the set-point. Consistent interruption of intimacy is how the set-point is maintained.

When partners are socializing as a couple, one may feel uncomfortable with the other's exuberance and attention to people. One becomes irritated with the other and directs attention to the cocktail waitress. The other partner intensifies his or her own flirtatious behavior. Ultimately, they lash out at each other.

When they get home, they argue to the point of rage and physical violence. This scenario will be replayed again and again. Hypnotic entrancement regresses couples to sensory stimulation and distorted perceptions of cause and effect in relationships. Couples lose the larger picture of what is actually happening in conflicts and everyday reality. The scenario of conflict, collapse, and reignition of the same old arguments and conflicts is quite characteristic of entranced couples in the addictive phase.

Many bored couples maintain their set-point or balance through inducing elements of the unknown (exposing vulnerable feelings, seeking to test limits of acceptability with members of the opposite gender outside the relationship, varying time together and apart, threatening to leave, impulsiveness, provocation, etc.). There is an entrancing quality to adventure--uncertainty--and the unknown which keeps partners living at the edge of reality, literally sitting on the edge of their seats. Never completely knowing what's coming intensifies moment-to-moment experiences that are absorbing, hypnotic, and, at times, erotic. Partners can at one moment be laughing then, almost like a flash flood, they turn on each other, arguing vehemently over who spoiled and ruined forever their perfect moment of ideal love. Such sudden shocks freeze partners in their hypnotic tracks, preventing growth and set-point expansion. Yet there is a perverse balance as partners tend to avoid too much uncertainty or risk, which would "snap" the limits of their relations like an overstretched rubberband. Entrancement's regressive and childlike-state-dependent conditioning obstructs mature dialogue and exchange. This is the controlling effect and purpose of hypnotic set-points.

There are taboos against healthy and sensitive experimentation in entrancing relationships as the hypnotic set-point obstructs meaningful intimacy. Wild and chaotic acting out and controlled no-talk rules prevent meaningful change and preserve the status quo. Such hypnotic set-points exist because the relationship hinges on fantasized visions rather than on actual relationship achievements of two adults. The adventure and unpredictability of the unknown keep them riveted and absorbed in one chaotic encounter after another. It is not unlike what Shakespeare (1996) suggested when he wrote, "Theirs is a tale told by an idiot, full of sound and fury signifying nothing!" The possibility that most, if not all, of the chaotic conflicts entranced couples experience may "signify nothing" can be quite annoying to them. Reality, sometimes, can do this to those living in the fantasyland of denial.

Entrancing relationships encompass a wide range of expressions from the low-key nesting couple tucked away at home to the manic, high-speed roller-coaster variety. Whether securely nested in for the winter or out for a wild summer's ride, they all have one common denominator. Entranced couples become frozen at a certain hypnotic set-point that prevents them from becoming genuinely intimate and open to each other.

Their emotional and physical risk-taking behaviors create equal but opposite controls of being on guard, walled off to real change and a generalized feeling of caution about their own chaos. These polarities serve to freeze the set-point of entranced couples to deeper and deeper levels of immobilization until the whole structure fractures, falling to pieces. The foundation of the purpose and meaningfulness of their relationship erodes.

The concept and definition of hypnotic set-point refers to the agreed-upon point of fusion or enmeshment of partners' identities to support their hypnotic fantasy. The set-point regulates how much denial and abandonment of each partner's self ("I" and "you") is absolutely required to fuse into a fixed set-point of "us-ness." This hypnotic set-point of "us-ness" is in the service of indulging the hypnotic fantasy. The degree of partners' fused identities is a measure of the strength of the hypnotic fantasy's pull. This hypnotic pull can override the integrity of each individual, subjecting each to the demands of the hypnotic fantasy. Thus, a husband may suffer his wife's extramarital affairs to maintain the illusion of unity. She may pursue affairs with other men in the hopes of reactivating an aroused fantasy response in her husband. She may unwittingly reenact a similar fantasy with other men.

The idea here is that the hypnotic set-point will regulate each partner's behavior and emotions, many times against their own best interests (and even against the better interests of the relationship itself). This will be done to service and enhance the illusionary nature of the hypnotic fantasy. It's almost as if keeping the dream alive were more important than the dreamers themselves. He may be out drinking and may spend a great deal of time working. His wife may care for the home and children, working part time. They rarely see each other. She may be assured of his provider status, keeping her fantasy of marriage and home alive. He may feel he's doing his duty, putting in his time at work, keeping the marriage going. He rewards himself by hitting the bars and having a few drinks. Clearly neither partner is enjoying this "fantasy" as they fight constantly when together.

The concept of imagining and fantasizing is really a hallmark of hypnosis. Unfortunately, the quality of the hypnotic, addictive relationship also seems to involve fantasizing. It involves imagining without any of the real sharing, investing, or building between two partners in the reality of everyday living. It might be added that hypnosis or hypnotic-like qualities have their healthier, more generative fruitful qualities in relationships that are loving. In their healthier hypnotic version, the quality of fantasizing and imagining involves genuine suggestions of bringing that dream to real life, not just dreaming dreams.

Such quality maintains integrity in enhancing each individual's sense of self and self-esteem. Hypnotic qualities can work together to help couples build a shared and loving sense of mutual give and take. It encourages growth among both individuals in a framework of an ever-expanding relationship. They continue to share in open ways. This allows them to grow as individuals within the framework of that relationship. Their relationship is open-ended and large enough to allow for personal growth and the growth of their relationships with others. This can happen without losing integrity of their sense of oneness together. The very hypnotic qualities that can destroy an entranced relationship, when harnessed through trance mastery, nurture healthy intimacy.

PATTERNS OF ENTRANCEMENT

In the entranced, addictive relationship, there is little sense of openness where partners can grow, prosper, or feel loving and intimate together. Sharing their relationship threatens each other with the outside world. It becomes an either/or proposition. They are either totally possessive and control one another, or they have little or no contact with each other as they separate into their own worlds. It is a highly closed, rigid relationship which may have the appearance of being loose and open but is actually quite limited. It is what we call a closed rather than open system. It is in this type of constricting relationship where two people discover themselves in a death grip.

Partners may feel entwined and go through periods of erotic numbness. If they do not do this, they will die. They have not yet learned how to master their personal trance experiences as loving, problem-solving adults to forge a loving relationship with its own identity. They rely on a fragile, emotional, and sensually charged exotic encounter as a substitute for genuine intimacy, feeling they have to cut off part of themselves to be free of the other. No wonder there is such a fear of loss!

For entranced couples, their core space is where dreams have turned to nightmares. They experience their core as a hole filled with nothing but emptiness. Entranced couples fear their core character is bleak nothingness and flee to their fantasy ideal, which only perpetuates such a sense of nothingness. Contrasting entranced relationships with healthier ones along the lines of hypnotic dimensions is similar to the figure-ground reversal of Escher (1989) art. The viewer's perspective of which pattern of the picture is seen in the foreground or the background will determine what is perceived to be real. The point is that contrasting entranced relationships to healthy ones demonstrates that hypnotic qualities are always at work. It only depends on which pattern (entranced or healthy) is perceived (and therefore utilized) to be in the foreground or background as to whether hypnotic qualities are helpful or destructive to an intimate relationship.

Parallel dynamics and phenomena of the hypnotic experience can be seen in entrancing relationships. Partners prepare themselves for romance with endearing dream talk. Pondering scenes of romance and listening to music lay the groundwork for induction (or seduction). These experiences are similar to the hypnotic, pretalk stage. The actual induction of entrancement can rapidly occur from the impact of the initial encounter. It can also happen over time where partners gradually "recognize" (or re-cognitize as in reconceptualize the other into their own, hypnotically ideal, image) their entrancing rapture and idealization of one another. There may be an initial surge of energy as mind, body, spirit, and environment begin to merge and fuse within and between partners.

Partners begin to merge physical stimuli with imagery and idealization of what they internally construct this physical stimuli to mean. For example, he sees her red hair, slim body features, and hears her self-assured commentary. He then constructs imagined scenarios of a ravishingly beautiful and powerfully classy lady he may have been waiting for all his life. His very construction is the absorbing internal dream that is parallel to the hypnotist's inducing dreamlike scenarios in his clients.

In the case of the addictive relationship, there is no one there to monitor how deep or beneficial such dreamlike states will be. Partners begin their runaway hypnotic dreams fueled by wild, erotic, and child-like imagery, idealizing their perfect partner based on personal attributes and past learning. They superimpose the physical attributes and inner imagery of who they construe their partner to be with idealized dream partners. They think they really know what they have in their partner. Yet these images and attributes are a camouflage for the true character structure of the "real" partner that remains hidden and untouched.

THE EVOLUTIONARY CONNECTION: ATTRACTION AND BEAUTY, HARD-WIRED IN

Remember that the relationship you are in has a creative logic that is, at times, hypnotic (trance logic). It doesn't have a commonsense logic. The relationship bond has nothing to do with any kind of logical, cognitive rationality. Rather, it has an irrational, mind-body cognition (sensory awareness) all its own that is connected to the dysfunctional condition as if you were trying to understand the logic of a dream. This is usually what hypnotically induced, addictive relationships are all about. In working through emerging mind/body images and sensations to understand and resolve relationship programs, it is powerfully re-sourceful to access the hypnotic, "irrational" logic of the relationship. In understanding such trance logic, it is important to remember that much of entranced learning is based on sensory stimuli and fantasized imag-ining fused with this stimuli.

Recent studies by Singh (1993) have suggested that men are predis-posed to become sensorially stimulated and intensely focused with cer-tain female physical proportions. For example, women who have a .7 ratio of waist to hips (27-inch waist to 38-inch hips) attract more men. The perceptual-neurological-hormonal connection is hard-wired into men, which feeds right into intense fixations and fantasizing. This heightens the probability of inducing and creating entranced relation-ships. Such hard-wired-in mechanisms of attraction and beauty have been further demonstrated in infant studies (Morris, 1997). Groups of infants were shown two types of pictures of both men and women. One type of picture illustrated men and women with symmetrical features in the cheeks, jaw, and overall facial structure. The other illustrated men and women with asymmetrical features.

The findings of the study were quite revealing. All groups of infants immediately smiled, made cooing sounds, and attended longer to pic-tures of men and women with symmetrical features. The same infants had shorter attention spans and no smiling or cooing to pictures of men and women with asymmetrical features. Infants by definition are too young and inexperienced to be significantly influenced at that age by social and/or cultural determinants of attraction and beauty. The interpretation is quite intriguing. Symmetrical features were cross-culturally regarded as attractive and asymmetrical features as unattractive.

The interpretation of the results suggests that there can be a hard-wired-in neurobiological basis for what is considered attraction and beauty between human beings. Such attraction and beauty between people is not always socially or culturally determined but may well be built into our very evolution and genetics. Evolution may have selected symmetrical features in men and women as prehistorically indicative of higher success rates in child-bearing and longevity of offspring.

The consequences of such a hard-wired basis for attraction and beauty is that it only serves to enhance and intensify entrancing forces already operational between partners. Learning to deal with and master the experience of mature relationships calls for the recognition that powerful energies and forces are operating beyond simple conscious, rational control of our intimacies. We need to appreciate how the mind-body connection of each partner begins to create and fabricate illusions and entrancements based on obsessive fixations of select features of the "other" and the quality of the relationship itself. Without reality checks and guidance it becomes a runaway system.

Partners have a responsibility to learn to master these neurobiological energies of entrancement through consciousness raising functions of a heart-centered value (true love is the love of truth) of personal integrity (Welwood, 1990). The illusion of willpower, rational logic, and ego control appears to fail miserably in the face of entrancement.

Partners may think they are in control of what's happening in the relationship. Yet they may well be responding to powerful sensory experiences of a very automatic, evolutionary nature. As the relationship progresses, they discover that what they are pursuing now pursues them. They find themselves drawn into their partner with the subjective feeling of "Gee whiz, at what point did I lose control?" They have lost relationship of "I" creating self-experience. Like a detached retina, the "I" is disconnected from a passionate vision of cause and effect. It appears to partners as if the cause of what is happening is coming from the outside. This misdirected quality is similar to hypnosis. Such similarities suggest that entrancement parallels hypnotic experience (see Figure 2.4).

Figure 2.4
Parallels of Entrancing Addictive Relationships (EAR) and Hypnosis

EAR		Hypnosis
I.	Eye-catching allure of arousing partner (also blinking or batting one's eyes at the other).	Eye fixation (focused stare at a point on the wall; eye-flutter is also a sign of trance).
II.	Partner begins to block out surrounding events when sees his or her ideal partner.	Narrowing of attention.
III.	Partner may feel sensations of arousal, heart palpitations, tingling sensation, and rushes of emotionalized imagery.	Sensory awareness and imagery intensification of relaxation/excitement spreading throughout the body, depending on imagery of a calm scene or stimulating one (riding a roller coaster).
IV.	Partner perceives his or her arousal to be caused by that beautiful partner just encountered, not his or her inner idealization. More distracted from self-awareness of what is actually happening.	Misattribution of cause and effect distraction of what is creating the sensory experience. Subject may misperceive that it's the hypnotist's suggestion for eye-closure rather than his own fatigue of staring that makes his eyes close.
V.	Partner feels somewhat swept away in a relaxed pleasurable euphoria while attending to ideal partner.	Physical sensations of relaxation and letting go of ego controls.
VI.	Partner experiences increasing sensory and physical arousals of an erotic and compelling nature.	Deepening and spreading of sensory absorption and intensity. Experiences of imagery seem more and more intense and lifelike.
VII.	Partner feels drawn into a dreamlike state of his or her fantasy ideal with the alluring partner.	Imagery and visualization of memories, achievements, dreams, and/or fantasies becomes more prominent.
VIII.	Partner experiences a coming together of the other partner's alluring physical attributes and how it fits the "perfect" partner ideal.	Mind-body enmeshment of physical sensations with cognitive distortions and imagery.

IX.	Partner gets caught up in image or symbol of what his ideal partner represents (with her bright-eyed, bubbly personality and beautiful blond hair means she must be as pure as an angel.	Symbolic thinking in images and fantasies while limited in objective problem solving. Symbols of past family members can be imaged and identified with the hypnotist.
X.	Fantasizing of partner in idealistic images and scenarios (having perfect lives together, always loyal and true to one another, happily ever after).	Use of imagery and fantasy to create altered states of reality (visualizations of pleasurable childhood dreams and experiences).
XI.	Partner experiences rush of negative emotions in enmeshed contact (loss, abandonment, betrayal, all-or-nothing reality of either perfection or disaster).	Release of emotionally blocked negativity through intense association of inner sensations (anger, hurt, guilt).
XII.	Partner loses track of daily tasks, self-care, etc. Diminishing attention paid to everyday situations.	Fading of general reality orientation.
XIII.	Partners lose track of time when together (time seems to stand still or lasts forever).	Time distortion (five minutes can seem like five hours or vice versa).
XIV.	Partners get together, pull away, only to become more intense and absorbed with each encounter, which can seem "new" and like meeting for the first time.	Fractionation (repetitively going in and out of trance). With each cycle, trance deepens more and more.
XV.	Whatever happens to partners is experienced as affecting and being affected by the relationship (if one partner has a bad day or not feeling up, the whole relationship can suffer).	Utilization in trance (everything that happens in the induction and deepening is included in the procedure; your head has dropped and that means you're going deeper and deeper).

(continued)

XVI.	Partners lose mature sense of judgment in making intelligent decisions and solving problems in relationships (overreact or make mountains out of molehills in their conflicts).	Loss of critical faculties and judgment where subject begins to amplify feelings of tension, relaxation, happiness, or sadness without rational, logical assessment.
XVII.	Partners feel that they , are compelled to be together, act impulsively, say or do things to and with each other and not know why (become enraged, enamored, or indifferently cold).	Involuntary control with experience of feeling detached or watching sensory or imaginary events happening on their own (arm catalepsy).
XVIII.	Partners seem to act and feel like kids in highly emotionalized pleasure/pain scenarios (she loves me, she loves me not).	Regression of adult level of functioning to childlike states.
XIX.	Partners exaggerate and get overwhelmed at minor irritations and infractions in the relationship. These seem larger than life.	Distortion and magnification of reality events (subjects can magnify cool sensations into frozen ones or warmth into blisters).
XX.	Partners lose perspective and clear thinking ability as a result of sensory and emotional overload. Beliefs take on magical qualities (we are meant to be together at all costs; I can make this relationship work no matter what happens).	Cognitive distortions of thoughts and beliefs in nonreality based directions (I can leap tall buildings at a single bound).
XXI.	Partners may distort reality so severely as to create images of what they actually experience as real (seeing partners as their prince charming and/or source of betrayal in visualizing or "seeing" them cheating).	Hallucinations: positive and negative (subjects can create unique imagery such as their arms are wings and they are now able to fly like a bird; they can also image that they are an awakened head with no body attached).

XXII.	Partners are quite suggestible to each other. Even when apart and temporarily "outside" the relationship, things the other one said stay with them and are remembered (how terrible life will be without you). This creates compulsive thinking such as, "I wonder what he/she meant by that."	Posthypnotic suggestions (subjects can be given posthypnotic suggestions for how sick to their stomach they will feel if they see a fattening food).
XXIII.	Partner feels healed or damaged by the "magical" touch, kiss, or rejection of the other.	Hypnotic events convey a magical quality of happening without causal agent (happening by themselves).
XXIV.	Partners are intensely absorbed and fused with their fantasy ideals of one another.	Absorption: self involvement and total concentration of attention on beliefs of achievement.
XXV.	Partners have the experience that they are both intimately absorbed and fused to each other. Yet they are able to observe themselves acting in fantastical and extremely extraordinary ways (adult partners watch themselves act and feel desperately involved with each other in ways that surprise and even shock them, such as spending exorbitant money, time, and concentration on the relationship).	Dissociation; watching self while acting and thinking in sensory and symbolic images. Subjects engage in split or parallel awareness of two or more states of consciousness.
XXVI.	Entranced partners install messages in one another to forget (amnesia) how painful their interaction is when apart by suggesting, "Just remember how wonderful he or she really is and forget how abusive we treat each other."	Posthypnotic suggestions for amnesia can be given to intensify trance phenomena in the subject's life situation when out of hypnosis.

(continued)

XXVII. Entranced partners experience intensive reliving of romantic times, places, and emotionalized events which are compartmentalized in romantic states.	Hyperamnesia or vigilance of vivid, detailed memory recall while in state-dependent trance.

In trance induction, the classic technique of waving a watch in front a patient's face implies that the watch is somehow going to make him or her go into trance. Prolonged attention to watch waving induces eye movement and fatigue. As the person's eyes get tired, the hypnotist's suggestions of "closing your eyes" creates the illusion that the cause of eye closure comes from the hypnotist and the watch. In reality, eye closure is coming from the person attending to the watch, which causes the eyes to tire and therefore close. The eye movement accesses sensory representational systems in the brain (James and Woodsmall, 1988) (visual, auditory, and kinesthetic) and primary processing of information, all of which increases susceptibility to suggestion for eye closure. Yet the person attributes and reframes involuntary eye closure to outside experiences and causes (to the hypnotist's power of command).

This type of illusion of control and shift from voluntary to involuntary focus is similar in quality to addictive relationships. These types of relationships have a fantastical imagery that induces mental and physical stimuli (draining energy, causing fatigue, and eventual compliance to fantasy pulls). Self-suggestive messages such as "This must be the beautiful woman of my dreams, anyone with such beautiful hair must be an angel" are now accepted. Partners feel butterflies in their stomach and can hardly wait to be together. Each has such a power over the other. Such comments indicate loss of contact with one's internal reality. In reality, these comments and feelings are our internal responses to our own idealized images that we are attributing to someone else. The source of these responses is actually coming from internal, self-programming.

Such self-misdirection and shift of attention to the other person causes a great deal of illusion (and illness) for ourselves. In this "self-hypnotic" experience, partners are entrancing themselves and entering into a trancelike, self-induced state by our own "magical thinking and illusion building imagery." We self-hallucinate an idealistic identity quality of our partner. It is self-induced, self-imposed. What we attribute to our partner actually resides in ourselves. Yet it is deep, buried, and out of our conscious reach except when we are entranced with our partners. Entrancing encounters can also elicit unconscious activation of each partner's own unique ideals, senses, and abilities within themselves. Yet partners may be blind to their own unique, personal characteristics, misattributing them instead to their entranced partner. In entrancement, individuals may not realize that the ideals they see in their partners actually reside within themselves.

As a consequence, the hypnotic dream partners have of one another may originate from their own unconscious dream for themselves. Even powerful, erotic associations that partners attribute to each other echo this hidden connection of self-ideals misattributed and externalized to the significant other. Erotic entrancement and seduction of the significant other partner suggest a self-seduction and compromise of one's own unique character.

Notice that in hypnosis the subject is asked to go deep into trance to have a hypnotic dream of some therapeutic or other beneficial experience. This may involve a dream of greeting a loved one, achieving relief from stress by envisioning a calm, peaceful scene, or imaging themselves as achieving wonderful outcomes. Ironically, every part of their hypnotic dream is actually a hidden manifestation of some part of their unique self.

This is identical to what occurs in a partner's dream of fantasy ideals. In addictive relationships, there is a dreamlike state where individuals appear to go into a sleeplike state. They are unwittingly attending to their unconscious associations of their "dream girl" or "dream boy." They begin to live that dream in what we call the "waking state." They think they are awake, but are in fact in a trance with their eyes open. Some people have referred to this experience as lucid dreaming, which is where one is "awake in their dreams." It is almost as if their relationship is a real dream. It seems real while they are in that dream. It is actually a hypnotic dream they are having at an unconscious level. Partners do not realize how deeply they are involved in this fantasy. They act as if their ideal dream is quite real. This is where they have lost their hold on a mature grip of reality. They are accessing what we would call a regressed state with childlike or even infantile needs. Many times, as in hypnosis, there is a form of age regression. The individual tends to go back to earlier times, earlier experiences, and even earlier needs that are more childlike in nature. Partners can become children to one another, having little access to critical faculties of judgment and problem-solving skills.

As the hypnotist regresses his client, so the entranced addictive relationship regresses both partners. Such regression is to a level of a childlike state. Inner and earlier childlike needs are reawakened. Primitive fantasies are evoked. Longings for that perfect love, that harmony, that blissful Garden of Eden experience, that sense of innocence, purity, and harmony are all part of the regression. There is a nurturant sense of womblike oneness reawakened by the hypnotic dream that emerges out of regression. It is important to remember how innate these core needs are. When they are activated, it is all too easy to attribute these normal human needs to our partner. That is, we misattribute our core nurturing needs for "mothering" to the mistaken notion that we have a core need for our partner (I can't live without you). It is also very powerful to notice that there is a sense of time distortion.

What this means is that hypnotic entrancements age-regress partners to earlier childhood levels of functioning (the lower part of the brain known as reptilian that is highly sensory but lacks cognitive maturity is activated in trance). Partners experience early emotional needs for primary parent figures because of this hypnotic entrancement, but do not recognize this within themselves (don't see that it is their internal entrancement that arouses neediness). They instead misattribute this activated, regressed neediness for care and attention onto their entranced partner. The significant other partner now is perceived to be both the cause and the curative source of nurturing gratification. Through hypnotic regression, the entranced relationship has created a time distortion where past image (nurturing mother) has now merged with present image (entranced significant other partner). Thus the other partner takes on such importance that partners feel they can't leave home without them or terrible abandonment will occur.

Time distortion has a powerful impact on a romantic relationship. Individuals can spend a weekend together and to them it can seem like an eternity. Indeed, these can be very wonderful experiences in healthy relationships. Unfortunately, in the addictive relationship these become lost weekends. When they emerge, partners have a sense of emptiness, a sense of abandonment, and a sense of impoverishment as if they have no self in which to return. Time seems to stand still or be frozen at the same point from where the relationship begins repeating itself. The euphoria of first encounter, as mentioned earlier, is stuck and never quite gets past a certain state of development. Consequently, time seems to run out too quickly when together and too slowly when apart. Partners in addictive relationships lose track of how much time is invested waiting for those few, fleeting precious moments of erotic encounters. Time distortion prevents the individuals from realizing the vast amounts of empty time wasted for such minimal returns. The combination of losing track of time and misattributing core needs generates a powerful and absorbing entrancement. No wonder these couples have such a hard time resurfacing and rediscovering their "I-self" relationship.

There is also a narrowing and a closing of attention. As in hypnosis, fixation and selective concentration require that individuals disconnect from the larger picture. They attend to intense, unique experiences. In addictive relationships, the individuals tend to isolate from the outside world. They too tend to feel that their relationship "just happens" by itself as both feel pulled in.

Ironically, their fixation progresses to such an extent that eventually they isolate even from themselves. Their absorption continues to shrink their worlds. They see fantastical, illusionary qualities in each other. She may have beautiful eyes and sparkling red hair. He may have a wonderful mustache and dark, ravenlike eyes. The two of them fixate on the parts of the physical sensory and illusionary charisma of one another. They are so entranced by one another's nuances that they do not see the whole character of the person in front of them. They have disassociated the personality traits, sensory allure, and illusionary charisma of one another from the total character of the person.

There is also a sense of parallel awareness. The hypnotist induces the subject to both visualize hallucinations and observe him- or herself do this at the same time. The effect is created that the subject is in two places (both hallucinating and observing this process) at the same time. A partner once said to his friend how amazed he was to see himself worry mindlessly over the other's possible infidelities; he knew it was a waste of time, yet he did it anyway.

Partners in addictive relationships almost have to pinch themselves to believe that their experiences are real. Yet pinching may not serve to awaken or validate their romantic interludes. In trance, individuals can be pinched for extremely long periods of time quite severely and not feel a thing. As in addictive relationships, the individuals are so absorbed, fixated, and disconnected into their experiences that they feel none of the real pain involved. It is a very numbing experience. Indeed, the addictive relationship has that powerful narcotic effect which is actually a hypnotic, analgesic fixation and absorption. That is, such intense absorption and fixation becomes a powerful painkiller. Entrancement distracts from painful reality (temporarily) and induces euphoria. This is actually the enmeshed quality of that "lost weekend" type of an addictive relationship.

Additionally, as in hypnosis, individuals who are in deep trance can hallucinate a vast range of images: people they miss, lost loved ones, and even experience riding in the front seat of a roller coaster. Such hallucinations can be seen in stage hypnosis where individuals act out roles of actually being able to think they can speak Japanese or have walked on the moon. They can negatively hallucinate acting as if their arm is missing, or that they cannot remember their last name.

These capacities of negative hallucination in hypnotic trance are also present in individuals with a history of severe mental and/or physical abuse. Negative hallucinations and other mental forms of disconnection from personal experience tend to occur with greater frequency among abusively treated partners. They act as if it had never happened. This makes it hard to confront the reality of the relationship. There could be severe verbal and physical battles followed by acting as though it never happened the next minute.

These experiences are negatively hallucinated and filtered out through trancelike somnolescence of deepened hypnosis. Abusive experiences are disconnected and disassociated through intense, fixated absorption on the internal sensations of the hypnotic dream. It is this very absorption into the dream which recreates the negated abusive nightmare. Extreme versions of this dissociation occur when partners are not together for two to three months at a time. They may have sexual relations with other partners, stating they are "out of love" with each other. They may think if only they could get together again, all would be forgiven. They negatively hallucinate the reality of their sexual liaisons, saying they do not count. They may argue or hurt inside, yet they always keep the dream memories alive (of something that never existed or was not genuinely allowed to exist for long).

The perverse nature of this "in" and "out" love experience is the very nature of going in and out of trance. Yet, being out of trance doesn't mean they are outside the influence of posthypnotic suggestions. They may be out of trance temporarily, but they have not fully awakened to their true self. As such, they may transfer their absorbing qualities to other partners when temporarily out of touch with each other. They may come back to their original partner but they are prone to drifting from one intense partner or experience of a partner to another. Partners are interchangeable like toy Legos simply filling in empty spaces. So long as the intense, absorbing entrancement is there, so is that partner. When trance goes, so will the partner if that is all that is there.

There can also be positive hallucination in the addictive relationship as the individuals begin to reassociate to the fantasy, and reidealize one another after the most abusive experiences. In a hypnotically induced addictive relationship, the fixation is on maintaining the illusionary fantasy of the ideal relationship that has bonded and buttressed both partners into a very binding, restrictive, enslaving, hypnotic dream. Any deviation from this dream, which is bound to occur, creates nightmarish horrors and demons of abandonment, loneliness, loss of control, and annihilation. Partners positively hallucinate (imagine they have a perfect, lovely, ideal bond) and return to recreating that magical quality of how beautiful their relationship is. It may never, in fact, have existed or have any manifest substance, yet the two of them will insist on the reality of their memories. It is as if people hallucinate memories that never actually happened in quite that way. This is the quality of the addictive relationship in its hypnotic form.

Memories can be distorted, deleted, or manufactured in trance experiences as a symbolic representation of present unhappiness. Partners can regress to early childhood memories of hurt, loss, and anger as a reflection of here-and-now relationship entrancements. The present can distort past recollections.

Partners will entrance both their outer experience of each other and the setting with their own internal representations. This involves the ideal matches and associations which self-select themselves inside partners' fantasies to reconstrue (or misconstrue, "miss what's true") in what their partner is all about. This ignites and merges selective qualities and parts of each other. They fuse selective physical and personality attributes (beauty and charisma) with their ideal picture of what their partner should be (and now is in their fantasizing mind). Their mind "reasons" that if their partner has these features, then it must mean that this is the one for me. This "if-then" pattern of thinking is quite hypnotic. Fusion of selective physical and personality attributes in entrancement evokes trance logic in perception and interpretation of what is meaningful.

Partners begin to imagine themselves more and more together, which is similar to moderate levels of trance. As they continue through the entrancement, they usually will experience more of a personal reality to this imagery of togetherness in the form of physical feelings of being together (whether they actually are or not). This subjective sense of fused togetherness can become more and more expansive and pervasive throughout each partner's daily routine. This is a sign of deep trance levels. Eventually, partners deepen to a euphoric, dreamlike quality of their ever-idealized connection or bond.

It is at this point that partners cross over into the land of entrancement. Instead of seeking to integrate the comparative differences and similarities of each partner's ideal contrasted with what's real, they collapse and compress the "reality" of each other into an ideal fixation. This fixation is now each partner's personal reference point for their subjective sense of what's "really real." When our subjective sense of what's real is intensely fused and confused with what we objectively sense is real "out there," we call this state a waking dream.

At this stage of entrancement, there is neither the sense of a partner's being uniquely him- or herself nor having a choice over who he or she really wants to be or not to be. Partners are simply submerged into fixations of dreaming about what's "real" and are actually dreaming or creating illusions of who their partner is to be to fulfill the fantasy.

When there are dreamlike qualities manifesting themselves in entrancing bonds, these are signs that the relationship has hit the dream-sleep level of trance. These dreamlike manifestations are experienced as a sense of "unrealness" where partners are seeking to be together. They can't quite put their finger on it (because there may be nothing of substance there to touch). It's the experience of "I have to pinch myself to see if this is really happening to me!" When partners go to work, engage in conversation, or are out on a date together, there is an odd sense that "We are in the same physical place." Yet partners feel vaguely detached and out of touch with themselves, with what is happening, or who they naturally, really are. There may be the opposite extreme where all the partners' senses are heightened and exaggerated so that even a simple walk in the mall takes on larger-than-life magnitudes of significance and importance. There may also be the sense of stepping into some set character or role where an individual almost sees himself or herself play out some act as if in a movie. These are all indications of dream sleep, the deepest of hypnotic levels.

The consideration of entrancement as a dysfunctional, hypnotic experience is suggested in professional, diagnostic references. Entrancement corresponds to the criteria of a trance state where there are temporary, marked alterations in the state of a person's consciousness. Partners in entrancement may feel that there is a partial or complete distortion of what it means to be themselves. Partners may feel like something has taken them over or possessed them because of how unusually emotional and intense their feelings and behaviors are. They may feel alterations in states of consciousness.

Have you ever known anyone "possessed" by love where they felt compelled to be or act in a way that challenged their everyday identity? Partners experiencing such unusual emotional altered states vaguely remember how or why they acted in such a manner. Partners are so enthralled and lost in absorption of one another that they lose track of time at work, ignore friendships, and forget responsibilities.

Entranced partners actually feel their own personal identity seriously compromised to the point of nonexistence. This can create fear, panic, and chaos in the experience. This also can create perverse passion.

Entrancing couples journey progressively through a deepening process. Their relationship progresses through deepening stages that parallel hypnosis (induction, deepening, and dream-sleep levels of trance). This deepening process through various hypnotic levels will be evident as we explore the nuances of entrancement states.

Couples will temporarily appear to come out of their entrancement. Basking in their heart-pounding experiences of idealized love, they awaken with the wondrous afterglow of newlyweds on their honeymoon. This ratifies their entrancement. They experience involuntary feelings of uncontrollable urges, compelling them to reunite and resubmerge ever deeper in their renewed entrancement. Notice honeymooners that seem almost love-struck. The morning after their first night together leaves them with that glassy-eyed daze as if they are still dreaming in the daylight. This afterglow readies them for the next, even more intensified, encounter. Entranced partners experience this honeymoon period, which initially serves to deepen their entrancement. They have deeper, intense periods, relax, lighten up, and then become even more enraptured with their next encounter with each other.

The hypnotist brings the subject out of trance only to put him or her back into trance at an even deeper level than before. The entranced ideal temporarily goes on hold only to be reignited to an even deeper level of absorption. While it may appear that subjects come out of entrancement, the posthypnotic suggestiveness of euphoria and wonder urges them to want more. What is this strange and unusual reality that beckons them? Remember, it is this very strangeness and wonder that is really part of the trance experience itself. Yet entranced partners may be quite unaware as their conscious thinking and attention span have been all but eliminated for anything else but their enmeshment.

In time, idealization gives way to disillusionment, which propels couples to deepen and recycle even further in pursuing their elusive butterfly--their ideal, fantasy partner. There is this spiraling downward recycling through the levels. Each time partners go through their idealizations and conflicts of eventual disappointments, they become even more absorbed and embroiled. They feel they cannot "not" be absorbed.

They obsess about and finally reproach one another until their sense of reality collides with the entranced depths of despair. They can feel as if they have lost most, if not all, sense of self. Their romantic ideals of one another have all but been completely shattered. They may wander aimlessly in an ever-deepening sea of worries, conflicts, feared losses, and longing for their elusive perfection of ideal love. They can develop a sadness and embittered rage for this paradise lost.

The recovery stage is the genuine posthypnotic awakening from this nightmarish dream sleep. It involves detrancing and true awakening. Hypnosis itself usually involves coming out of trance with posthypnotic suggestions for change. Genuine awakening involves elimination of all posthypnotic suggestions for enmeshment. The danger is if this cleaning out of suggestions does not occur, then when entranced couples separate the relationship could continue, with each longing and left wanting for the ideal of the other. It is almost like what amputees feel who have lost a leg but can still feel it in some special way, which is called the phantom limb phenomena. So for trance, even when the formal trance is ended, there are posthypnotic suggestions that keep the feelings alive long after trance ends. We could call this programming. The relationship (and the trance) can continue long after the formal appearance has ended. Partners may think they can control how close or far they are, only to discover they fall right back together even deeper.

That is why it is so important to completely awaken and detrance from this entranced programming. We need to transform our lives according to that self-hypnotic process of being true to our own inner purpose sensing our unique self. This sense of unique self is referred to as unique motif. That set of unique qualities that conveys each person's special core and nature has an artistry of its own. Such a unique artistry is referred to as a sensory motif. This parallel of awakening from entrancement in both hypnosis and addictive relationships appears to be one and the same. As we awaken, we discover our own self-hypnotic transformation through that inner character and motif which has been referred to as the "unlived life."

   This recovery stage is where the individual comes out of trance with various hypnotic, self-affirming suggestions. Self-hypnosis for transformation is installed at this point. While it is true that all hypnosis is self-hypnosis, the reawakening stage empowers and educates the subject in taking personal control for this process. Unfortunately, addicted partners are constantly "self-inducing" entrancement with one another. The process is controlling them as they are lost in their own self-imposing imagery and don't know it or how to control it.

   It is clear that addictive relationships appear to follow a hypnotic format. The progression and stages of addictive relationships parallel those of the hypnotic process. Again, I define addictive relationships as those where there is a narrow, highly absorbed closed focus where partners become absorbed not on one another enjoying themselves in the relationship but on how they should, ought, or must be to maintain the fantasy ideal. Partners can exert pressure on each other to talk a certain way (do not mention other people's names) and obsess over each other's small deviations from idealized behavior (one wants to be alone for awhile).

   Such absorption creates a fixation and a rigid kind of imagining about what their ideal relationship ought to be. The resulting contrast of the ideal compared to real-life experiences energizes the addictive thrust in the first place. The gap between the ideal and the real results in a conflicting tension that entranced partners resolve by losing more of themselves in enmeshment. Indeed, enmeshment is exactly what begins to happen in an addictive relationship where two people are not really sharing themselves with one another. There is no sense of oneness or shared relationship. They don't share their unique interests and talents in the relationship. Rather, they seem to lose themselves in one another's hallucination, unable to discover more of who they really can be.

   It is important to understand the severity of how engrossed and enmeshed partners can become in these hallucinations. In this enmeshment, symptoms emerge in the suggestible (as in hypnotically suggestible) partner who is being influenced by the dominant or aggressive partner. The passive partner will have had a long-standing enmeshed, submissive relationship with the more dominant partner. The theme of persecution and need to respond to a perceived shared threat from the outside world permeates the relationship. The hallucinations and other symptoms serve to further isolate the couple and intensify the enmeshment. When the partner is removed from the influence of the entranced enmeshment, the delusional beliefs and symptoms will spontaneously fade in time.

Entranced bonds operate in quite similar ways. Both partners develop a delusion and paranoia of "outside forces" (both in their milieu and themselves), seeking to destroy their perfect love and illusion of oneness. Even times of naturally being themselves can be perceived as threatening their own fantasy bubble. One partner may have an innate desire for exploring the mysterious and unknown but be chastised by the other for taking risks. The other partner may accuse her of asking for trouble, running the risk of rape, and violating their bond. Many entranced couples act out and rebel at their own delusions and fantasies of this "perfect love." This only serves to heighten and "prove" the "real" dangers threatening their perfect love. They become self-threatening, a real danger to the illusionary "self" of the relationship. They tighten the controls and enmeshed isolation even further. Extracting partners from this "psychotic" entrancement means true reawakening from the trance. The threats of so-called outside forces usually originate from within the partners themselves, subtly pressing to assert their real self.

In a healthy relationship, there are real people. There is the "you," there is the "I," there is the "we." In the addictive relationship, there is actually no one person present. It is neither "you" nor "I" as the "you" or "I" is a pure hallucination/fantasy of the illusionary "self." There certainly is not a "we" because to have a "we" implies there has to be two healthy, unique individuals to begin to share that third quality of relatedness and bondedness. There is a lost self seeking confirmation in the other. This is similar to the hypnotic subject seeking guidance from the hypnotist. Indeed, Martin Buber (1958) in his profound book *I and Thou* talks about the I-thou relationship where the "I", the "thou" (which is of course is "you") and the hyphen between the I and thou which is the relationship. In the addictive relationship, there is no real encounter or hyphen as there is no relatedness between two unique people. There is an enmeshment of one person into the other and vice versa. It is a fusion of parts and attributes selectively combined to create the illusion of a whole relationship. It's as if we took pieces from different puzzles that had the same shape at one end and tried to make a whole, meaningful picture out of it. How do you solve a puzzle when you're not playing with all the pieces?

It is not the sense of two people sharing their worlds. It's rather having one person's world shoved down the other person's throat or vice versa. Of course, there are varying degrees of this. It is not an all-or-nothing experience in terms of the degree to which this quality of shared versus "shovedness," if you will, operates in various relationships. In the classical addictive relationship, the primary emphasis is focused not on a relationship but on a relegation of one person subjected to the other person's will and vice versa. Both people feel (or will feel) essentially ripped off, betrayed, discouraged, and unrequited as a result. This unfortunately tends to be a hallmark of many romantic songs, stories, and at times the classical Romeo and Juliet version of chronic misunderstandings and confusions between two loves.

The individuals in the situations described discover that their liberation comes not by eliminating the hypnotic quality but by utilizing that hypnotic quality. They learn to access and articulate their own self-hypnotic discovery of their unique character as indicated in the recovery stage. This is the inner motif of their own exciting, invigorating flow state of self. They discover their own unique purposes, interests, joys, and fascinations. They can become "hypnotized," if you will, or hypnotically involved with their need to genuinely be themselves. Such a need is to express their own true nature or artistry, which I call their motif. They discover the love within themselves to bring this motif to life. This is the hallmark of what we call utilization where that which seems to cause the problem becomes a resource that resolves it.

The initial hypnotic stage of pretalk presents what is, ideally, to happen in the hypnotic induction. Pretalk parallels the initial impact of addictive encounters. Addictive relationships have this quality of idealization and fantasizing of the significant other. Partners "pretalk" themselves into absorbing how wonderful their partner is developing a certain attraction or idealized fixation. They talk to each other and themselves in a preparatory way, orienting and fixating one another in an inductive involvement. Now begins the orienting and planning stages of how they will "fall" in love without realization. Partners embark on one whale of a roller-coaster ride. It is imperative to understand that this ride places them at risk of losing their sense of self.

In the swirling energy of their whirlwind entrancement, there is a temporary suspension of each partner's sense of time and reality regarding day-to-day routines, as is typical of trance behavior. To grasp this sense of lost self it is necessary to discover each partner's core character of sensory motif.

CHAPTER 3

TRANSFORMING MOTIFS

ARTISTIC FORMULATIONS

The hypnotic framework of entrancing, addictive relationships emphasizes the potency with which hypnotic dynamics influence couples.
Thus far it may appear that partners are like sailboats being blown cha-
otically about at the mercy of these forces of nature. However, such is
certainly not the real state of affairs.

Imagine the motion of a spinning gyroscope. After winding string
around the center rod and pulling, the inner spinning wheel keeps it up-
right. Whether it is held in the palm of the hand or on the tip of a pencil,
it sustains its position and orientation for the length of time the spin
lasts. Human beings also may have their own, unique spin and gyroscopic movement that keeps them on some life course, resilient against
outside influences. This unique inner gyroscopic movement having its
own unique signature is what I have termed the sensory motif.

Artists have motifs in the way they move their paintbrush or sculpt a
statue. It is the unique artistic movement and design that allows us to
distinguish a Picasso from a Michelanglo. Each has his own motif.
Motifs are not static. They evolve and shift, as exemplified by evolving
states of Picasso's or Chagall's work.

Each individual human being is actually a marvelously unique, artistic motif with his or her own movement, way of being, possessing a
unique signature of self. It is that inner movement of motif that gives
such gyroscopic stability and structural design in anchoring individuals
on their life course. The inner movement of such a gyroscopic motif is

actually a signature and formulation (having some uniquely personal pattern and/or design that manifested itself as a highly individualized shape and form) of each human being's core self.

Such a signature of self is illustrated in unique character themes and patterned behaviors persistent throughout the self's developmental stages. Persistence of an organizing motif (the self's signature) developmentally emergent throughout an individual's lifestyle has been suggested by previous studies. Pearce (1985) uses Piaget and Inhelder's (1964) work on early childhood development (concrete to abstract formal operations) suggesting emergence of a postbiological ego identity (Erikson, 1950). Pearce states that this identity emerges through development of sensory-motor connections and emotions toward a fluid mental world of creative power and expression. He notes that this organizing identity exists from the beginning of life but in a latent form that awaits, as a growth blueprint, stage-specific attention and development. He stresses the critical importance of models (motifs) essential for development of this identity blueprint or organizing principle.

Pearce suggests that early developmental learning of language actually occurs in the womb, where small micromuscular movements parallel verbal sounds of the mother. Condon and Sander (1974) found through sophisticated analysis of high-speed sound movies of scores of newborn infants that so-called random movements immediately coordinated with speech when speech was used around the infants. Computer studies verified a complete and individualized repertoire of body movements for each infant synchronized with speech (moving a left elbow slightly on hearing a *k* sound as in *cough* or *cat*). Their studies of older children and adults revealed patterns of synchronization to be permanent and universal. They found movements in adulthood had become microkinetic, detectable only by instrumentation but still unique to each person.

These findings are consistent with other studies (Bernard & Sontag, 1947; Brody & Axelrod, 1970; Klaus, 1972). The only exception to this were autistic children, who showed no body-speech patterning. This exception may only mean suppressed performance of synchronicity, not absence. What is essential about these findings is that the newborn has a distinct, unique repertoire of movements (motif) with the synchronicity occurring within twelve minutes after birth. Pearce accepts the compelling logic that twelve minutes is insufficient time for synchronicity to develop. He therefore suggests that the infant structured this patterned response at some level of design while in the womb. He suggests the drive for this patterning be considered innate. That driving intent (or purpose) within needs only content (stimulation) from the outer environment with which to interact and thus take manifest form and shape. Here is a fundamental example of intent or purpose preceding the ability to "do." This and many other types of in utero learning are documented by Verny and Kelly (1981). This inherently unique structuring character of self emerges in varying degrees of refinement (interdependent on environment, early childhood experiences, physiological conditions, etc.) (Dabrowski, 1967, 1970). Chomsky (1967) proposed that language was innate, built into the genes.

Briggs (1988) reports research on nuances of feeling-tone "themes" in creative people's lives. Below the level of language and cognitions lie the complex nuances or shades of feelings between love and hate that organize events along these themes. Briggs indicates how metaphorical and imagery language could access organized feeling nuances of lifestyle themes that are oversimplified in thoughts and language. It would seem that there is a nonverbal structure or lattice below the level of language and thought with its own set of organizing principles. Jung (1964) referred to the presence of archetypes operating in the self.

This nonverbal structure could be expressed in sensory motifs. Motif is an evolving formation of design. The sensory quality in motifs (visual, auditory, and kinesthetic) serves as a fundamental expression of thematic or symbolic ideas embedded in the motif. The motif's design may first be expressed at the sensory level (a child's attraction to handling and molding clay into bold, colorful shapes and designs). As the motif develops, it can emerge at the emotional level (child's personality begins to become colorful and charismatic, molding and boldly handling life tasks). The motif can then emerge into cognitive and spiritual expressions. These developmental stages parallel the concept of the tribune brain (MacLean, 1973), which depicts developed brain structures that are sensory (reptilian), emotional (limbic), and cognitive (new mammalian).

The preceding material implies that individuals are inherently designed with a motif and intent to harmoniously organize their lives to be healthy and whole. Dabrowski (1967, 1970) and Dabrowski and Piechowski (1977) describe personality development as a progression of five ascending levels. They describe dynamic dimensions facilitating this ascendant self-organization as guided by a personality ideal, creating harmonious unity and integration. The inherent guiding unity of this personality ideal is characteristic of innate motifs and their intent toward unifying wholeness. The unique character of sensory motifs represents the personality that is ideal for that individual self.

Sensory motif is an inherent kind of structural schematic that determines the shape or design of what makes each of us unique. It is ever unfolding. The motif seems to operate as a highly individualized field of energy characterized not by a single pattern or even sets of patterns (in terms of personality and/or behavior patterns), but rather generates what is referred to as a family of interacting patterns. Human beings can be quite complex and no single pattern or sets of patterns adequately describe the uniqueness of self. That is why most individuals resist being categorized. I advocate using the model of a family of interactive patterns as a step to grasp this complexity.

Such a model suggests that human beings operate in inherent patterned ways, modifiable at the behavioral level yet essentially unchangeable at the core level of self. It is rather like the structure of a tree. The core pattern of the trunk is innate, yet the way it grows and branches outward is modifiable. The unique subtleties in inherent patterns of behavior (speaking, walking, working, loving, relating, etc.) in various areas of an individual's life overlap in their similarity yet express their own specific variations. Such a system of interactive patterns is referred to as a family of interactions. Our work behavior patterns will affect and interact with our patterns of relating at home. Yet the way we operate at work is not identical but only similar to our behavior patterns at home (we may be high achievers at both home and work, but be more active at work and passive at home). Our early childhood behavior and belief patterns interact with and affect the way we function as adults. Unique ways in which patterns in one area of our life affect those in other areas (thought and behavior patterns of love and intimacy learned in childhood affecting and being affected by those adult learning experiences) demonstrates the interactive affects of sensory motifs.

The wholeness of the motifs lies buried in the myriad of patterns and events of a person's life. It is not unlike puzzles that ask how many faces can you see hidden in a pictured collage of objects and figures. Sometimes standing back, releasing old fixations and opening up to creative ways that reformulate how and what a person is perceiving allows these motifs to emerge. That is why perceiving the family of interactive patterns is so essential in grasping how the motif is perceived. This allows the configuration of the motif to be visible.

These configurations are like the ripple effects of dropping a pebble into a pond of water. As patterns of waves spread out, some hit the shore and bounce back into oncoming patterns of waves. The interaction and interference effects of these colliding waves create shapes and configurations that repeat themselves in similar but different ways. Such similar but different configurations are called a family of interactive patterns. As motifs are not learned but are inherent structures to be developed, these interactive patterns are the distilled, pure manifestations of what is already innately present.

A very simple example of this can be seen in your own signature. Each time you sign your name, there will usually be some kind of small or large variation in the way you signed. However, you can always recognize your signature from anyone else's, as there are characteristics and shapes that emerge from the patterned variations of all of your signatures combined.

The sensory motif manifests itself in such a family of interactive patterns. Motifs imply unique configurations based on movement. We are always in movement whether just being in one place or quite active. Without movement, there is no life. However, the type of movement to which I refer is a special one known as flow. Csikszentmihalyi (1990) discusses how flow occurs through focused sensory and mental interaction, creating qualities of various form and design (a tennis player's flowing back-and-forth movement creating form, skill, and art). All people may find their self-existence in flow experiences that evoke qualities of form and art where they say they really feel alive and exist as their true selves. The sensory motif's existence in self is essential for each person's unique sense of meaningful existence. It is equivalent to the essence of self.

Motifs most clearly demonstrate their unique configurations and characteristics in these flow states. Interactive motifs usually, but not always, involve exchange in various activities--either alone, as in reading a book, or with someone else, as in playing ping pong or making love. Flow is a process that is conducive to generating a family of interactive patterns. That is why such a process is so intrinsically rewarding and gratifying. As a result, there is a powerful sense of purpose generated in these states.

Resonance between an individual's unique sense of self and the way one's lifestyle is manifested has been measured as meaning in life. Ebersole and Quiring (1991) discuss meaning in life depth (MILD) as a cognitive content process by using a five-point scale to measure depth of meaning. They indicate that the more precisely interactions of self and environment resonate to that person (design qualities or motifs), the greater the sense of meaning. It is postulated that the self has unique form and design qualities that necessitate resonant interactions (art, music, etc.) idiosyncratic to that self's motif. Experience takes on meaning in terms of what one discovers as identifiable external forms that are symmetrical with internal organizing principles. As the individual experiences a matching of external and internal organizing experiences, he or she feels a sense of meaning and purpose in life.

Frankl (1963) in logotherapy has emphasized the importance of discovering meaning and purpose in life. Each person's organizing properties seem to have a unique differential signature (or designation) such that some experiences will resonate more with some individuals than with others. When there is resonance, the individual feels like there is purpose in his or her self-experience. This, therefore, can be referred to as a purposeful self that resonates or relates when symmetry is discovered in experiences that present properties of their organizing principle. This ordering process, although unique to each client, is essential for the joy of flow experiences to occur in such unself-conscious manifestations (Csikszentmihalyi, 1990). At such times, the individual has a sense of joy, absorption, or fascination.

Motifs can be expressed in flowing, artistic forms that are sequenced in unique, sensory syntax. The particular shape or configuration of a person's motif will have unique expressions. For example, some people may use such phrases as "see how they feel about ideas," or "get feelings off their chest." They then begin to share them verbally or auditorily. This could be their syntax of experience.

However, motifs are more than how the senses are sequenced. Motifs are an intricate and articulated type of design that partners begin to manifest in their own life characters. Motifs are beyond mere interests and hobbies. They are the structurally unique signatures of self. Motifs are the templates that generate within us an innate sense of order and beauty. They serve as the organizing gyroscopes that order the syntax of experience. They are fluid, not fixated. They involve a subtle, flowing order and creative design. As a result, they create a sense of purpose. This sense of purpose emerges as these flow states are experienced and transformed into their own unique artistry, form, and style of expression. Motifs can be seen in people flowing through some interaction. Yet motifs are more than a style of interacting. There is a unique signature and blueprint in their characteristic ways of moving through life.

For example, some people may become very absorbed and intrigued in abstract symbols of ideas. Albert Einstein was one of those. In developing his theory of relativity, he would become absorbed and intrigued in what he called "thought experiments." That is, he would imagine what the effect of time and space would be if he were riding a beam of light to the ends of the universe and back. His motif was one of manipulating abstract symbols in relative frames of reference where time and space are fluid. Such a motif involved contrast and juxtaposition of different levels of abstraction. Notice the interplay of an absolute, universal oneness contrasted against his emphasis on how relative the universe can be. Indeed, he sought oneness throughout his life as evidenced by his search for a unified field theory of universal forces. His penchant for relative frames contrasted beautifully with his search for pure truth and a universal constant ($E=mc^2$). His motif utilized a paradoxical structure as he pursued unification through relativity. It is interesting that his motif of enjoying the relative nature of a holistic universe never got him to dinner on time with his wife. He was late, but then it's all "relative." Einstein enjoyed the motif of juxtaposing parts and wholes in contrasting designs.

Other people may be much more concrete in their manifestation, such as engineers or tool and die makers. Their focus may utilize motifs in a setting involving physical forms and concrete imprinting. The nuances in these motifs may have their focus more in engineering and maneuvering their ways into physical, manifest forms. Musicians enjoy the tactile feel when playing chords, harmonizing in syncopated rhythms, and the varying interchanges of patterns and arrangements. While these structural patterns may be most visible in certain areas such as music, they are found in many fields. These designing features have a kind of architecture (or arche-texture of feeling) in that they act as self-organizing templates. They serve to catalyze and guide the formulation and precise articulation of how these unique patterns can be expressed and experienced in the here-and-now situation. Each person has an intrinsic motif or family of interactive sets of qualities. To the degree to which we are congruent and aligned with sensory motif as an organizing principle of self, the more empowered, harmonious, and robust will be our relationship with ourselves and with others.

Developmental stages through which motifs self-organize and emerge is not necessarily without hazards and difficulties. There are many cases of deprivation in early childhood or in later years (trauma, oxygen deprivation, marasmus children, etc.). Many hardships certainly can be viewed as impeding developmental interactions for growth and change. Yet as Frankl (1963) demonstrated, in many cases meaning and purpose can manifest under the most adverse conditions. It would appear that because of how traumatic and deprived life conditions can become, it is even more essential to access one's unique motif in life. As both Frankl (1963) and Csikszentmihalyi (1990) imply, it is in times of greatest adversity when individuals may need to be at their very best, and a sense of meaning and purpose evolves through flow experiences as individuals are compelled to engage their sensory motif. It may be an alcoholic hitting bottom, a child abuse victim confronting a perpetrator, or an earthquake victim discovering firmness in his or her own resilience to survive. In all these cases, it is that immutable sensory motif that empowers each person to dare to risk and move through their terrors. It is their motif that allows them to enter into a flow experience, discovering meaning and purpose in their adversity.

The organizing, empowering experience of motif allows the fears, terrors, and anxieties to peak and then become incorporated into a larger, holistic, self-organizing identity. One's sensory motif is the experience of an immutable, unshakable reality of self at the core level. It therefore empowers and energizes awesome capabilities of belief, positive expectation, and creative imagination for problem solving. It gives one a sense of permanence in an otherwise chaotic world of trauma and turmoil. The degree to which the self can access and resonate with its own character or motif through outside interaction (Csikszentmihalyi, 1990) is the degree to which meaning and purpose are fulfilled.

Impairment of developmental growth through trauma can result in dysfunctional, state-dependent learning. The concept of state-dependent learning (Rossi, 1986) indicates that what is learned, remembered, and enacted is state-bound. In reaccessing one's psychophysiological state at the time of experience, memories, learnings, and behaviors organized in that state emerge. Cheek (1981) found that severe stress leads to altered states, identifiable as a form of spontaneous hypnosis encoding state-bound problems and symptoms. Lienhart (1983) formulated a theory of multiple personality based on state-dependent learning. She indicated paradoxical messages and chaotic confusion of memory sets both in time and context of events. In treating traumatized clients (Erickson & Rossi, 1980; Rossi, 1980), it was found that by circumventing "learned limitations" and accessing response potentials, integration could occur.

This bypassing of interference from state-bound material required a special design in which creative reorganization could occur. Erickson (1980) used age regression to bypass present, resistant, state-dependent learning. The client's dysfunctional behavior has its own "functional autonomy" when state-bound material persists against the client's will or ego (Rossi, 1986). It is therefore necessary to invoke that special design or motif to provide the integrative function. When Erickson tapped the client's resources, he could well have been using the motif that has a therapeutic "autonomous function" of its own. The motif, being developmental in nature, occurs at preverbal stages, empowering it with cross-context, state-dependent learning. Motifs can provide the common, unifying denominator in reintegrating dysfunctional, state-dependent learning. Smith and Jones (1993) indicate that traumatized clients can reintegrate with experiences that reverse fear of the "new," allow opportunities for personal choice, and restore security in the continuing sense of being one's self.

The developmental nature of motifs provides the capacity to reorganize states of chaos and confusion into integrated experiences. Motifs serve to reorganize and reintegrate dissociated, state-dependent experiences. Csikszentmihalyi (1990) refers to higher-ordering effects that emerge with absorption in pleasurable flow experiences (making love, watching a child sleep, sculpting clay, etc.). The flow experience is an inherent feature in each person's unique sensory motif.

The motif is an open system responsive to fluctuations in nuances, sensations and feelings, perceptions, memories, and cognitions. It seems to emerge as an interaction between the inherent organizing character of the individual and the environment in which learning occurs.

The therapeutic value of sensory motifs emerges when their unique design is accessed with clients "stuck" or fixated in limiting life conditions. By accessing the coding and organizing features of sensory motifs, thoughts, emotions, and behaviors can be liberated and creatively used. Development of these sensory motifs serves to nurture emergence of powerfully embedded life themes critical to the client's sense of meaning and purpose. When the client accesses these motifs, creative, organizing, thematic processes are set in motion (creating music, growing flowers, building houses, coaching teams).

The intricate organizing principles of sensory motifs can be seen when people are doing their life work. Whatever their field of experience (music, art, business, machinery, etc.), their choice expresses their unique internal organizing principles and manifests their movement in a flow state of purpose.

The experience of this organizing movement within the client when accessing such uniquely personal experiences is a feeling of "I cannot

not do this." When there is a love of repairing old cars or painting sunsets, there is the sense that one could not avoid doing these activities even if one tried. There seems to be a match or congruence between what the person is loving to do and an internal organizing structure or principle of self. When this match between activity and internal organizing forms or structure exists, there is a sense of alignment. As the artist paints a version of a sunset, there can be an experience that all is well with the world (Csikszentmihalyi, 1975).

It is this principle of self-organization as manifest in sensory motifs that aligns the client's resources. This is similar to what Pearce (1985) indicated when discussing the need for models to develop identity. It is alignment and resonance within this larger organizing field that facilitates the individual's empowered mental and sensory integration. It is all too easy to focus on a problem area to be resolved and thus miss the inherent organizing motif.

RESILIENT MOTIFS

The interactive affects of motif with the family and social milieu are well researched in studies of resilient children. Resilience is the ability to recover the unique, psychological shape of one's self after having been twisted and bent out of shape due to adversity. Emma Werner (1992) presented research findings in *Overcoming the Odds* regarding a 40-year longitudinal study of 210 resilient children on the Hawaiian island of Kauai. The findings reveal a complex interaction between child and environment. It appears that resilient children utilize both internal and external (extended family and social connections) resources. The internal resources of resilient children involve vitality, a sense of confidence, and self-righting (able to recover psychological balance) qualities. As many resilient children had to help out in dysfunctional family situations, they learned not only self-reliance but also self-knowing of their intrinsic core abilities and talents. Stripped of conventional family resources, they had to develop and hone their own inner, unique core abilities and characteristics to survive (abilities and skills such as creative writing, art, dancing, or carpentry). Such a collision with lost resources left only their inherent, core motif standing. Emphasis on their unique talents and abilities generated a sense of vitality and charisma in these self-directing children. As a consequence, these energetic and self-initiating children were perceived by adults as highly attractive and likable. The synergistic effect of these children's adherence to their own unique motif was not only to develop a sense of mastery and competence, but also to make them more attractive to potential mentors.

Being attractive and likable increased the probability that these children would be "adopted" or sponsored by the right type of mentoring adult to help them succeed on their unique life paths. Werner's research confirmed that resilient children were more likely to recruit the appropriately supportive mentor who would empower them into a positive life trajectory. In addition, such a recruited mentoring intervention could occur at any stage of the individual's life cycle (the person could be four years old or forty years old, it was never too late for such mentoring).

External factors such as mentors, guides, coaches, teachers, 4-H club leaders, and so on assisted resilient children in achieving and overcoming obstacles. Resilient children appear to have "good luck" in selecting mentors. For example, one resilient teenager with exceptional interpersonal skills knew how to talk and charm the mother of his girlfriend and was invited to move in with them as a protective shelter home. It seems that resilient children learn to "make luck happen" as they are good at selecting mentors as a consequence of having to be self-helpers.

Resilient children are challenged to rely on intrinsic self qualities, honing and sharpening their inner talents and uniqueness. This honing and shaping process etches out the unique design and structure of the resilient child's motif. I'm reminded of how engineers can strengthen and reinforce the resilience of very thin steel plates used for automobile hoods by stamping in unique angles, shapes, and lines to create texture, design, and resistance to impact and damage. In much the same fashion, resilience is enhanced by the challenging times of dysfunctional families where children learn to hone and shape through adversity their unique inner designs and motifs. They only need supportive mentoring to bring this to life.

Resilient children have a sense of coherence and trust that they will overcome obstacles. They seem to have a clear, private sense or shape of who they are and attract abundant support for their motifs and unique abilities. While resilient children are said to be able to "snap back into shape" after adversity, notice that this is more than just a metaphorical way of speaking. The shape and form to which they innately adhere is actually the shape and form of motif. One could say that resilient children snap back into motif. They resume their uniquely structured, resilient form and shape which is actually that of their sensory motif.

The powerful attractive qualities of someone making the effort to work their motif recruits the right mentor at the right time. Witness, for example, African American males with specific athletic talents rising out of dysfunctional settings through the recruited support of a coach or big brother. In this way, a self-righting or gyroscopic balance through-out life is maintained in aligning with their inner core shape or motif which extends, through mentor attraction, into the external environment.

The interactive aspects of resilience (internal resources of vitality and competence stemming from a coherent sense of core motif and ex-ternal resources of recruiting supportive mentors and enhancers) is similar to the motif's family of interactive patterns model. One can see intricate, interactive patterns of motif both within the individual and between the individual and his or her environment. They are mutually reinforcing and reflexive to one another. The more inner motifs are developed and relied upon, the more self-righting or balanced is the individual in staying on a positive life course.

There is a honing and refining of inner motifs with an interactive support and encouragement from significant others. This interaction assists in this shaping and sculpting of the individual's unique design and core motif. The idea of maintaining one's shape and being able to bounce back from adversity suggests that a coherent, core consistency is operating to bring one back into form. That core consistency is the sen-sory motif operating as an inner and outer gyroscope allowing a resil-ience and return to unique form.

The interactive, perpetuating nature of motifs is that they attract and generate on-going development, support, and enhanced refinement. In this way, motifs can be healing and self-correcting in the face of adver-sity utilizing resilient qualities.

SELF-ORGANIZING AND DEVELOPMENTAL MOTIFS

Motifs need to be nurtured and developed from early childhood and throughout life by attending to their unique organizing qualities. The developmental nature of motifs is that they have the capacity to organize and guide the evolutionary development of individuals' lives. Motifs provide the capacity to reorganize states of chaos and confusion into more meaningful experiences. Motifs serve to reorganize and reinte-grate what are called dissociated, state-dependent experiences. Indi-viduals who have been hurt either physically, sexually, or emotionally in childhood have separated or disowned different parts of themselves and repressed certain memories. These disowned parts, wounds, and memories are anchored and fixated to state-dependent experiences that, when accessed, arouse the trauma (sexual intimacy can arouse states which embody memories of abuse).

Motifs can help by enabling the person to discover the artistic talents, intrinsic interests, and organizing features of his or her own fascinations and joys. Accessing such powerful organizing structures assists the individual in making personal sense and meaning out of life experiences that intellectually are in conflict. Traumatized clients, for example, can begin to work through and reintegrate painful and detached parts of their life experience and repressed feelings by first accessing empowering, core motifs. This can access the joy of their own organizing, artistic talents whether they be music, art, poetry, or even the artistry of engineering, mathematics, and the like. Motifs offer an inherent scheme or structure that organizes their life experience. While life experiences may not logically make sense, motif has its own unique, creative "logic" that is nonlinear (not a simple cause-and-effect model). This inherent, self-organizing signature of the core self serves as a filter through which conflicting and nonsensible personal life events take on a continuity or meaningfulness all their own.

Many personal losses and rejections, when filtered through one's motif, can assist in meaningful reorganization of such events as times in which one had lost touch and adherence to one's own true self. When relationships suffer it can be indirectly related to becoming rigid and narrow in one's demands, not being true to one's own principles of mutual growth and expansion. Partners discover that many of their intimate relationship problems leading to entrancement are clearly related to being distracted from their own unique motif in life. When congruent to one's motif, partners feel whole, complete, and enjoy personal freedom they are able to share.

Motifs clearly have an internal gyroscopic structure that assists in the organizing and development of our personal growth and development. They are actually the formative nonverbal structures or templates that affect the shape and form of what we believe and how we make sense out of our world. Computers offer an intriguing model for understanding how this template process works. The computer uses a special template design to rearrange and reorganize written material from its original form to a specialized format. The text will not be changed, just the format, guided by the template. Whatever their chosen field of endeavor, individuals, in discovering their own organizing themes, can experience a coming together and healing of traumatic issues.

Many traumatized people struggle with intrusive memories and denial at the same time. That is, self-repeating ideas and images of painful losses and fears of helplessness in personal relationships may seem to involuntarily come into the individual's awareness. There usually is an attempt to deny and suppress such inner mental experiences. Entrancement is usually operating at this point. Motifs assist the individual in coming out of entrancing, recurrent mental experiences. Motifs empower self-organizing management of an individual's inner, mental experience. Motifs allow and create organizing self-experiences of intrinsic wholeness. As a result, they provide a powerful, organizing "motifating" model that gives a safe, stable structure for resolving conscious/unconscious traumatic struggles.

Ironically, the therapeutic aspects of trance occur more readily with uniqueness and individuality as absorption seems to be facilitated by novelty. There is a higher ordering of affect or emotion which emerges through absorption into those pleasurable flow experiences. These are unique to each person's motif. While making love, watching a child fall asleep, or sculpting clay may vary in priority for each individual, they each offer a sense of flow experience reflecting each individual's inherently unique character structure. The motif is an open system responding to changes and fluctuations of feelings, sensations, perceptions, memories, cognitions, and external conditions.

Manifestations of motif seem to emerge as an interaction between the inherent organized character of the individual and the environment in which learning occurs. Differentiating unique signature qualities of one's motif from such interactions assists in identification and access. When Madame Marie Curie was pursuing the discovery of a radioactive substance now known as radium, she had to sort through tons of ore and dirt. She sifted, filtered, and distilled hundreds of pounds of excess material, resulting in only a thin, pure concentrate of radium. She had interacted with tons of material mixed with hidden traces of radium. Pursuit of one's multifaceted motif involves distilling through a myriad manifestation in which it is embedded. Pattern manifestations of motifs are all-pervasive in every area of one's lifestyle (work, love, friendship, etc.) and need to be recognized and differentiated as they overlap from one area to another. Motifs emerge at the overlapping interface of where lifestyle patterns interact. They are like a multifaceted, crystalline structure where multicolored lights can shine through, yet the purity of the crystal structure is preserved.

Therapeutic values of motifs emerge when their unique design is accessed with individuals stuck or fixated in limiting life conditions. By accessing the coding and organizing features of sensory motifs, thoughts, emotions, and behaviors can then be reorganized and utilized. Development of sensory motifs serves to nurture emergence of embedded life themes critical to the partner's sense of meaning and purpose. When partners access these motifs, creative, organizing, thematic processes are set in motion. For example, creating music, growing flowers, or building skyscrapers can access unique, inherent abilities and talents, helping partners get in touch with a core sense of self. In entranced relationships, this very core motif of self is what has been "lost" in the chaotic whirlwind of entrancement's fantasy-ideal. While it, of course, is still present, the motif is now hidden and camouflaged by the luster and fusion of entrancement.

Regaining that musical motif within creates a harmony. Such harmony allows a genuineness or resonance with that person's ability to be themselves. This in turn allows resonance and harmony in their relationship. Just as there is a psycho-bio-physical connection to relationships, there also exists this structural hierarchy of motif in each of us. Accessing the sensory motif taps into these organizing structures at the mind-body level. For example, while men generally may have a hardwired-in perceptual-biological-physical response to female proportions, it is also clear that each of us individually has our own inner concept and aesthetic of beauty. These idiosyncratic perceptual-biological-physical wired-in responses to beauty are as much inherent as well as learned. The inherent, structural design of what we find individually beautiful is our sensory motif in action.

Accessing sensory motifs of one's talent, art, ability, aesthetic interests and so on opens doorways to unique character-designing empowerments. These unique, organizing structures suggest what we love to do, play, or even become. Sensory motifs provide foundations for identity and self. Knowing that you may have an innate, organizing structure of spatial positions with your hands and fingers, for example, can help you pursue relevant encounters (piano, typing, writing, etc.). Motifs can suggest broad areas of endeavor from which refined manifestation of these inherent structures and forms can take shape and expression (from brain surgeon to computer technician). The challenge is to discover these inherent motifs and their specific applications and manifestations.

Growing and developing dexterity, for example, can be discovered and manifested in the way a person lives his or her life and relates to others. An individual may develop greater finesse and become adept at "handling" complex relationships. Recovery from entrancing relationships requires access to self-organizing structures already inherent within ourselves. Indeed, it is for want of developing our unique, character-organizing motifs that we can fall prey to hypnotic entrancement. It is at this juncture that the entranced partner's fear of loss of identity is actually a movement toward discovering their core self, characteristic motif.

However, the unique characteristics of entranced partners' artistic motifs may be allowed expression only through selective hypnotic experiences. These usually take bizarre and, at times, frighteningly twisted manifestations of their genuine form. In their own way, partners manifest their unique motifs in distorted caricatures and cartoonlike versions of their genuine artistry. Their wild roller-coaster ride threatens the loss of their identity as they know it. However, it is this very process which can lead to the discovery of their real self or characteristic motif. Partners orchestrate their relationship like dramas or scenes from a Shakespearean play. Out of their most survival-oriented and need-based functions (control, power, fear, etc.) partners encounter symbols of their own motif imbedded in one another's physical and personality features.

Partners are oblivious to concrete, commonsense and everyday reality. They prefer a private, illusionary, fantasized reality even if it means drawing on the dark, mystical quality of their own inner minds. This kind of fusion of fantasized reality in that hypnotic dreamlike relationship can wreak havoc when seeking to work out relationships with friends, families, children, and special occasions. In the hypnotically induced relationships, these kinds of real-life issues are lost to partners fused in hypnotic mind-sets with a logic and fantasy all their own. Their problem-solving abilities in real-life issues are as impaired as their perception of real life.

Finding one's life work (purpose in life) through utilization of motifs can be healing for entranced relationships. Whatever the field of endeavor, the choice and application express unique, internal, organizing principles. Accessing internal organizing principles assists the healing process in providing a sense of balance and stabilization for partners lost in entrancement. Such aligned congruence between what the person loves to do and the internal, organizing structure or principle of self can provide a healing sense of integration very much needed by entranced partners. The expressive motif of unique style and structure allows partners to reestablish their unique sense of identity.

It is this principle of self-organization as manifested in sensory motifs that aligns individual resources. It is alignment and resonance within this larger organizing field of structure, design, and inherent "architecture" that facilitates the client's empowered mental and sensory integration. It is all too easy to focus on the problem of the addictive relationship to be resolved and thus miss the inherent, organizing motif already operating within each of the partners.

As mentioned previously, motifs are profoundly manifested, especially in flow experiences which occur through focused, sensory and mental interaction, creating qualities of various form and design. Flow experiences, which activate the unique, transforming design and structure of motif, activate the sense of self within partners. The sensory motif's existence in self is essential for each person's unique sense of meaningful existence. It is equivalent to the essence of self. Engaging partners in unique flow states assists them in their experience of meaning and self-worth.

It is postulated, using the concept of sensory motif, that the self has unique form and design qualities. These require aligned interactions (with the inner and outer world) such as art, poetry, music, or machinery that is idiosyncratic to the self's motif. This is not simply a particular state of consciousness or mood, it is an innately designed set of traits and attributes that are formative expressions of the motif of self. Just as Picasso had his own artistic motif, so do each and everyone of us. That means that it is important that we find a medium that matches and reflects our unique qualities, talents, and artistry. The danger is that in addictive relationships, instead of reflecting our uniqueness, they tend to reflect our hardened, stereotyped image of what we think we should, ought to, or must be. Rarely is this what we are.

As a unique expression of motif, the flow state takes on an experience of meaning. Partners in flow discover identifiable, external forms that are compatible, symmetrical, and reflective of the internal, organizing principles of who their self is. When partners are in sync with each other and have a rapport, they seem to have a sense of mutually shared harmony. They are able to be and move as unique and sensory selves in the way they talk, act, and even dance together. Partners in flow manifest a particularly unique, back-and-forth timing and movement. This movement is the external flow experience of each partner's unique, internal sensory motif coming together to create a synergy all its own.

When a person is doing his or her life's "artistic" work, it could be said that he or she feels a sense of meaning and purpose in life. One does not have to be a painter to be an artist. Indeed, a mechanic can be very artistic in his work rebuilding rusty old engines. There is a sense of resonance where meaning and purpose in life emerge. The internal motif is aligned with the external world of manifest interaction. We express our unique, inner motif in whatever media, field, or life profession and/or endeavor that allows a meaningful, flowing expression of this motif. Even the interests or hobbies we choose--for instance, steelworkers who enjoy hunting, fishing and woodworking--are expressing their inner motifs with their hands-on experiences. The more developed each partner's motif is, the greater opportunity couples have to learn to share and integrate their relationship, thus creating flow and synergy.

Realize that each person's organizing properties seem to have a unique, differential signature or designation. That is, some experiences will resonate more with some partners than with others. This is because certain experiences will more closely reflect the unique, inner motif of partners who have design features similar to the experience at "hand." An example of this is the steelworker who positively responds to "hands on" activities such as hunting, but not to activities that involve sitting and listening (such as the opera). When there is resonance, it can be said that each partner feels as if there is purpose in their experience together.

At that point, one can refer to what might be termed a "purposeful self," which resonates and positively responds when symmetry or balance is discovered. Resonance can occur not only with partners, but also with tasks at work and play. This occurs in experiences that present features similar to qualities and attributes of a partner's inner motif. Partners feel more comfortable and together when their motifs have similarities that allow for internal, organizing experiences. In other words, some partners might enjoy the schematics of an engineer's blueprint because they relate and find a certain symmetry and harmony with their own internal, networking design. Compatible partners can enjoy and embrace each other's differences because they actually share a similar template or motif which is made more complete when interacting together.

Symmetrical motifs of each partner interact in flow, creating purpose and organization of an inner experience unique to each. Such symmetry is essential for the joy of flow experience to occur. We become unself-conscious when we immerse ourselves in healthy life-enriching, identifiable ways of expressing our inherent self. Partners have a need for a creative variety and flow that occurs in these experiences. There is a sense of play and sense of purpose. The flow state is essential in accessing these motifs of design and order. Indeed, matching the unique designs of inner motif with the outer flow of movement and energy creates a sense of power and change for abundance in the future.

In the previous chapter, reference was made to the process of the birth, life, death, and rebirth life cycle. Entrancing partners go through these very phases where they meet and conceive of being together, live out the course of their relationship life, terminate, and reemerge in more enriched ways. Working through the hypnotically "fixated" stages allows them to give rebirth to their artistic motif from within.

The birth of a unique motif experience is not without pain or a sense of loss (witness a mother's labor of love during childbirth). The birth of the motif may involve three phases similar to that of the artist and his or her creations. First, there is accumulation of ideas, visions, and data to gather information to start and explore the "project" discovering one's motif. Second, there is saturation where the artist is taken over by the vision and intensifies his or her work, going through determined discoveries. These discoveries are journeys of the artistic work. It allows this entity to build and shape itself within the character of the artist (witness the exploring and accumulation of Mozart's efforts in writing classical music; he became obsessed with its dictation to him at the age of five). Finally, there is explosion or birth where completion and emergence of the artistic vision and design take on their own reality. This is manifestation of their work in some form (painting, writing, music, an accountant's audit, etc.).

As partners work through their vision, obsession, and completion of entrancement, they can emerge as unique "works of art" in their own individual lives. The partners can integrate the discoveries and obsessions of their experience in the relationship. They can emerge and take on their own unique realities. Termination of the entranced relationship can mean the reawakening, birth, and manifestation of motif. Each partner can then give birth to that unique, artistic motif of who they are, allowing its design and character to show through the many facets of their lives.

The following two cases illustrates the healing and therapeutic value of motifs. By identifying, accessing and utilizing unique design architectures of each client's motif, resolution and recovery are the creative outcomes.

APPENDIX: CASE PRESENTATION

The following two cases illustrate empowering effects of accessing client sensory motifs. Therapeutic effects of alignment with this organizing field demonstrated how resonance with this field generates the joy of flow experiences. The clients were seen in an outpatient setting for eight to twelve weekly sessions in short-term outpatient therapy. It is interesting to note that when the concept of organizing experiences of life purposes was introduced, all clients involved seemed to accelerate in their treatment progress. Clients struggling with a variety of presenting problems seemed to report optimism and energy when accessing experiences of life purpose. They seemed to deal with their issues with a sense of self-acceptance and self-esteem, and in each case resolved their presenting problems. The follow-up to these cases was limited to the time frame of the therapy itself.

CASE 1

The client was a married subcontractor referred for treatment by the probation department for stress and creating a public disturbance. He had become quite irate and incensed by a contractor, so he stole some of the contractor's tools and machines as compensation. In the sessions that ensued, many issues were explored: (1) feeling powerful, (2) how he seemed to attract conflict and chaos into his life, and (3) how codependent his relationship was with his mother. The client became livid, almost explosive, in one session, expressing how frustrated he was in being deprived of his financial compensation. He also felt limited and constricted in his relationship with his mother. It seemed as if he were enjoying perverse pleasure in being deprived of his earnings, which allowed him to go off into one of his expressive tirades.

When asked what he enjoyed doing, what seemed to be purposeful and flowing in his life, he expressed how much pleasure he derived in being able to use his expertise in adhering to building codes. Indeed, his real pleasure in life seemed to focus upon construction: building and arranging and rearranging component parts in construction and reconstruction-like processes. As a child, he enjoyed taking his building blocks apart and rebuilding them into new forms. For him this meant freedom, power, and expression. He loved this process and said he could "do it all day." He seemed to even carry a visual image or map of an erector-set-like motif that, like Legos, allowed him to symbolize the layout of the internal structure of wires, plumbing, skylights, sprinklers, and the like. He was even able to draw this structure with horizontal and vertical lines, triangles, and right angles resembling the skeletal structure of electronic circuitry.

He would use this map as his reference design for what he had created as representative of the ideal building safety feature. His schematic design was creative and he was quite capable of revising this image as needed. He felt everything had to fit, and he loved discovering new arrangements. He played with these toys for hours in the attic. He very much enjoyed working with the minute building blocks which he called chips, as he could construct or destruct his creations at will.

When he tapped into this dynamic organizing principle for himself with its sensory motif of building and construction, he realized that much of this emotional rage and frustration represented his misalignment with not living more congruently with this mosaic design. It was suggested to him that he obviously emphasized through his rage and uproar a tremendous energy for being able to "build up" to a certain peak experience and then explode and "tear down" whatever was created in his path.

He seemed to like the idea that he was powerfully able to map out his sense of design in critiquing how his contractors deviated from the "correct blueprint" of their agreement. He began to feel less helpless and outraged. He took perverse pleasure in intensely focusing on how to build up a price design or schematic of how an agreement, building, sprinkler system, or wiring should be structured and then stripping away all the "fat" and "excess" material.

As he identified with this organizing patterned motif in its sensory form, he seemed to integrate many issues related to power, personal integrity, and differentiated self. Accessing his organizing motif in a sensory format seemed to liberate him from enmeshed contacts and allowed a healthy detachment invoking humorous responses instead of intense rage. As continued suggestions occurred as to how this motif may be operating in his life, he gradually became more centered and focused.

The outcome manifested itself in terms of relief from stress, coping ability, and an appreciation of his own freedom and power for self-nurturance and validation. He seemed to be impressed with his own internal structuring process as if he really had "something to offer" and could let go of hidden dependency needs on motherlike oppressors toward whom he formerly acted out his anger over his alienation from his own purpose. The stress in his life and conflicts with others seemed to diminish in light of his new attunement to the interweaving process of purpose and flow throughout his life.

CASE 2

The client was a forty-year-old nurse who came to therapy to deal with her divorce, feelings of lethargy, and thoughts of suicide. She had a fifteen-year-old daughter who was on the move in terms of her own adolescence and youth. She was unhappy with herself, felt she couldn't keep up with her wealthy friends, didn't seem to enjoy her nursing, and felt frustrated in not having a boyfriend. She exerted only half-hearted efforts in her job and relationships.

She felt her life was going nowhere and there was just no point to it all. She seemed down, listless, and feeling she hadn't got much going for her, even though she was an attractive woman, in good health, and had a good job. She was raised to be very educated and intellectual. Her father was in a country club, yet she felt she didn't belong there. She felt that she didn't fit into this kind of lifestyle.

It was suggested to her that while she really didn't buy into this intellectual, upper-middle-class value system, she was fearful of taking a stand about what she really wanted. She feared her father's disapproval and her mother's rejection.

She said she didn't know what she really enjoyed except for a stage comedy skit where she played one of the *Saturday Night Live* comedians. She loved performing, the spontaneity of the moment, and dramatizing life events to enhance them to larger-than-life experiences. (She dramatized her plight in therapy sessions in a very theatrical, dramatic way.) She referred to herself as Scarlett O'Hare of *Gone With The Wind* and seemed to be acting this part out in real life. She also loved mystery and challenge. Her drama of her problems really embodied her solution in that she loved to act out her depression or any kind of role or character. She wanted to be an actress where she could enact many of her vital creative scripts. She exhibited a motif of a multifaceted diamond needing to enhance each unique facet to some dramatic extreme edge. Acting allowed such enhancement to occur.

Rather than being pathological, this orientation could be pathfinding of her purpose in life. She could be creative, artistic, and bring her art to life through performance. Her mother was a former artist who killed herself at age forty-three. She felt her mother was full of self-doubts and stopped living up to her own artistry.

It seems likely that the client feared that she might act out her mother's plight and needed to learn to affirm her purpose in the arts and creative acting. I suggested to her that she started out in her life with a negative emphasis on an artistic way of life. She could be more artistic if she let herself attend to and purposefully flow with her own unique art-forming process. She perked up and realized that she could decide to access and experience the joy of acting as it resonated with that deeper sense of self. She needed encouragement to follow her truth and purpose.

She also liked psychology because it allowed her to deal with people who were "acting out" their pathology, which is what she was familiar with in her own family. She found that when psychiatric patients acted out their wild dreams, bizarre delusions, and distortions, it gave them a kind of vitality and expansiveness. Such expansiveness was expressive of her motif, which required varied enhancement of her multifaceted nature. She deeply harmonized and related to this. She needed to act and perform creatively in her real life, creating exaggerated dramas so that she could give meaning and purpose to her life. Actually, the presenting problem of acting down, forlorn, and depressed was the "resenting solution" of revealing her need to act out and bring to life her many emotions and images.

It was suggested that she really wanted to be an actress. She then sat straight up, smiled, and said she needed to study and emphasize acting as an artistic experience. This seemed to change her current experience of how she could bring to life hidden dreams and yearnings for realizing her private self-expressions. This allowed her to appreciate the harmony, symmetry, and organizing motif of a multifaceted personality and how rich and colorful it could be.

CHAPTER 4

LET THE DANCE BEGIN

STAGE I--PRE-FRAMING AT THE ENTRANCE

Individuals go through life, to some degree, with preconceived notions, expectations, and motivations as to the kind of idealized partner with whom they would like to spend the rest of their lives. Constructed in early childhood, these images and expectations emerge at nodal points in time such as adolescence, the early twenties, or even at midlife. Those images and fantasies of the idealized other begin to surface and manifest in the types of partners chosen. Between three and five years of age, primary idealizations are most manifest. However, they are continually updated and refined.

It is fascinating to observe how two people can encounter each other with similar yet complementary motivational needs for bonding (security, comfort, belonging, etc.). Each has a set of expectations of how their partner ought, should, or needs to be in fulfilling certain preset ideals and fantasies. Partners seek individuals who meet the relationship criteria they have established in terms of physical beauty, personality type, intellectual levels of stimulation and arousal, spiritual levels of inspiration, and so on. When someone steps into their life by some "serendipitous" event (though it may not be serendipity) who seems to fit their image and hits them at just the right point in their lives, they can experience a phenomenon called "falling in love."

LET'S MAKE A DEAL: "I'LL BE YOUR DREAM AND YOU'LL BE MINE"

Whatever kinds of images, illusions, and fantasies are hallucinated is exactly what partners fall in love with. It's the image, illusion, and fantasy. The important quality here is not so much that they have fantasies, images, and illusions. What is important is that they believe and interpret the presence of that image and illusion as meaning that this person embodies all the wonderful personality characteristics, qualities, and values they ever wanted. In their emotional rush, partners tend to misattribute their desired idealized qualities onto one another because of the other's physical and/or charismatic attributes. That is not such a surprise. What may be a surprise is what partners begin to embark on when they encounter that unique surrealistic, sparkling mate (at least in their mind-set). Compulsive thinking can initiate insistent feelings of having to have such an individual as a partner. What partners do not seem to understand is that the association of this stimulating encounter with the illusionary image in their mind's eye is the beginning of fixation. It's not necessarily pathological, but it is a fixation that can lead them into a very powerful, hypnotic trance.

Individuals tend to ascribe certain traits and characteristics to prospective partners based on their features. The way partners construe physical attributes, the meanings they are given (sexy, intelligent, good, and bad) may have a biological as well as cultural basis. In evolutionary terms, women with proverbial hourglass figures may be desirable for child-bearing purposes. Desire by men for such features appears to be hard-wired into their repertoire of responses. The imbued meanings attributed to sheer physical appearances (much less the emotional-personality features discerned) in potential partners strongly suggest that excitation of the sympathetic nervous system by strong, sensory stimuli can trigger intense feelings, attributes of idealization, and attraction fantasies. It is important to realize that the bio-psycho-social basis of attributing meaning and quality to physical and personality characteristics is essentially a process of misattribution. That is, individuals may be beautifully and "factually" convinced their partner was the "best thing" for them. Is it any wonder partners have so many confusions in relationships when their "thinking" is done by their senses, not their transformational brain.

EUPHORIA, ROMANCE, AND PARADISE

Partners say the perfume was hypnotizing and the personality mesmerizing. These statements are not just euphemistic terms. They access the powerful fixation and self-inductive quality of their own self-hypnotic image of what smacks of beauty, aura, and charisma. Indeed partners create their own self-induced trance without knowing it.

In this self-talk, self-inducing trance begins a powerful journey into the deepest recesses of their own, unconscious mind. It is indeed an instantaneous, rapid induction. In the Broadway play, *West Side Story*, Tony sees Maria across the dance floor, and the sudden, unexpected shock effect of that "perfect vision" entrances him into "love." They begin to induce a mutual spell between the two of them. Gazing into one another's eyes is the type of eye fixation that occurs in the beginning stage of hypnotic induction. The hypnotist says to his subject, "Let your eyes focus on some point on the wall. As you continue to stare, your eyelids could become heavy, so heavy that they may close, and you might feel more relaxed about going into trance whenever you are ready, either now or in a few moments."

This motivates and entrances, responding to the idealized person as a resonation of an individual's internal, idealized thinking and imagining which is now activated, projected, and fused onto the other. If one senses and discovers another person with his or her own unique and mysterious qualities that match one's idealized fantasies, instant rapport and absorption can develop. Everyone has some internal construct of an idealized partner. That one becomes absorbed into one's own internalized image, and fantasy expectations of who one projects that person to be constitutes remarkable self-deception. Such self-deception is further enhanced when an assessment of a partner is based on physical features of body shape and size. The fusion of body image with personality attributes matches the fantasized ideal projection as one and the same. The boundary between our inner and outer worlds has now merged into one and the same. What was perceived as fantasy is now "reality" to partners. While one sees a princess, the other sees a very plain-looking girl.

There is a slow but sure inductive quality between the "I" and the "other" which begin to mesh because of matching projections (misattributions). They make their entrance into that inductive quality of meshed oneness which has the quality of selective attention, seeing only the best in the "other" as our ideal partner.

In hypnosis, there is the suspension of critical faculties of judgment, analysis, rational thinking, will, power, choice, and objectivity. Critical faculties are replaced by the use of subjective experience as the criteria for making decisions and pursuing pleasure. What this means is that partners follow their romanticized sensations of entrancement, mindlessly pursuing their fulfillment like children led astray by the enchanting melody of a pied piper.

Those critical faculties utilize everything partners have ever learned and understood about the qualities of a mature adult relationship. These adult faculties are unavailable in entranced relationships as they become suspended in trance. The fusion of one's partner with one's fantasized projection generates entrancement and is perceived to be real and thus becomes real. There may be experiences of regression that activate childhood and/or child-like emotions, memories, and behaviors. Impulsiveness and demands for immediate gratification may ensue as well as fears of abandonment and loss. With the suspension of critical faculties, partners are vulnerable to regressive influences and become poor problem-solvers and decision-makers. This abandoning of reason, reality, and healthy caution is a sign of entrancement and the beginning of addictiveness in the romantic interlude of hypnotic induction. Partners, in a sense, become selectively focused, filtering out only those qualities that do not fit the fantasized and diluted image that they have of their partner. What is important here is to recognize that this is the beginning of trance.

Most partners will say that nobody is going to take over their mind. They feel no one can tell them what to do. They may say that nobody is going to run their life. The amazing thing about it is that partners who are strong, individualistic, and rugged in their determination to be their own bosses and captains of their own ships, cannot wait to suspend authority and control over their lives and, with reckless abandon, give them away to strangers. Partners become desperate and are willing to give themselves in this entrancing experience to that idealized other.

Entrancement is the strange kind of inductive trance with its own illusionary voice that beckons like Ulysses' sirens of a fantasy island. Well, this type of entranced, inductive language pattern is a way for partners to not only suspend critical faculties but to suspend control of authority over their lives. It creates a desperation to give themselves over in this entrancing experience to that idealized other. Entrancement's hypnotic influence can lead the way to partners abandoning family, friends, and work. In this honeymoon period, partners are engrossed in "love."

Without realization, this honeymoon period is a powerful induction in which suspension of their own personal identity can occur. To love and become one together may involve a suspension of reason and reality testing temporarily. Healthy loving is a mutual give-and-take extension of each partner's selfhood reaching out to the other.

Entranced relationships are quite different. Couples in relationships dominated by entrancing qualities suspend consciousness of not only their roles in everyday life, but also the center of who and what they are. They rarely know how to get "back to earth" or become grounded when their journey falls short of their ideal. Partners in entrancement do not reach beyond their boundaries, they lose them. Their integrity and character are swept away in their rush to "hit" their ideal moon. Intimacy for them is not a journey to cultivate and enjoy, but rather a hurried rush of adrenaline shock to get there now. They do not learn from mishaps and miscues that miss their ideal mark in relating to one another. These are perceived as unforgivable betrayals rather than realistic indicators of how far they may have progressed on their journey together.

This is not to say that such fantasizing and romanticism and experiences are not without many benefits. The temporary suspension of critical faculties (otherwise known as temporary romantic psychosis) can be a period of enormous growth, exploration, and discovery. Conventional boundaries and everyday limits which define us are temporarily perforated and diminished.

As boundaries collapse, opportunities for new learnings and discovery can now occur. Tragically, in cases of infidelity, the prices paid for such learning opportunities are painfully high. Nonetheless, entranced romantic relating can be an exciting period where couples may immerse themselves into new roles and displays of heretofore suppressed passions. The danger exists, however, that we mistake these romanticized fantasy adventures for absolute reality. Entranced partners do not know how to freely move in and out of them. They are willing to give their lives, hopes, dreams, sometimes even families, friends, and their own futures to keep this quality at all costs.

Partners may need a ritual space for these adventures. Yet, without access to a mature self-character as a criterion to make healthy judgments about their course of action, partners fall prey to being lost in unverified illusions that could violate their core character. This is where trouble begins. When fantasy becomes mistaken for fact, there is a pro-

longation of "romantic psychosis" (alluring, sensory entrancements creating a shaken, somewhat fragmented sense of self, with a partial loss of
impulse control) in the relationship with a real potential for psychoti-
clike experiences (the coherent sense of self-identity begins to significantly disintegrate; the person feels completely vulnerable and susceptible to fantasy/nightmare illusions, impulses, and sensations).

What begins to happen is that mesmerized partners, already suspending critical faculties and authority over their lives, impatiently invest all their time, energy, and emotions in the relationship and are indifferent to anything that could realistically keep them apart or hurt them.
It is important to note that not all of a partner's actions are a sign of
"romantic psychosis." As mentioned previously, there are some definite
personal growth needs that each partner has that are genuinely rooted in
their core character. Relentless pursuit of these growth needs reflects
the irrepressible quality of core character in itself. The unhealthy psy-
choticlike quality of self-fragmentation emerges in the entranced way
partners have thrown themselves into such a whirlwind relationship,
mindlessly ignoring the serious costs to self and others. While the goal
may be self-growth, the means can be quite self-annihilating.

In the initial thirty- to sixty-day encounter the induction is quick,
fast, and deep. Partners become absorbed in daily thoughts of one another. They entrance themselves through selfhypnotic thought patterns,
which embed commands of being with each other. When partners are
entranced, they are so close that they can think and act as if they are two
people sharing the same mind and body. They are intensely fused to one
another (joined together at many levels of thinking, feeling, and habitual
ways of behaving). Such beautiful rapport is disguised entrancement
and is at the heart of the problem. Partners lose their own distinct character and unique self. They act as if they can mind read each other, pre-
dicting the other's every move and thought. Yet both are prisoners of
enmeshed entrancement.

Make no mistake about it. This hypnotic pull is a powerful force
field with a reality of its own, drawing the two into an ever-deepening
entrancement. It's all part of the induction. In that initial phase, individuals hypnotize and rehypnotize each other and themselves. In hypnosis, this is referred to as fractionation. The hypnotist brings the subject
out of the trance for the purpose of being able to have them return into it
at an even deeper level. Each time subjects reenter trance, they experience a deeper, more profound depth.

Entranced relationships appear to present similar cycles. When partners come together, are engrossed and entranced intimately, they at first experience euphoria. As they part, going about their daily business for awhile, they seem to come out of their entrancement feeling some loss and skepticism about how good and/or real that experience was. Partners may take the attitude that the contact phase of their entranced relationship was too good to be true. They may doubt the reality of their relationship. As they get together again at some future time, partners discover an even more intense euphoria emerging than previously existed. They may now assume an attitude of enthusiasm and ecstasy at their wonderfully renewed dream relationship. Each cycle of engaged contact, parting, and resurfacing and reengagement serves to strengthen the entrancing bond.

Entrancement is maintained in both the engaged phase (partners sharing time and activities together) and the disengaged phase (partners resurface and part). This has important ramifications for couples seeking to significantly change or end their relationship. Partners may feel that by changing the type and amount of time, activity, or communication, significant change may occur. Yet, such surface changes may only result in an actual increase in entranced bonding for the couple.

Partners repetitively reenter again and again, coming out, questioning their sanity, only to go back down even deeper than before. Partners pinch themselves, test reality, checking to see if their fantasy love is real. Entranced partners are poor reality testers. What prevents sharing of their relationship is the entrancement itself. There may be no emotional space or time allowed for others. They are so engrossed in each other that friends and relatives may seem more of an intrusion than inclusion to their experience.

Partners immerse themselves headlong into an entranced course of action determined to make the relationship work no matter what. They have already made an agreement (implicitly in their own mind's eye of consciousness) that this connection is something that must be maintained. It is a "till death do us part" level of entrancement. If they happened to go on a cruise together or go out to dinner, the event becomes a magical memory that stays in their minds and influences their brains in the deepest, most hypnotic way. It is as if a child were having her or his first memories of seeing Prince Charming in Disney's *Cinderella*. The point in all this is that entrancement alters each partner's perception and meaning of simple, everyday ordinary events. While at first this may have a charm and romantic appeal about it, the blinding, charismatic effect of entrancement distorts the reality of honest, personal preferences in the service of maintaining the magic of the moment.

Partners in this early phase of entrancement are willing to deny themselves, their personal needs, and even values (participate in activities that violate personal standards such as substance abuse and erotic behavior) so as to maintain the magical oneness of entrancement. It is not so much that partners are afraid to assert themselves. It is more that they are invested in protecting that special sense of all-encompassing oneness so characteristic of entrancement. Partners may feel an enriched sense of rejuvenation and rebirth as each encounter seems to energize them with a special sense of wonder and meaning lacking in their everyday reality. Their incredible (as far as these couples are concerned their experience is larger than life) periods of interlude induce a powerful, sensory trance that opens them up by diminishing their identity boundaries. There is a mixture of both real and unreal.

It defies logic that in sixty or ninety days that partner could be everything we ever dreamed would fulfill our needs. Somehow, there is this magical quality. In this illusion, one partner suspends and transcends all the laws of physics, time, and space reading the other's mind, attending to feelings where one's wish is the other's command. The magic begins to unfold. She reads his mind. He knows (or thinks he knows) what she is thinking. He knows what she is desiring and passionately anticipates it before she asks. This kind of magical, illusionary rapport between partners is akin to the wide-eyed wonder of a child on Christmas morning. All these gifts appear by wishful magic out of nowhere. Entrancing relationships operate by a special clause or rule of entrancement in that perfect love and harmony should magically just happen. Resolutions to normal relationship trials and tribulations are expected to just materialize out of nowhere by some mysteriously benevolent powerful figure. The entrancement rule in relationships leaves no room for trial and error (this is perceived as failure) or imperfect resolutions. Their magical formula is "your wish is my command." The magic is absolute oneness of the partners. Neither exists independent of the other. There is no "coexistence." There is a total mesh with no space or time between the two. The "co" is gone in their coexistence.

The hypnotic quality of such magical thinking and imaging can be seen in the perception of the hypnotist's induction of the subject. Notice the hypnotist's words speaking to the subject "as you listen to my voice, you will go deeper and deeper and have a wondrous feeling of soothing comfort spread over your body, even now with every word you hear, and these feelings will spread deeper and deeper throughout your body with each breath you take. With every moment that passes, you can grow deeper and deeper, truer and truer." Such an induction conveys the message that it is the magical, powerful voice of the hypnotist that creates, out of nowhere, a deep soothing and comfortable state. Yet it is the focused imagination of the subject that empowers the hypnotist's voice.

As with the skilled magician or hypnotist, there are no more powerful words than when two lovers entrance themselves and one another with "love talk." There is fusion of imagery, longing feelings, and physical hormonal senses. This fusion of stimuli from various sources occurs too quickly to tell the mind from body stimuli.

Entranced into their romantic interlude, they are enraptured with the set belief, as their feet are planted firmly in midair, that this relationship was "meant to be." Sadly, they begin to discover in the future that they have induced a powerful, mutual trance upon one another. When they come to each other, there is something special or unique. It seems to vibrate a "reality" or entity of its own.

It is human nature to attribute positive qualities to features we find attractive in others. This attribution is really a mistake or misattribution. Research has shown that many people attribute intelligence and leadership to tall men, simply because they are tall. Men attribute certain qualities to women who have certain hair colors. Women may misattribute qualities to a man's quality by virtue of the car he drives and income level. Such stereotypical criterion for loving, long-term romances are key indicators of entrancement.

When we attribute qualities to special features and parts of real, whole people, we split both them and ourselves off from the totality that gives that man or woman a real self. The total person is blurred and lost in that specialized part of self mistakenly confused for the unique wholeness of self. Where, for example, seeing that attractive young brunette sitting with that curl in her hair sparks attributed thoughts and fantasies of who she might be and what she might be like. We draw on personal references to make sense and meaning out of our experience. We associate, compare, and, at times, fuse what we see with what we think we see and interpret it to be.

These hypnotic mixtures can be associated or paired in learned ways with words, songs, social events, people, places, and things. Such associations can arouse the deepest, most inductive, trancelike responses. Just a word or phrase can cause a person to recall and recreate thoughts, images, and fantasies organized and associated with the felt sense of the relationship. Both the mind and its reality's boundaries begin to blur. Reality is fantasy and fantasy is now reality. The euphoria is seductive and partners don't care what is happening to them until the "honeymoon" ends.

While this phenomenon is presented in many romantic novels and manuals about relationships, there is rarely a clear, accurate depiction of the very powerful hypnotic dynamics operating between two human beings. These euphoric experiences may be passed over as neurotic or dysfunctional and not recognized as universal field forces common to all. Human attractions such as these can propel us deeper and deeper into a trance where we partially or completely feel like we are losing critical control of our own conscious choices. Partners sabotage their genuine identity. Their nature and purpose are distorted into a cartoon quality of this fantasy that we mistake for the real thing.

This is not to suggest that all romantic relationships are characterized in this way. Not all romantic relationships are entrancing to the extent of having lost that very special, volitional part of ourselves. It happens when couples get locked in this phase through lack of awareness and distorted illusions of what genuine, mature love is. This creates addictive relationships where we lose that sense of caution that allows us to wait a minute to see if this is going too far. Partners find that they cannot work, though they need to work. They find that they are not taking care of their own family as they'd like. Partners delay spending more time with their kids and find the bills not getting paid. Partners know it is time to shape up and get their finances back in order, but fail to act. These kinds of experiences indicate that one has lost some degree of control, perspective, and boundaries.

It may be temporarily wonderful and beautiful to be so enraptured, but one knows it's time to come back. This awareness indicates a healthy relationship where one can enter into and pull back as needed to maintain the reality functions of everyday living.

Partners in these relationships know how to move in and out of trance. Being stuck in entrancement is more a problem with those individuals who see their partner as the absolute one and only. They have fallen in love, but they do not know what it is to be loving.

They feel they cannot live without their partner. They feel that they cannot function without each other. When one person has to go out of town for a trip, both may go into a melancholy and depression. At first it may seem, "I can function without this person." As time goes by, their entrancement becomes deeper and deeper. They discover that without their partner, life seems to have no meaning or purpose. Partners develop perceptual blind spots and filters to each other's human vulnerabilities, which are key indicators that the dynamics of entrancement are operating.

The inner charisma radiating from an entranced partner's personalities blinds each to the genuine character of one another. Such illusionary pathways tantalize partners to believe they have discovered remarkable truths in each other. Nothing could be further from the truth. Partners do not differentiate when in an addictive hypnotic relationship.

Character issues are not distinguished from sensory attributes. Someone with beautiful hair, a charming personality, and a certain kind of pomp and circumstance must be someone who is special. Each partner attributes (or misattributes) intrinsically valuable qualities to one another. The self-inducing, internal messages to ourselves suggest this person has all the qualities any man or woman would want.

Through self-talk and imagery, immature idealizations of perfect partners are accessed in trance states and may reflect regressed childhood needs for an idealized parent figure felt to be in some way deficient. Partners are raised, to one degree or another by imperfect parents and entrancement regresses partners to mistaken assumptions that totally perfect partners are now possible and even necessary. Entrancement disempowers adult capabilities to function in healthy, adult reality.

Children want "more" of something they enjoy (ice cream, cookies, etc.). Entranced partners act like mesmerized children who always seem to want more of what feels good. Being entranced with the prospect of having "more" of an idealized partner creates entranced regression and creates susceptibility to the merging of physical and personal characteristics with childhood fantasy needs. All of this comes together in a kind of self-inducing statement that says "if I have this person in my life, then I will feel I have meaning and purpose." To entranced partners, their sense of meaning and purpose has been embodied (literally) in that now-idealized partner. Is it any wonder that, with these complex, interwoven connections, it is so difficult to let go when the time comes for this to happen?

The irony is that such idealization denies the partner's sense of self and human needs. It denies the partner who is doing the fantasizing in terms of his or her own needs as a living, breathing, human being discovering his or her own identity, interests, and uniqueness. Both partners are captivated by the hypnotic fixation of need focus rather than achievement, purpose, and life focus.

Addictive self-induction starts when partners are perceived to possess an exotic, charismatic personality associated with selective attributes that are now entranced into that addictive image of the other. Physical, sensory, and personality characteristics that partners attributed to one another create hypnotic induction. Partners see the other person as someone who reflects a fantasy of having it all. Partners are not seen as only models of fantasy. Rather, partners experience each other as a living, breathing manifestation of fantasy come true.

Embedded within entranced fantasy ideals partners have of one another lie hidden elements of envy. While one partner may admire and idealize the other, that partner may also secretly wish they too possessed such valued attributes. Such hidden envy for the other's attributes is highly intensified in entrancement as a result of lost self-identity boundaries.

Entrancement tends to create such paradoxical, dialectical tensions in intimate relationships. The power of the hypnotic pull is the envious absorption and consumption of what the other has, not who the other might uniquely be as a person. They equally lose sight of their own unique characters, falling prey to the fused, paradoxical themes that permeate entranced relationships. Partners experience conflicting pulls, feeling on the one hand they cannot live without each other, and yet on the other cannot stand to live with the other.

Entrancement encourages each partner's self-boundary toward diffusion and disintegration. Partners lose the ability to maintain a separate and distinct integrity that attributes to each their own unique characteristics. Each becomes absorbed into the other's attributes. The consequences are fear, jealousy, and a lost self.

Overidentification (partners seeing themselves in each other to the point of losing their own sense of self), plus exaggerated admiration and envy, can mean that partners develop fear of the very unique qualities they so dearly love in each other. Partners' fear of intimacy is actually the fear of one's own uniqueness. Without uniqueness, there can be no intimacy. Entrancement creates the illusionary reality that intimacy is its own outcome. Romantic entrancement espouses the allure, passion, and heat of embrace. Yet the paradox presents itself that entrancement creates the very fear and avoidance of each partner's unique qualities that are essential for intimacy. Entrancement, therefore, stands in its own way toward the path of intimate relating.

ENTRANCEMENT: REALITY DENIED

If entrancement interferes (by creating fears) with itself in the pursuit of intimacy, the resulting distortions create a reality denied. Entrancement is an illusion appearing real, forever denying a partner's fulfillment of its false promises. Illusions induce surrendering a sense of control and authority in each other's life.

There is a rapid connection and induction characteristic in this kind of relationship. The problem in the beginning, as in all addictive relationships, is that the fantasy is expected and demanded to happen instantly. It is not seen as a journey with a desirable outcome to be nurtured and developed. It becomes a should, a must, an "ought to happen now." It becomes an irrationality of pressing partners into this neurotic, illusionary shape, fitting into the needs of the hypnotic pull. This results in denying both one's own self and the other person's identity.

Herein lies the true nature of the addiction. There is insistence that this fantasy be embodied in partners as a means of gratifying life fulfillment. The boundaries of inner thoughts and images become blurred and vulnerable to confused fixations. Partners attribute "super" powers to the other that can now supposedly change our lives.

This kind of omnipotent thinking and imaging is powerfully entrancing. It is designed to fulfill the complete induction of merging into an all-consuming, all-encompassing, larger-than-self bonding and nurturing. What is fantasized inwardly (both on a need and idealistically based fantasy) is fused outwardly with external physical and personality attributes of our partner. There is a submergence and entrancement of inner and outer worlds fused into one. Addictive fusion through this self-induced hypnotic state begins to corrupt character.

With a suspension of critical faculties, entrancement activates mistaken beliefs stemming from distorted early childhood learning. It also engenders a suspension of volitional control where partners act as if they cannot help what they do. Entrancing experiences create a sense of being illusionarily taken over by the magic and wonder of this enmeshment of inner and outer worlds. It now takes on an entity all its own, so powerfully real that it now displaces commonsense logic. There is no reasoning with partners at this point.

They cannot sort out fact from fiction. Entrancement demands perfection. As quickly as times between partners seem beautiful and wondrous, they just as rapidly can turn sour and stormy as a flash flood. The slightest deviation from perfect role playing of the ideal fantasy could result in raging jealous outbursts, accusations of betrayal, and violent attacks (verbal, emotional, and/or physical). Such are the regressive effects of entrancing relationships.

These are the kinds of disqualifications of each other's fantasy needs that begin to emerge when the two of them have so mutually induced a trance with one another. They evoke turbulence in pulling apart, only to dive deeper into enmeshment. A temporary pulling apart creates a fear of loss, which causes partners a loss of balance (a key feature to increasing susceptibility to trance), and serves only to deepen the pull of entrancement. They are not deviant people. They are not sick. They are not ill. They are entranced. Very few people grow up without some painful, personally damaging experiences. Partners in these types of relationships do not necessarily qualify for psychiatric treatment in and of themselves. Such relationships, if not detranced and genuinely awakened, will drive both to the point of frenzied emotional, spiritual, and eventual physical bankruptcy.

It is especially important to emphasize a unique factor of the idealized state. As in hypnosis, both parties begin to discover that by being in this type of relationship, they can now be someone that they always wanted to be but previously never believed or dreamed they could be. For example, one partner believed that, suddenly, he had found somebody who gave him all the love, admiration, and attention previously denied him. Such idealization reaches a peak level of entrancement, narcissistic by nature of its self-centeredness. It results from a pyramid effect (a hypnotic technique) of one positive suggestion of specialness building upon another and another until partners believe they are each other's God.

Such fantasizing, preframing and larger-than-life image construction is exactly the type of hypnotic experience that occurs when people go into trance. When going into trance, the hypnotist deepens the subject's experience by pyramiding or building upon one positive suggestion after another to intensify or peak the presence of various hypnotic phenomena. Hypnotic subjects discover that they can construct amazing images, acting as if, for example, they are encountering creatures from the moon who speak Japanese. Both hypnotic subjects and entranced partners become fantasy characters in their own lives.

Whether it is stage hypnosis, or the staged hypnotic experience of the idealized, imaged, addictive relationship, one factor remains true. The most appealing and attractive quality of these relationships is that it creates a larger-than-life other worldliness where previously frustrated dreams can now come true. Partners are transported from the boring, everyday mundane, the tedium of daily routine, to a fabulous world where dreams can come true. Something magical seems to fill the air. Actually it is fog (confusion is a hypnotic technique).

The quest becomes whatever sense of excitement, stimulation or drama serves to create and enhance entrancement. Whatever allows movement into this altered, addicted, hypnotic kind of "beyond me" caricature of a role is the order of the day as long as it maintains the entrancement.

As partners become entranced, they become fixated and absorbed. They substitute hypnotically indulged euphoria fed by mind-altering, endorphin-stimulating, entrancing caricatures and distortions of their real self. The ensuing emptiness and lack of genuine substance of character in these relationships further fuels the hypnotic pull for intense clinging and ever deeper entrancement into the self-abandoning world of larger-than-life caricatures.

Partners encounter the distortion and illusionary affects of having been emotionally drawn into and hypnotically interwoven with their projected, mythical characters. They have created the hero and heroine they always wanted to be. His might be strong, courageous, and virile. Hers could be regal, heavenly, and angelic. They see nothing but the beautiful and lovely illusion of their idealized other.

Many people never really learn about enmeshed or entranced qualities in relating and thus continue to repeat the same or similar relationship mistakes, in one variation or another, over and over again throughout their adult lives. Their central mistake is that they do not know how to "stay awake" in intimate encounters. By that I mean they "fall asleep" into that euphoric, dreamlike entranced bonding, falling "head over heels" in love with their idealized partner. Both partners' true characters fall into a suspended animation state no longer meaningfully operative in entrancement. Partners can live many years and have numerous kinds of relationships and never awaken to their true character in loving relationships.

Entranced relationships experience deviation from fantasy roles, human quirks, and flaws. Each revealed flaw means the unraveling of their relationship. In entrancement, there is no core character and partners firmly believe that once the ideal fantasy falls apart, so will their bond together. As a result, they hang onto it for dear life.

Partners step into euphoria through repetitive experiences, which allows them to step into characters of princess and prince charming.

Suddenly, walking by the pond becomes associated with a trance induction of creating a larger-than-life reality. This is exactly what happens in a trance.

Notice similarities in trance induction. Subjects can step into a dream state by watching a swinging pendulum or listening to a relaxing voice. The hypnotist tells the subject to hear his voice, feeling waves of relaxation spreading through one's body. The hypnotist links his voice with feelings of pleasure by saying, "As these waves spread, you could discover deep, wonderful experiences, enjoying how comfortable it is being in this wonderful, pleasurable time and place." These types of paired, external foci (sound of my voice and walking by the pond) develop into deeply personal, inner meanings for both partners. Such personal connections (inner voice) within each partner to externally shared experiences (walking by pond) now become imaged sources of pleasure, empowering these associated phenomena as rituals.

Dwelling and repetition of rituals and trance inductions power the addictive relationship, transporting partners to a reality appearing larger-than-life. Partners are lost in an enhanced, self-magnification. As the reader will come to see, it is this type of enamored enhancement of larger-than-self caricature, beyond the wildest dreams of what partners believe could be, that creates so much misery and pain. This kind of other reality, this surrealism, is exactly what makes it so hard to maintain the relationship and eventually leads to its demise. The relationship will collapse as partners come to discover the inherent fallacies of the hypnotically induced fantasy. Partners learn what can and cannot be with this person. Partners can arise from the collapse of this overinflated, house-of-cards relationship if they release each other from the confined prison of entranced idealism. Only then can each partner's unique character and beauty be freed to love and be loved in real-life embrace.

CHAPTER 5

PASSAGE TO THE LAND OF DISILLUSIONMENT

STAGE II: INDUCING PARADISE, LOSING GROUND IN DREAM SLEEP

When we discover that our partner is not who we want him or her to be, we realize we never had accepted ourselves or him or her as any of us truly are. It becomes very difficult to let the relationship continue in its present form because to do so we have to let go of that larger-than-self image of each other's own mythical character. We are then confronted with having to accept the "everyday" reality of who each of us seems to be (which may not be as impressive or dynamic as our fantasies of one another). Indeed, it is not the loss of the other person that we dread so much as the loss of our mythical, heroic, larger-than-life-itself "character" that we have come to believe in so fervently. The agony of loss in a relationship can stem from losing such a powerfully, entrancing resource which feeds into our bigger-than-life illusions and delusions. In the light of such a loss, our everyday lives pale by comparison.

The loss of such a grandiose resource can be quite depressing (depression is usually the strongest emotion partners report in ending a relationship). When flaws and cracks appear, disillusionment sets in. There is a progressive, deteriorating quality of the idealized, addictive relationship. The proverbial bubble begins to break through the jagged edges of human flaws.

Such is the beginning of the disillusionment stage. While there is some "coming down to earth" in healthy relationships, the fall from paradise is not nearly as far or as shattering as in entrancement.

Each partner has an unrealistic illusion of how they must and should be with the other. It is considered a violation (according to entrancement thinking) when either one steps outside the fantasized boundaries of the hypnotically constructed relationship. Any break in such a constructed bond initiates a sense of anger and resentment. The beast and beauty phenomenon begins to emerge. He wants to see a loyal, loving, dedicated sidekick (commonly referred to as a codependent) who is always perfectly aligned and focused on his needs. She wants him to provide that secure, stable presence no matter what happens (Cinderella complex). Each has a facade to maintain in entrancement critical to their self-images of grandiose narcissism. Disillusionment and accusations are triggered when partners deviate from their "perfect" roles and fall from grace.

The domineering partner varies depending on who is in the "driver's seat" of who's accusing who. Such accusations of mutual imperfection are quite stressful. Both partners discover a need for personal space and time to be alone. This typically involves healthy areas of their lives where they are better able to be their real selves, whether on their own or with their own sets of friendships. This can become, however, another point of conflict. It is interesting that partners, trying to keep their euphoria alive, sense this has left them wanting. Boredom has been juxtaposed with perfect love, which is why conflict is needed and readily available to keep them interested. Boredom may seem strange for two people who are "euphoric" with one another. However, like any kid with an ice cream cone or any wonderful dessert or any trip to Disneyland, after awhile there is a feeling of being spent. Too much of anything creates saturation, and the potential for boredom in entrancing relationships is high if no variance is introduced. This is especially true if partners have to keep up the same old perfect image or front.

What happens when people have been making mad, passionate love all weekend is that by Sunday night they are saturated, feeling like it is time for something a little different. If sex goes on, it becomes more than just boring. It begins to bore a hole in the relationship and creates a certain amount of antagonism and emptiness. It can even reactivate old, negative childhood memories, which are indicative of how abusive the entrancement is becoming.

The restrictive qualities of this induced, fantasized relationship prevent creative expression of personal, individual time and activities. Restrictions lead to frustration and restlessness. Such conditions of the relationship cannot be asserted or commented upon for fear of violating the unspoken rule of the relationship that they are to be perfectly in love together all the time. They are stuck and fixated in imaged role-playing with each maintaining the illusionary, entranced bond.

This results in the need for more stimulation. A partner's fixated, perfectionistic role demands create boredom and tension. It is only a matter of time before problems erupt. Stepping out of character risks awakening from entranced bondage. Such premature awakening without each partner's establishing a confident sense of individual character is painful. Confronted with this double bind, partners are left with escalating needs for distraction and excitement. Whether pleasurable and/or painful, the goal now becomes discovering brief, temporary releases from an untenable, restrictive relationship. The irony about their endless pursuit of stimuli and exciting, unique experiences is that their entrancement is at the heart of creating the very confinement it was designed to eliminate. The real excitement is about whether the entranced relationship will live or die (she loves me, she loves me not?). The double-binding, no-win predicament provides perverse excitement.

Real variation (role differentiation) offers faceted strength and discovery in healthy relationships. Couples have the opportunity of growth and intimacy in a deepening way. In a healthy bond, partners can freely "step out of character" without feeling they are stepping out of the relationship.

In an addictive relationship, these variations conflict with a compulsive quality to maintain the euphoric fantasy through adherence to a fixed ideal outcome. The necessary compliance to the contract must be maintained in all conditions, at all times, with each person present. If it does not happen, there is a perception on one or both parts that one partner is not being perfect or fair in the way he or she is treating the other.

INTENSIFIED DYSFUNCTION

Entrancing dynamics intensify and perpetuate each partner's difficulties in establishing relationships. Some partners may fear control and manipulation. Others may agonize over abandonment. Entrancement exacerbates such vulnerabilities to heightened levels of dysfunction. Partners in addictive relationships view intimacy as intimidation and mutuality as a form of "get even" relating. They are trapped in an entranced double bind that creates impossible demands and chaotic turbulence.

The fear and compulsive nature of entrancement makes partners feel that if they, as a couple, ever come out of rapport in the relationship, they will lose the beautiful creation. There is anxiety and fear of each partner not being able to fulfill his or her deepest, most inner needs that may have persisted since childhood. Such needs are reactivated in entrancement. These may be needs to be loved, to be the center of attention, to be praised, to be genuinely cared for and loved for themselves. Ironically, each wants to be accepted and loved for himself or herself. Yet, in this type of relationship, they each press the other to act out illusionary, self-distorting roles to bring that acceptance about. This creates pain disguised as pleasure. Entranced partners base unconditional love on such role fulfillment.

The pain-pleasure dynamics of addictive relationships are actually extremes in emotional states with a zero-sum effect. No matter how wildly pleasurable or agonizingly painful couples' experiences are, they usually end up right back where they started, only deeper in entrancement. Each mood swing serves as another turn in the ever-deepening spiral cycle of entranced bonding. Confusion deepens with each spiraling cycle. Pain is pleasure and pleasure is pain. Both are now of equal intensity for hypnotic absorption. Partners fear the loss of euphoria when they act outside their perfect role depictions. If one partner perceives the other as out of compliance with the romantic role caricature, that partner rationalizes (uses entranced thinking) that the other is "falling out of love." That partner either has to provoke the other back into role caricature or act defensively to potential loss by breaking out of his or her own romantic caricature. This latter move is unlikely, as it would entail breaking out of entrancement.

With the progression of entrancement, partners find that they can only get so close before they "fall into conflict" together. This serves to deepen entrancement. The point of only being able to get so close is called an intimacy set-point and emerges in the disillusionment stage.

Partners discover that they move back and forth from pleasure to pain, oscillating around an intimacy set-point that determines how close and how far they are to be. Partners become confused as to how and why perfectly wonderful moments seem to end in disastrous conflicts and rage. They wonder why their times together fall apart, work out, and then recycle. Such oscillations are signs of disillusionment and the intimacy set-point in operation. This functions as an endless loop of induction, entrancing them ever tighter and deeper.

Oscillation can be driven by core needs for unconditional love contrasted with an all-pervasive doubt of lovability. Induced fantasy is supposed to resolve the conflict. The idealized fantasy (embedded in induced trance of the Garden of Eden), is discovered to be a precariously balanced "resolved" conflict lost at the slightest break of rapport. Because of the fragile and artificial illusion of the bond, anything less than total connection and attunement is terrifying. Fear is chronic of one or the other partner stepping out of character.

If this perfect state of love and "unconditional regard" and acceptance is broken, it threatens to reveal the inner conflict of unlovability. The trance becomes lighter and lighter as he or she awakens to reality.

As partners unknowingly come out of trance, they discover falsehoods hidden in the sense of blissful harmony. As partners have nowhere else to turn (no sense of self or identity at this point without fantasy), to come out of entrancement is to return to a world of emptiness, loneliness, and fear of being unlovable. The only perceived choice is for partners to loop back into entrancement, plummeting even deeper together into the stage of obsession.

It is important to note that when one partner is threatened emotionally by "too much" intimacy (time together, loving gestures, etc.), this begins to violate set-point boundaries of intimacy such that one partner withdraws by acting indifferent and detached, provoking the other.

CHAPTER 6

ATTENTION: ALL YE WHO ENTER, PREPARE TO ABANDON SELF

STAGE III: DEEPER OBSESSIONS AND NIGHTMARES

The disillusionment stage now becomes obsessive. The movement from disillusionment to obsession in the addictive relationship becomes a very powerful one. In order to repel the threatened rupture of the fused, entranced relationship, there must be worrying and ruminating. Obsessing about one another, even negatively, allows partners to feel connected, even if painfully. Pain now has become "pleasurable." Obsessive worrying occurs over how perfect the relationship is, should be, or could be. Minor irritations of how the partner has talked in the past about members of the opposite sex and other subjects may be reflected upon long after conversations have passed. Partners test one another to see if the other is the "genuine article" (will stand lovingly by their side through difficulties). This may come in the form of extorting guarantees of fidelity and eternal love ("I will always love you"). Obsession reflects the lost sense of self-reality which is a genuine loss. Obsession involves a loss of control. When partners cannot leave each other alone, constantly dwelling on one another, a sense of identity is lost. Confrontations, worrying, and suspicion erupt as to partners' whereabouts.

Desperate, verbal assurances of love ensue. Yet they see each other less and less. Partners may question why the other did not call sooner. Wondering who the other is with reflect fears of loss. Infidelity is perceived as the ultimate violation of hypnotic entrancement. Many times, promises made may not match actual behavior. The fear of loss may be real. The entrenched nature of this stage of the addictive relationship intensifies obsessiveness. Obsessiveness can be the mind's effort to ward off the threatening realization of the relationship's emptiness.

Preoccupation now deepens into a pervasive critique regarding the relationship's quality. Maintaining the fantasized imagined quality of perfect love and partner (almost perfect mother) that never existed becomes essential. There are tremendous feelings of loss, abandonment, and enormous amounts of depression that begin to set in at the slightest imagined or real perception that the other person is no longer holding up his or her end of the fantasized, inductive bargain. Partners experience narcissistic injuries when either one or both is not holding up to his or her end of the fantasy.

In the obsessive stage, partners temporarily resurface from the trancelike euphoria of oneness and connection with one another as they just start to feel comfortable. Confronted with awakened difficulties, they become even more deeply immersed in worry, obsession, and trancelike dialogue. What is happening that prevents that fantasy rapport from maintaining itself? Remember that one of the ironies of entrancement (that which is supposedly the most intimate of all relationships) has a built in set-point that retards the development of genuine intimacy. Partners have a very difficult time just enjoying their relationship and not trying to constantly "fix it." Ironically, the more worried, confronted, and argumentative the two become, the deeper entrancement and the more euphoria shifts to shock and pain.

Partners move from a once dreamlike state to what now becomes a nightmare. They find themselves arguing and conflicting over what would be considered minor in a healthy relationship. Mild disruptions in rapport are perceived, under the magnifying-glass effects of entrancement, as major cracks and faults in the integrity of their commitment. As a consequence of obsessive worrying and increasing insecurities, an intense shift in the absorbing quality of their relationship takes place. Partners increasingly resurface from euphoric idealization disillusioned, and repetitively submerge into an absorbing, obsessive negativity. The shift in focus has moved from seeking to maintain their fantasy ideal toward one of obsession over relationship imperfections and inadequacies. Partners are entranced in an obsessive cycle of surfacing from idealized, euphoric moments of intimacy, resubmerging into obsessive worries and negativities. Such a shift in cycle takes them deeper into the nightmare of entrancement.

In comparing this entrancing process to hypnotic processes, it can be valuable to consider deepening techniques utilized in standard hypnotic trance. Many dynamics are involved. One is called fractionation, which is another word for describing how to deepen trance by focusing and relaxing, going into experience, coming out, and going back even deeper than before. It repeats itself so the person is coming up and going down deeper and deeper with each successive cycle, until a deepened, total somnolescent (deep-trance state) has been reached. Such is the state of affairs in obsessive surfacing and submerging into ever-deeper entrancement.

PARADOXES IN PARADISE

The shifts in obsessive focus involve shifts in pleasure and pain. A paradoxical effect operates such that pleasurable experiences now become painful. The couple argues over the lost states of euphoric pleasure and becomes hypnotically shifted to euphorically painful, intense obsessions over who's to blame. If such a couple sought professional help, the therapist could talk about different psychiatric diagnoses for such behaviors, but actually these people can be very healthy in many areas of their lives. As most of these people are raised in imperfect homes with imperfect mothers and fathers, normal imperfections in personality development will be embedded in these people. Entrancement can bring out normal imperfection in anyone's upbringing.

People involved in these types of relationships may not necessarily be dysfunctional in the clinical sense, but faulty logic in their belief systems makes them vulnerable to hypnotic enmeshments. Partners need help to deal with this type of induced relationship. Partners begin to develop obsessive rumination over the intentions and motivations of the other's behavior. Suspicion and mistrust begin to intensify. Entranced partners demand support and unconditional love no matter what one does to the other. Absorbed in fantasized ideals, partners presume that each should always be there for the other.

PERFECT LOVE--A MUST

To achieve this innate acceptance of always being there for another no matter what requires the one thing with which fantasized, perfect love interferes. It requires the presence of a partner's core love. The core of love emerges from that core character and integrity which is the foundation of each partner's genuine self.

Entranced couples' very fantasy blocks access to the inherent character within each other. As a consequence, both constantly try to get the other to prove unconditional acceptance through provocative, even sadistic, punitive maneuvers. The seeds of doubt that each carry about themselves are being planted and grow in negative, suspicious interpretations and sadomasochistic treatment of one another. The equation being formulated is perfect love would now mean perfect agony.

I WILL ALWAYS LOVE YOU . . . NEXT

Partners have their own style, personality traits, and characteristics. However, individuality of partners does not fit the artificially simplistic fantasy of perfect union and harmony. The consequential disharmony resulting from two unique personalities having to deny their uniqueness in coming together becomes threatening and stressful. Instead of recognizing the need for dialogue and creating a healthier version of relating, differences are labeled a sin or violation of perfect love deserving of punishment.

Partners may regress to childlike states, eliciting intense passions and drives which shock, frighten, as well as delight one another. In time, such intensity can become overbearing and restrictive. Partners can instantly associate (regress in trance) to how controlling and/or suffocating their parents may have been. Partners vacillate between attraction and repulsion in their uncertainty about being with each other.

Partners no longer see one another in idealistic, impeccable frames of reference in such regressed states. What is perceived instead may be revolting to each other. What is now perceived are the natural human "deviations" to constricted love fantasy. Perfect love fantasy comes into conflict with manifesting the larger uniqueness of character.

The unique complexity of character has been restricted to rigid fantasy role requirements. Creative, spontaneous qualities of each partner become rigidly distorted and classified as either all good or all bad. Entrancements can be nested and dependent. Others may be high stimulus and need constant excitement. In either scenario, entrancement is oppressive at the individual level as it conflicts with partners' unique and unsharable sense of self.

NARCOSIS, MERMAIDS, AND NYMPHS

Whatever qualities attract us to our partners will, if not reviewed in a more mature perspective, begin to drive us apart. This is not because one partner or the other has changed. Rather, it is because both have become entranced with this kind of rigid demand of how they are now to be to maintain this absorbed state. As the entranced relationship progresses, more of what was previously viewed as desirable and enhancing now becomes grist and material for the critique mill. Every critique and fault-finding ironically deepens both partners into entrancement, which only intensifies pathological behaviors. Every deviation becomes another absorbing experience of what should not be present.

Qualities that take partners out of the absorbed state are threatening, as they may awaken one or both from entrancement. Such awakening qualities and behaviors are reframed and relabeled as dangerous, unloving, and rejecting. Paradoxically critique not only crushes and negates a partner's character, but actually deepens entrancement of what is allowable. Selective restriction of what is allowable intensifies entrancement. The more exhausting the energy drain, the more absorbing and entrancing the relationship becomes. Every denial of real, unique differences entrances partners deeper into an unreal world of terror.

Instead of facing realistic differences, partners begin to argue, twist, and bend one another, seeking to maintain that illusionary reality. The resulting disharmony now becomes familiar. It is their paradoxical (and pathological) way of having "harmony through disharmony." Partners conflict to such intensity, they discover that obsessive arguing becomes their way to love. Conflict, pain, and exhaustion become the entranced partners mode of operating.

The obsessive quality continues to emerge as partners constantly analyze each other's flaws, labeling the other's dynamics and imperfections (called character defects). Each believes that the other has the potential to eventually be his or her ideal mate. Each partner may believe that it is just a matter of time before the other "changes." The expectation of change in the future only intensifies the entranced absorption. Partners may debate arguments in their own mind while alone. Each may wonder who the other one is with, what the other one is doing, and so on. This obsessive self-dialogue is a form of self-hypnosis which further deepens trance.

Obsessive trance talk acts like hypnotic suggestion. Constant self-talk preprograms and prepares partners for the next encounter. What becomes increasingly evident is the developmental and evolving nature of the obsessive stage. As the obsession continues, they become more entranced by discomfort and pain. In time, the stimulation of pain becomes hypnotically enticing and develops into perverse pleasure.

Partners learn about one another's vulnerabilities and sensitivities. These become targets for annihilation where deadly blows, insults, antagonisms, and tauntings are delivered. As obsession progresses, allowing joy and pleasure becomes more difficult with shorter and shorter periods. Obsession involves control through pain in the couple's relationship. The entranced relationship begins to shift toward an ever more intense, darkened labyrinth of paranoia, suspicion, and fear of the unknown.

After one particularly pleasurable and fulfilling erotic evening together, one partner became more and more paranoid over the possibility that the other secretly had another lover. She feared losing control beyond hypnotic set-point limits of the relationship. Real joy could jeopardize the balance (of intimacy) of how much release from the entrancement was allowed.

The irony is that undue pleasure is now threatening. It exposed her to the reality of being loved, raising doubts of her lovableness. The greater the fear of love, the deeper the entrancement into negativity and darkness which increases doubts of lovability.

Obsession takes the form of coming out of fantasy, then going into it with an even deeper fervor and determination to "get at" what is "interfering" with intimacy. As time progresses, so does their obsessing, worrying, and complaining. Entrancement provides a sense of control where partners predictably know where they stand in their chaos. Genuine loving experiences threaten to lighten entrancement, exposing partners to real freedom of the unknown. It is the unknown that can be most intimidating. The paradox of love, letting go to hold on, gets lost in entrancement. This daring act exposes us to anxious uncertainty of what the future may bring.

The only way to keep a nonsubstantive, fantasy relationship alive is to constantly deepen the trance. Partners do this within the hypnotic framework or magical illusion of obsessive worry and fearful thoughts of loss and abandonment (they mistake vigilance for keeping vigil). "If I dwell on what might take her away, I'll be able to stop it." There is the belief that obsessing will somehow change reality. In an unhealthy way, it does. The more partners dwell on such obsessions, the more they "dwell" or live there. They act as if they are trying to get to the bottom of something that does not exist. That is the irony of the obsessive quality. Partners become more obsessed with something that is not there. They look toward one another's defects, one another's "imperfections" (as they are called anyway), which are what makes each person a unique individual. Imperfections here refer not to such real problems as alcoholism or abuse, but rather to uniquely personal variations violating set roles and fixated behaviors.

The implicit tragedy of the obsessive stage is that the harder partners struggle to work things out, the more issues are stirred up and the more they have to deal with to maintain trance. One partner confronts the other's lack of attention only to discover that in doing so he challenges her integrity and the ideal of their bonded entrancement. No sooner does one issue get "resolved" than more complicated issues arise, pulling them down even deeper. There are always more "defects, dynamics, and flaws" to deal with. They become ever more deeply enmeshed and involved in attempting to sort things out.

Their conflicts keep them at a distance, yet still tied to their fantasized ideal. Their absorption is deepened in pursuing ideals they sense are beyond their reach. As the obsessive quality continues, it becomes clear that other facets of their lives are coming into play. For example, time is moving on and they find themselves increasingly alone even with one another. They may experience stomachaches, headaches, and various forms of intestinal disturbances or have flashbacks of childhood memories depicting various forms of abuse.

While the past is something that stays with us, many times the past reflects the present conditions we are in. Not only does the present reflect the past, but past memories can also reflect present, abusive relationships with which we become obsessed. The tragicomedy of the obsessive stage is that partners are trying to get at the "defects" and "work out" painful experiences so they can somehow enjoy the relationship. Yet the relationship is based on having defects and problems to work out. The illusion of ever working out defects hypnotically deepens the relationship through its obsessiveness.

Partners struggle trying to make meaning and purpose out of something that for all intents and purposes doesn't have any. Tragic in their plight, they talk to their friends. They may even date other people, but may not call it dating. They call it confiding or having chats. They may try temporary breaks in communication. Whatever reprieve they use to take a break, they begin creating a separate life outside of their relationship, only to return to the "cocoon" of entranced (or entombed) bonding.

The irony is that the relationship is still seen as their center. While they may talk and spend time with other people, their minds, even unconsciously as with any trance, has with it a kind of posthypnotic or posttrance suggestion that "if only I could be with this person, then my life will be that wonderful, fantasized, nurturing oneness that it was always meant to have been."

It is at this point in the entrancement that the fantastic ideal of myth fulfillment is at its peak. Entrancement has equated having that special partner with having everything that could ever meet each other's deepest dreams and illusions of perfect harmony. Such embodiment of dream fulfillment in having that special partner requires the utmost protection and security of this scared bond. While on the surface partners desperately seek to keep up pretenses of this sacred connection, below the surface of permitted awareness lurk fears, insecurities, and unhappiness. Partners are losing themselves to protect their entranced sacred bond and dread such awareness.

As a consequence of an entrancement that obscures genuine self-awareness, partners seek to have supportive and supplementary outside relationships to meet their deeper needs. Such peripheral relationship contacts are necessary to keep an unreal entranced bond alive.

Yet new relationships are not really "new." Partners now begin to entrance other people so that others are as entranced with their entrancement as they are. Notice how people love talk shows on dysfunctional relationships. You might call it a group hypnotic induction and deepening.

Entrancements perpetuate themselves like an addiction with ever-widening involvement. Partners (and others drawn in) are not able to truly experience who they are. Only a distorted caricature and skewed version colored by obsessive fantasy are allowed to illuminate how that person ought or must be.

The essence of obsession in entrancement is that partners are not so much obsessed with each other as they are with whether or not their partner is adequately maintaining the correct representation of their fantasy ideal. Partners do not realize how they are walking around in a certain trancelike state. They have a trance vision of what success is, a trance vision of what love is, a trance vision of what family is. They even have a television to communicate with other visions of how life should be.

It is an entrancing quality where partners become caught up with that magical concept of how life ought to be. Partners, without thinking, buy into a certain entranced, ritual myth about relationships passed down to them from their own family heritage, their childhood experiences, and their own bio-psycho-social-cultural background. The truth is that partners become obsessed with each other because they become obsessed with themselves. The obsessive quality is a very selfish quality and even narcissistic.

There are important points to remember about the obsessive stage. The first point is that by definition, obsession is a loss of control. It is a loss of control in the sense that one becomes automatic in what one is thinking without true self-awareness of this process. That is to say, you might find brushing your teeth, curling your hair, shopping with your children, and having thoughts, ruminations, and negativity about that relationship without realizing it. You might find yourself digging into issues, analyzing your partner, even speaking out loud to yourself as you obsess in mental self talk. It is upsetting to discover how illusionary our thought control has become.

When partners are confused between inner world and the present reality, they lose awareness and access of ability to chose which thoughts to think and which not to think. Partners lose the boundary between their inner, mental self-talk and the outer world of the here and now. They are lost in their fantasized thoughts and immersed in that entrancing nightmare that has come to take over their life.

Reminiscences of early childhood experience in the obsessive stage are very common. What begins to emerge with the feeling of loss of control is reliving unlovable past experiences. Regression accesses for each partner their early family dramas. That life script is thus reactivated. There is nothing that deepens the trance experience more than regressing into past experiences brought to life by here-and-now obsessive ruminations. The more partners obsess and ruminate about the relationship, the more it brings them back, like a time machine, (like a hypnotist age-regressing his or her client) to a time in which they first experienced powerful, emotional moments in their lives with significant others.

A second point about obsession is this reliving of intimate, dramatic family of origin experiences. These can overwhelm and totally undermine the quality of the already fragile relationship. Such reactivated early childhood family dramas can be beneficial to the extent that they challenge partners to deal with past issues. What is not so wonderful about them is that partners do not know what is happening to them.

They do not realize that they are being taken back. They do not realize that they have stopped looking at each other as people and begun to project past memories and scenarios onto each other through their own hypnotic, regressive childhood experiences. She may be tempted to call him Dad. He may be tempted to call her Mom. They have stopped seeing what little individual character of which they may have been aware. They have stopped seeing it within themselves so how can they see it in their partner? They have almost completely lost themselves within the obsession, which is another important point.

There is a loss of self in obsessive ruminations, worries, and nightmares how the other is not giving what is needed as dictated by entrancement. With this loss of self, partners cannot give to each other when disabled in giving to themselves what they need. Partners forget to remember what they love to do. It is difficult to enjoy good conversation and experiences with people, places, and things when the body is present but the mind isn't.

A third point to remember about obsessive relationships is that the more one tries to resolve them, the more dissolved one becomes in them. The more you struggle, the deeper you get stuck. The more partners slam into, blame, or accuse each other, the deeper entranced they become. Ruminations become more intense and obsessive with the passage of time.

There are depressive memories of what no longer is wishing and longing for what was once their wonderful Garden of Eden, the illusion of euphoria that they had in the idealized stage. They become immersed in an ever-deeper trancelike experience. In a deep trance, people act as if they are asleep, even though they are very much awake in a more selective sense. They are in a highly focused state of concentration (attention is selectively directed toward ideas, feelings, behaviors). That focused concentration creates an illusion of things happening by themselves. That is because selectivity of attention causes us to ignore the source of what is influencing the situation. Yet partners are always creating their own experience mostly without realizing it.

One is not always aware of what one is creating. One seems to be living the entranced drama of the relationship so intensely that it becomes a reality all of its own. Such an intensely focused state is created in entrancement and is called a somnolescent state. There are some lessons to be learned in and about that somnolescent, "sleeplike" state. If you asked them their names, if you tried to talk to them as people while they were in that state, you would only get the kinds of responses that would be consistent with that state.

The images, beliefs, and fantasies partners experience in entrancement appear virtually real to them. That is the experience of being in deep trance. It is as if the unbelievable experiences one could only imagine are now happening in real life. In a deep trance state, one does not feel one has any control. One does not feel one has any real boundaries. The entranced fantasy is so real, so consistent, that it echoes and brings to awareness deep-seated (or seeded) needs that partners may have always had. How motivated are they to come out of something that promises, even remotely, to fulfill those aroused, inner fantasy, childlike needs? Whatever experiences could awaken them from this trance are discarded and lost in that out-of-control, very vivid, very real, four-dimensional mirage.

It is this fourth-dimensional, fixated ideal frozen in time that obsessively loops each partner's efforts to change back into himself or herself in an ever-intense, deepening entranced relationship. Entrancement is the never-never land of Peter Pan, where partners cannot grow up. Partners become almost like lost souls. Each may go through the motions of their everyday life. They seem to be alive, but they are not. Partners are focused selectively onto one hopeful but elusive fantasy that has turned into a nightmare. Just as if someone dreams of home but can never go back. They can never return to that euphoric, perfect, ideal state.

In the obsessive stage, an individual laments that he or she can never return to the pure harmony of ideal, perfect oneness. Sensing this, the best one can do is to substitute obsession for idealized love. In the pursuit of what one feels one cannot have is the ironic intensification of striving ever harder to obtain the mystical, magic of the initial euphoria of the past. If individuals can't achieve the future growth, then they somehow adjust by pursuing the past. There is an intense attending and obsessing over what once was. Partners progress in getting themselves stuck in the past. If they could learn to move forward in time, seeing each other as human beings with variations of good, bad, and unique, they could rediscover a more realistic magic.

The loss seems too great. It becomes all-consuming, all-entrancing, and all-deepening. As time progresses, both begin to go through periods of confusion and diffusion. They feel like they do not know where they are. There is a sense of going through the motions. They feel very confused and wonder what they are doing. Such vague and confused experiences numb their feelings of being alive and excited about life. They are lost in trancelike states. Now the growing reality has come to pass that their fantasy is not going to be. They both dread the inevitable reality.

Such foreboding awareness causes an enormous amount of depression. It causes a deepening, not a lessening, of intense wanting. In a healthy relationship, in a relationship in which two people discover a lack of compatibility, they would simply, perhaps with sadness and with some pain, accept the inevitable and move on. However, in a fantasized, addictive, hypnotic relationship between two lovers, such is not the case. Instead of being able to make adult assessments with critical faculties available, the individuals make blind decisions. There is just criticism of one another.

There is a lack of good judgment about what is happening to each of them. Indeed, they are so critical of one another, they have passed the point of knowing what is good for one another. They have lost an important reality orientation of judging what is in their own best interests. Even if they could have had a decent relationship, they have so muddied the waters that they are prevented from seeing who the other one is to develop the love, respect, and character so critical for healthy, loving relationships. Instead of loving one another, they are, for the sake of love, "in love," they are entranced.

That is why they are not amenable to logic, reason, or willpower. It is not that they are so happy with each other at this point that they would like to stay forever. Ironically, in an addictive, hypnotic relationship the worse it gets the more entrenched they become. As partners experience their fantasy ideal slipping away at every turn, their desperation increases at an exponential rate to hold onto it. They become entrenched in the age-old principle of wanting more of what they are getting less and less, which is the fantasy ideal.

The perplexing nature of wanting what one can't have becomes ever more entrancing. The more lonely and miserable partners are, the more longing there is for the other person. Rather than letting go and finding another who can fulfill his or her needs (starting with themselves), each moves to an even more tortuous stage: rapprochement.

CHAPTER 7

PRISONERS OF WAR (LOVE) AND SADOMASOCHISM: WHEN IT'S KILLING ME TO LOVE YOU

STAGE III: EVER DEEPER

The rapprochement stage has now begun to emerge. The relationship as it was originally idealized has, for all intents and purposes, been eliminated. The dark focus is now what is keeping the partners entranced in what may be called the nightmare or shadow image. Such a focus is the exact opposite of what they had in the beginning. Instead of the unbelievable ideal, it is the unbelievable ordeal which has now become the nightmare. The absence of beauty has created an expectational set of longing for the past, which strengthens the depth of that trance to a degree that becomes magnetic. Partners feel helpless, out of control of themselves and their relationship.

In rapprochement, partners believe the other is at fault for destroying their magical, once-in-a-lifetime fantasy bond. This rupture strikes at the core of their innermost yearning of everything they ever wanted in perfect love. Both begin to engage in various punishments that the other now "deserves" in the form of abusive mistreatment. Intensive critique is constant, reaching a fever pitch of contempt and revulsion. What emerges is almost sheer condemnation of the other's "deviant and deviating" qualities.

The movement has progressed (or regressed) from an all-loving perfection to an all-consuming rage. At this stage, the hypnotic pull of entrancement shifts with a fury, spiraling downward into darkened wounds of emptiness and loss. Partners are so fixated and sensitized to the pain of loss, that any show of love or affection seems like mockery.

There is no room in such a nightmarish entrancement for loving gestures which are painful reminders of what they believe will never be. The depth of entrancement is beginning to reach the depths of despair.

The core woundedness of each partner involving hurt, fears of abandonment, loss, and shame are all about to surface. Each partner's most dreaded nightmares are about to be confirmed in the rapprochement stage. What is being tapped is the shocking realization of paradise lost surfacing through rage, anger, and self-projection.

It is essential to note that this surfacing is the product of the entranced relationship, not the cause. Partners perceive one another as from the dark side. Each is now viewed to be the incarnation of evil itself. The incredible rage, disdain, and contempt partners have for each other in this context of rapprochement takes on a vehement and violent quality.

RAPPROCHEMENT AND PARADISE LOST

The sadomasochistic dynamic has now surfaced full-blown where partners trade mortal blows of verbal and, at times, nonverbal violence and aggression. Partners may resort to this as they feel impotent and desperate. They are in a death grip like two bull elk on a snowy field with horns locked to the death. Each impales the other to the point of inflicting what is believed to be much-deserved pain. The transgressions of "major violations" now "justify" righteous rage in each partner's mind. Each blames, accuses, and attacks the other for destroying perfect love. In defending against depression of loss and abandonment, partners project onto each other the cause of their entire life suffering.

As the wounds surface, each partner takes his or her turn hurting and being hurt. Inflicting pain on our partner expresses the compensatory desire to "get back" what was lost. The deepest level of entrancement has now been reached.

Infantile age-regression (rage regression) may occur back to earlier years where perfect love, magical in quality, was wished for in the parent-child bonding but was sadly missed. Because of how intense and real this hypnotically induced, trancelike regression is experienced, no amount of pain and agony is too great a punishment for the other's offenses. Both present and past offenses are compiled together in the "betrayal" of our partner.

It is important to understand that the quality of this "relationship," if you will, is intensified through fixations from parallel past experiences

of unrequited love. Individuals progress in getting lost in each suc-
ceeding regression. Partners go deeper and deeper into absorbed trance,
reopening old wounds which create holes in their character. Old wounds
of hurt, rejection, and abandonment tear at the core of each partner's
unique character, blinding them from perceiving their inherent identity
and wholeness.

These wounds are time-bound. The deeper the trance, the farther the
time regression. Partners cease to function in the adult state. Partners
trance-gress (commit a transgression or mistaken discernment of reality)
to childlike resources. Transgressions seem bigger and more terrifying.

Partners alter their perception and interpretation of reality while
regressed in entrancement. Entrancement is a mind-altering experience.
Depending on the trance state accessed, events can be construed to mean
what partners "choose" in that state. Choices are limited by the state
they are in at the time. Entrancement magnifies emotional investment in
partners to the irrational extreme that life without the other seems to be
meaningless and unbearable. The partners' agony is now their ecstasy.
Their pain is now their entrancing pleasure. Could this be part of the
dynamics of wife abuse, stalking relationships, domestic violence, and
the like? Partners can be relatively normal, though not necessarily
healthy. They are normal to the extent that people regressed to early
childhood could discover some moderate to severe traumatic experiences happening at that time.

The point is that the regression accesses painful experiences in each
partner's life. It propels partners to drive wedges into the "hairline
fractures" that exist in everyone's character armor. As the regression
goes deeper, this penetrating wedge creates an ever-wider gap, releasing
a flood of anger and hurt. This is what is being unleashed in the rapprochement stage.

As the individuals go deeper and deeper, they lose even more of
their own personal integrity, character, and identity as to who they are as
adult human beings. What level of maturity they may have had is soon
deteriorated and washed away in this emotional flood of hurt, rage, and
excess baggage. Not only do partners begin to blame one another, they
begin to blame themselves and their relationship. Everything comes
under attack.

What is about to be discovered is a pyrrhic kind of victory where
partners essentially begin to destroy all three parties: the relationship,
the self, and the other. The hypnotic entrancement is heightened and

brought to critical mass in emotionally and physically explosive episodes.

Each partner is at the point of vehement and nauseous rage toward
the other. One cannot describe the sense of despicability that the two
people begin to feel toward one another. Partners can feel trapped and
captured like prisoners of war. "All's fair in love and war" goes the old
adage. This sentiment is never more utilized than in addictive relationships. The entranced rage war is fueled by "fusion" power. That is,
partners become enmeshed or fused together in one another's perfection
demands of love. The concept of two individuals becoming fused into
one is well touted in romantic literature and songs. Such fusion obsessively magnifies an idealized partner's normal cracks into fatal flaws.
Their Garden of Eden's perfect love has eaten the forbidden fruit of self-
knowledge, which is their sin of originality.

FORBIDDEN FRUIT

Rapprochement emerges and leads partners on a journey discovering
core beliefs and needed confirmations that may have been hidden
throughout the script of their lives. Partners may have always wanted
these hidden fantasies (forbidden fruit) to come to life but not believed
them possible. As a consequence, partners aren't fully awake but instead live in hypnotic entrancement, longing for unrequited love, feeling
deprived. Partners may long for a home. They may want to go home
but are never able to achieve such a place. This can be taken to mean
many possibilities in this context. Never going home refers to never
being able to get to that perfect love, bond, womblike experience. This
lost perfect love comes in many forms.

Whatever version of this idealized perfect harmony, oneness, or
giftedness with which we hypnotically and mythically go through life,
partners in entranced relationships are convinced that only this dream
will make life perfect, whole, and wonderfully complete. The rapprochement stage reveals the dream to be a field of barren fruit infested
with false promises of fulfillment. Partners insist on their fantasy ideas
coming to fruition only to discover emptiness in unexamined ideals.
Hidden fantasies may or may not embody the relationship's fantasy ideals but, left unchallenged and entranced, fester. Forbidden fruit, when
exposed through honest self-expression for what it is, reveals the seeds
of revitalizing character.

The character of each partner's sense of self has its own unfolding reality that when denied, unacknowledged, or at times distorted creates a dark, nightmarish side of ourselves. When partners do not live their lives aligned with their inherent character, they have lost a core anchor of identity. It taunts and haunts them as to why they are not living it, pursuing it, and bringing their own personal truth to light. It is what is referred to as the "unlived life." When partners are living in the fantasy of ideals, of what they have come to misconstrue and misperceive as their real life or self, they become angry not only at the relationship for not fulfilling their needs and those of the fantasy, but also at themselves for not being who they truly are. If partners could awaken from entrancement honestly examining hidden fantasy ideals, they would divest such flowery illusions from the seeds of their core character.

Unexamined and entranced, love is experienced as intrusive and imprisoning. Intrusive love is the real violation of self and other. Loving one another now becomes an act of violence. Needing to differentiate and to mature as adult partners are now emerging as critical issues. Much of the anger and violence has to do not only with the fantasy of not being fulfilled, but also with the rage and anger of feeling trapped in the fantasy and having to fulfill it.

That quality of feeling entrapped or encased in the fantasy of ideal love and the effects of being shut out from one's own sense of identity, uniqueness, and life purpose is a critical indicator of addictive relationships. For now, suffice it to say that part of the rage is related to denial of self. Because of this enmeshment and induced deepening of hypnotic fantasy, partners can become enraged and fearful of being cut off from their own true purposes, their own true selves.

To that extent, it may be a very healthy rage even though the expression of it in terms of addictive relationships can be extremely dangerous and destructive. Many acts of violence and physical and emotional abuse may be distorted, symbolic gestures that are a sign of self-alienation and loss of true character. Many of these destructive acts may be a form of self-attack, expressing self-contempt for violating one's own personal integrity.

EATING YOURSELF ALIVE

The fragile structure of entrancement caves in when partners are confronted with sharing their relationship at healthy, community functions. An odd set of dynamics unfolds. Partners may lament not having this fantasy fulfilled. They find one reason (or excuse) after another to justify not being able to be together. They create an odd kind of paradigm of "I'd love to be with you if only the schedules could be worked out."

The reality is a remarkably creative hidden agenda which operates to prevent powerful intimacies of the entranced relationship from unfolding. Partners in entrancement prefer to live in this fantastic kind of apparition or hallucination, heroically "striving" to be together (what is Romeo and Juliet?). They attribute inability to be together to mysterious forces beyond their control (what is Juliet's father?). Such forces may, in part, be their own inner raging against themselves. In light of day-to-day living together, the relationship would be exposed as shallow and adolescent, lacking genuine sharing or intimacy.

The fantasy ideal's conspiracy is a disguise that distracts partners through convenient adversities, preventing both from being able to enjoy healthy, personal, social situations together. Such a conspiracy protects the entranced bond from being exposed in the communal light of day. It prevents the fantasy of "oneness" from ever being exposed as to its falseness and frailty. When partners feel hurt and/or angry with each other over small arguments and conflicts, such negativity is used as a facade and distraction to justify why they cannot be together in community activities. That is their mutual conspiracy to hide the reality from themselves that they are really fighting over "nothing." There is no substance to their relationship, which is the abuse. The intoxicating hypnotic pull of "substance abuse" that entrances and entraps them in the prism of their illusionary castle in the sky is filled with black knights and dragons to slay.

The two of them arrange in their own unconscious, protective functions to avoid intimate times together that could build a genuine, hopeful relationship. Such events would be risky and vulnerable as the individuals would be challenged to step outside of their narrow fantasy world. Their fears of intimacy and losing control perpetuate distance. Such fears keep each partner's life compartmentalized from one another as is so often the case in addictive, hypnotic relationships. Entranced partners usually lament that they gave their all to the other. While investing intensity, what they gave was everything they had (including their real self) to narrow, fantasy roles of what was supposed to be. Partners lack self-awareness and self-honesty to realize how constrained and piecemeal their efforts are.

Blinded by fear induced by entrancement, partners dread the loss of the other yet fear the loss of self-fusing. This bind is "resolved" by half-hearted efforts. Partners only get (or give) a piece of this person here or a part of that person's time there. It looks as if it is an adult relationship, but in actuality it is the old "divide and conquer" principle.

Fragmentation of relating is hypnotic as illusions of part-time sharing induce the whole (hole) magic. Absence of genuinely holistic relationships makes the heart grow magical in that piecemeal approaches to relating creates an incomplete picture with missing gaps leaving the rest to imagination and mystery. In the absence of good sense, entrancement filters out all but the brightest of stimuli to our senses; we draw upon the nonsensible. We mythologize our partner's flashy points into eye-catching figures of idealistic beauty.

Paradoxes of this stage involve rage and fury at the "other" for not fulfilling his or her fantasy's need where unfulfillment is actually designed to protect them. In sensing emptiness in their entrancement, partners have growing fears of being hurt from intimate involvements threatening to bring closeness.

There is nothing but fantasy. This "sense of nothing" beyond the entranced relationship is what activates the binding dynamics of being caught between the fear of abandonment and the fear of smothering. Adding salt to the self-inflicting wound of lost self is the dreaded discovery that this much-needed fantasy is nonexistent.

Partners have fears that one or the other is dying. Such fears reflect their vague awareness that the fantasy of entrancement is a near-death experience. The hypnotic quality of the relationship is so entrenching and entrancing, it blinds them to their own self-destructiveness and self-abandonment. To protect themselves from this revelation, they must increase their assault and attack. The rapprochement then hits crisis proportions. The fantasy/nightmare becomes self-mutilating and eventually self-annihilating.

The rapprochement stage has a cycle of vacillation where partners move close, fuse together, and then withdraw. One or both parties will act as though they do not need this relationship and could live without it. When they do separate, one or both may enjoy and feel a kind of domination over their partner.

Partners may feel insecure and fearful that without even the shattered dream of the fantasy, they have nothing. Partners fear they have gone too far. With this fear, they collapse back into addictive, hypnotic relating. Such hypnotic fractionation (coming out of trance and going back into it deeper) intensifies entrancement. It is a continual process throughout the hypnotic quality of the relationship.

Entranced relationships appear to reverse reality. Outside is inside. Partners have lost their boundaries of when they are inside their own self or dealing with external, interpersonal reality. Partners are unaware of inner feelings and images they have of each other, believing they are responding to each other's needs when it is their own to which they are attending. This paradoxical nature of entranced relationships is reflective of the difficulty partners have of getting outside of their narcissistic, self-mirrored position, genuinely seeing the other as a flesh-and-blood human being. This might be called static bonding where the relationship does not progress past a certain point toward greater intimacy.

There is no "inside" or "outside." Entranced relationships foster a sense of mutual stagnation and fixation with go-nowhere, repetitive cycles. There may be periods of lucidness when the absorbing trance is not operating. Hypnotic fractionation gives each partner a temporary sensation of taking a break from the hypnotic self-and-other absorbing entrancement. As this temporary break occurs, couples are in their surfacing phase, feeling more individuality in their lives. Offering only temporary respite, they reenter to greater absorption.

Rage emerges when partners are trapped in these positions. The impasse and fixation intensify and deepen entrancement. Deepening intensifies their fantasy ideal, feeling they must have each other now more than ever. Any deviation from fantasy ideals is magnified and perceived as threatening, and nightmarish attacks ensue.

Remember that the hypnotic quality of entrenching ragelike experiences comes from the collapse of two individual personalities into hypnotic fusion. In perfect love is the painful discovery of unreachability. Rapprochement peaks to an ultimate loss. There is frenzied rage and fury as partners approach awareness of desperately desiring what they will never have. What "sweet suffering" for the sadomasochistic romantic. Compelling their relationship to "work" contributes to what we now term as stalking, fatal attractions, and sadomasochism. The emotional and physical abuse can reach suicidal and/or homicidal proportions.

It is in entrancement that enmeshment becomes so strong. It is important to realize that these entrancing experiences bond partners together in a progressive, intolerable love and rage conflict. It is similar to two gang members in a knife fight with one wrist of each tied together and a knife in their other hand. Partners are tied together at one hand

and yet they have weapons of death in the other hand. In this trance experience, they are both pulled closer as they are tied by the fantasy, but they cut into each other as a way of cutting into the fantasy so they can separate not from each other, but from the fusion of the fantasy that binds each.

The focus in the rapprochement stage is not to maintain the fantasy, but ironically to maintain that point in unavailability. The perception of permanent elusiveness distinguishes the rapprochement from the obsessive stage.

Rapprochement is riddled with rage, fury, and conflict. This might imply the collision of opposites in partners. Paradoxically, entrancing relationships press partners to be identical to each other's romantic idealism. As a consequence, far from opposites colliding, it is the rapport of sameness that causes such explosive, self-destructive rage. A closer view of rapport reveals some interesting features. If rapport is characterized by moving, feeling, and thinking at the same level and pace, what could be more of a rapport than two partners becoming the same carbon copy of each other's fantasy. They have such intense rapport that they could almost be superimposed on each other.

When partners lose their boundaries and range of variety and uniqueness, they confuse their identity with being identical to the fantasized ideal. This extreme rapport, if you will, is completely restrictive. Partners impose the same wave length on one another to the extent that rapport is lost in fusion. What may pass for open-ended rapport is disguised disengagement devoid of intimacy. Partners are different people. The crux of their conflict is due to sameness demands of fantasy. Rapport evolves into rapprochement as partners caricaturize one another into entrancement. Conflict develops from hypervigilance and sensitivity to unique variations in each partner's self-expression.

A variation of rapprochement rage is the dreaded fear of abandonment. However, abandonment takes on a very different meaning and connotation in this context. When one partner is deeply entrenched at the moment, feeling bonded and attended to in fantasy, the other suddenly reverses position, emerging out of trance.

Partners take turns feeling like they are left alone carrying a torch for the one who abandoned them. The ensuing rage that emerges from being left in entrancement comes from abandoning one's personal reality and primary preferences in day-to-day experiences for the sake of "being with their partners in bliss."

Restrictive and abusive bonding is most evident in the sexualized component of the addictive relationship. It becomes clear that the most powerful, entrancing qualities prevalent are highly charged, sexual pre-occupations. Issues of jealousy, insecurity, and control take form in sexual manifestations of the relationship. Sexualization is a major pre-occupation in an otherwise null and void relationship. Sexualization of relationship manifests absorbing and entrancing qualities.

Entranced couples substitute erotic stimulation for genuine intimacy and appreciation for individual character. Restricted limits of time, shared activities, and disallowed emotions beyond certain points shift the focus from loving to lusting after one another. Partners are not after one another but after the pursuit itself. Partners fill emotional emptiness with erotic passion. The fixation and hypnotic high of the sexual stimuli orient the focus of the couple. Each partner seems to function like a chemical factory for the other to produce the endorphin, narcoticlike, hypnotically induced effect. These effects are ill-fated attempts to pro-tect against the insecurities, fears, and terrors which continue to surface in ever-greater manifestations.

Partners shift from two transforming individual characters growing into relationship into a twisted reality of a "lost in lust" trance. The orgasm becomes a pitiful substitute for an intimate bond. The two see one another as exclusively theirs to possess and jealously guard. Part-ners are deluded, seeing one another as an extension of themselves. "My partner is me and therefore is mine." This is the ultimate character of the possessive, jealous, narcoticlike relationship.

Becoming jealously preoccupied in an entranced, hypnotic pursuit of "what's mine" justifies in their mind rage and abuse. Each partner's possessiveness creates its own insecurity and is self-threatening. It shatters the quality of character bond necessary for commitment. Pos-sessiveness or feelings of being possessed are characterized by extremes (all or nothing) in commitments of time, energy, and material invest-ments. Entrancing hearts and souls (and bodies) creates vested interests and feelings (owning and being owned).

Entrancement engenders extremes of intense or diluted commit-ments of personal resources. Intense overcommitments create fears of being engulfed. As a consequence, the overcommitted partner will ei-ther withdraw or provoke conflict to create distance. The push-pull hypnotic dance has its own perverse rhythms.

Partners are used hypnotically like designer drugs. They induce each other's fantasy euphoria and thereby try to give meaning to a sense of emptiness in life's realities. The sense of emptiness is now painfully extended to both partners. They are now both "protected" from discovering who they are and how to function in the world. They rage at one another like tyrannical children having narcissistic, self-centered temper tantrums, not getting what they want, when they want it. They avoid and fear taking on the challenges of life in terms of nurturing a mature, intimate, one-to-one relationship. They take "food" from one another instead of giving nurturance to feed the relationship. They become regressed in entrancement to childlike needs, wanting to be fed but fearful.

The sexualization doesn't always mean physical sex. It may involve focusing obsessively on a partner's infidelity, acting out with physical abuse, punishing one another in sexually related ways. Partners may violate their own values in their indulgent assaults on one another. Entranced couples both sexually entice and terrorize each other.

The hypnotically induced effect of this sexual, chemical high cannot be ignored. The presence or absence of sexual intercourse is not so much the issue as are the abusive, rageful preoccupations surrounding it. One might say that there is a sadomasochistic sexualization of emotions and thoughts as partners become more preoccupied with subtle (and sometimes not so subtle) ways of wanting to hurt and be hurt in sexually related events. Mutual abuse and degradation of each other provide cruel, painful sadomasochistic experiences to their entranced bondage.

What at first starts off as part of a sexually romantic relationship becomes an all-consuming compulsion. Sex becomes the core matrix of what's romantic in the relationship. The powerful, hypnotically induced, and deepening effect of chemical sexual activity becomes the illusionary magical, all-soothing painkiller. It provides the salve of personal, interpersonal, and character difficulties that each person struggles to assuage in his or her life. It also creates the inner loneliness and painful emptiness its inducement is designed to fulfill. The emptiness can be so intense that even sadomasochistic moves are a perverse but welcome relief to no self at all.

There is an important mind-body connection here. As the mind pays attention to pleasurable physical sensations that come from sensual activities, it associates those activities to the people, places, and things that were connected to those sensations and activities. The mind (what we have in our heads to make meaning and sense out of our world of experience) learns to attribute magical, powerful qualities of potency to these people, places, and activities because they are associated with the pleasure hormones of our body chemistry.

In reality, it is we who are pleasuring ourselves. Because of the blinders of hypnotic entrancement, partners misattribute the source of physical and emotional pleasures to external events. Such events are artificially empowered, disabling a partner's critical faculties to make sense of their relationship.

A gap results between experience (sensational pleasure or pleasure from sensational pain--e.g., sadomasochism) and awareness of the experience's source to which one could accurately ascribe or attribute it. This gap or invisible space is actually created by partners ignoring their own resourceful character structure which gives value to their sensations. Partners become out of touch with their own resources and feel things are happening out of their control. This is a sign of a trance. Character is lost in entrancement as is empowerment. It is "my love" of orgasm that empowers it, not the orgasm itself. In entrancement, the origin of partners' energy and power is not attributed to their inner characters but rather to outside sources.

Displaced power to outside sources contributes to feeling vulnerable and insecure. Sexual chemistry (experienced as an "outer force" within) is actually a biochemical induction to hypnotic entrancement. Submergence ends only when the chemistry which induced such a powerfully euphoric trance state has expired. Hypnotic effects, accelerated by chemical highs, create all-powerful magical illusions that one cannot live without the other in the relationship. When one partner withdraws, the other is left (abandoned down there) going through painful withdrawal with no self to return.

Terror and fear of surfacing only serve to intensify the mind's attention being drawn to sensual realities, connecting pleasure with what appears to be outside itself. Partners believe the other's presence is what makes them feel good inside. The mind is motivated to connect two points to determine one line of thinking. This is the "romantic" version of Pavlov's dog drooling at the sound of a bell which has conditioned it to food.

The mind commits a perceptual mistake attributing control, pleasure, and pain to outside sources, missing the gap of its own character structure that is valuing and giving value to the experience in the first place. The mind, absorbed into bodily sensations, loses connection with itself and its unique structuring process of what it finds lovely, beautiful, and pleasing (which is intrinsically what is lovely, beautiful, and pleasing). To correct this error is to reconnect with that experience of character structure already located within the mind's eye. We need to learn to attend to the uniquely beautiful and artistic framework of viewing and perceiving relationships. The mind could then reconnect itself to its own body sensations in how it views "self" and centers "self."

Such lost consciousness creates fleeting illusions of physical and emotional sensations without conscious self-awareness to experience it. The consequences are raw emotions and sensations of pleasure and pain with little or no internal point of reference. There are efforts (by partners and those trying to help) to reassociate different consequences (both positive and negative in effect) to change behavior. Such efforts treat people like animals pairing bell sounds with salivation or entrancing sensations with eroticism. Recognition and respect for choice by the unique character structure that lies within the soul of each person is abdicated.

Resurfacing and withdrawal are frightening, abandoning forms of reality. There has been a fusion of mind-body experience, which is what happens in hypnotic induction and deepening techniques. Physical changes like relaxation and cognitive thoughts such as "getting calmer and calmer feeling the relaxation spread" begin to merge into a sense of one unified experience. The mind of words fuses with the physical sense leading to entrancement. In such a process, there exists the illusion that experiences are happening by themselves. An individual finds, for example, relaxation occurring involuntarily as a product of word-feeling states. The individual may feel it is not "me" actually doing it. This is similar to what is happening in the sexualization process of hypnotic induction through hormonal chemistry.

There is the implied suggestion that each will feel better about themselves through these sexualized emotional states. These fused states of euphoria create an illusion and a sad perversion of what is the truth about intimate relationships. Intimacy is the sharing of unique selves. On the other hand, the hypnotic fusion of mind-body in an absorbed state involves a loss of unique self and fuels the need to seek relief through endorphin-generating, sexually induced experiences. These experiences serve to deepen the hypnotic illusion of love. Such experiences induce desire in each partner to pursue an ever-deepening effect of submerging identity, reality, and life into that lost weekend of sexual gorging and indulgence. The rapprochement experience intensifies when two people are having a passionately induced feast upon one another, discovering they are ever more starved than before they started.

They are more depleted emotionally, intellectually, and spiritually. Their genuine sense of who they are has not been nurtured. The loneli-

ness, alienation, and sadness left in the wake of their perverse indul-
gences serve only to deepen the hypnotic pull of the empty euphoria.
They engage in a frantic chasing to make up for their increasing sense of
losses. When they do surface from that hypnotic blackout, they discover
a bleak, cold loneliness where only provocation and aggression can fire
their deadened feelings of being themselves.

Partners may provoke one another in demanding more loyalty and
prolonged sex while accusing each other of lewd and whorish thoughts
and fantasies. Such a combination of sexual demands coupled with accusations of whorish activity can be one of the ways partners excite and
arouse the sexual fires of an otherwise emotionally empty encounter.
Shifting from verbal, emotional, and ultimately to physically abusive
sexualization creates a wild, hysterical turmoil of feast and famine with
hypnotic love lost and found. Drama and arousal are just a hypnotic
breath away.

The mind-body effects of such highly absorbing sensory-emotional
mood swings induce an ever-deepening trancelike fixation of rage, hormonal stimulation, and the all-too-familiar levels of excitement, drama,
and crisis. This varied intensity maintains the hypnotic deepening and
submersion into an ever-progressive (or regressive) stimulation or eroti-
clike experiences. Threatening and aggressively abusive to one another,
such acts intensify entrancement. Excitement has an entrancing quality
all its own.

There is an assault to the psyche and/or physicality as partners criticize and debase one another in a mutually destructive pursuit. Such a
pursuit is a paradoxical way of creating the "final solution" of relationship annihilation. Partners can continue until they "erupt" out of trance
because the pain of reliving the pain has reached epic proportions. At
this level, their very survival is at stake. The purpose is not to establish
any kind of healthy contact or even to revive the lost idealism or the
romantic interlude of the first stage of the relationship. The underlying
agenda of this rapprochement stage is the annihilation of the very premise of the relationship itself. Partners attack the very foundation of that
which drew them together which now tears them apart. Partners appear
repulsive, intimidating, and violating of that special "loyal, loving" relationship that had purported to have been in existence from the beginning.

Partners are lost in the hellish illusions of infidelity and betrayal.
Instead of taking responsibility for their own decisions to have space and
time apart, they blame the other for such shifts. Entrancement by defi-

nition means abandoning awareness of internal self-control. The delusion is that of an alcoholic who rationalizes "controlled" drinking. The involuntary nature of denying what one is doing while beginning to do it is quite hypnotic. It is this double bind of "I'm not doing what I'm doing" that identifies hypnotic dissociation and involuntary control over events happening "outside" me. This is also a form of self-deception which creates a smoke screen, clouding the "game" partners now play.

In provoking confrontations, partners rekindle the enmeshed, hypnotic bond of reengagement so that they can feel a "sense of contact." These exchanges involve hidden or nested loops of messages of a highly provocative quality. They are nested in that confrontational accusations and labels are embedded or buried in the partners' verbal exchanges. They loop each partner back into the same endless, entangled entrancement. Such embedded loops serve as a perfect type of hypnotic induction.

He is vehement as he attacks her while denying that he thinks in a negative way about her. He has fulfilled her suggestiveness to punish her for her projected guilt. This also punishes him in that he has to live another hypnotic hallucination of how he is being betrayed and belittled.

The hypnotic sadomasochistic quality becomes tortuous for both partners. Partners entrance each other into creating their most terrifying scenario. Partners engage in the hypnotically absorbing rapprochement stage attempting to change, cajole, and blame the other one for not fitting into a fantasized scheme of things. This only confirms the futility of being close. Partners now can lament this futility and will use it as further evidence to fuel rageful attacks. Indeed, it becomes so exaggerated that the reality of what happens is forgotten and lost in the nightmare of how each is being unfair and cruel.

The hypnotic language patterns partners utilize with each other are a form of hypnotic transaction that constantly suggests and induces a sense of blame, insecurity, and sickness upon the other's part. A very real characteristic in these hypnotically induced addicted relationships is how absorbed these relationships are with inducing pain. Each partner is so absorbed in emotionally empty interactions that there are ever-increasing, painful feelings of helplessness and futility. There is a constant polarization of being either totally absorbed or totally abandoned.

Even if partners become healthier as a more self-directed person, they might still become enticed by the other's slanderous sabotage. If one partner engages in provocation about the way one thinks about the other, that partner could relapse back into hypnotic entrancement, which could again cause all kinds of backlashes and angry retorts. This can reignite the enmeshment and entrapment for both. The hypnotic pull is too powerful to be ignored. Without a healthy respect for this force, partners are quite vulnerable. Each confuses his or her emotions with the other's.

The entrancement blinds them to their own self-identities. They do not have honesty and integrity between the two of them as hypnotic entrancement fuses intimate partners. Through provocation, innuendoes, and attacks, hypnotic bonding is maintained. Each justifying maneuver and countering move creates an ever-tightening, painful lost weekend, a lost soul.

Progressing from minimal to intense contact with ten or fifteen calls one day and none the next, severe imbalance swings exist. Partners are not able to fully enjoy themselves as unique people in their relationship. The hypnotics of the addictive relationship are keeping both in bondage. It is either an enmeshed or disassociated trap. Even when partners are not together, they maintain illusions about the other. Entranced partners are never quite free to be themselves with one another. Relationship entrancement prevents partners from owning their behavior. Partners buy into entrancement which is what prevents them from acknowledging their needs. Partners love the fantasy ideal but loathe the nightmare it becomes.

To use the word "cure" in entrancing relationships has a special meaning. It means to eliminate the illusionary foundation upon which the relationship was formed. To eliminate the fantasy ideal involves the death of entrancement yet allows rebirth of genuine character between partners. The erratic high, the illusionary magic of wonder and idealization begin to come crashing down around their ears. Attacking and demeaning whatever decent quality may have existed are sadomasochistic ways of extinguishing the entrancement. Every asset now is a liability threatening to draw both to their demise.

The hypnotic pull threatens to collapse both sides of the relationship in a collision course of mutual annihilation. It is critical to understand that the love, rage, and hate in the rapprochement stage are designed to terminate the very structure of the relationship. Each individual senses the falsehood and perversity in the nature of the relationship. Neither knows of any other way out of such an absorbing fusion of heart, mind, and soul. It's as if a wolf with its leg caught in a trap must chew it off or stay there and die. The point here is that partners are so trapped with each other that they may have to release something valuable between them to have their own freedom to live.

Partners in hypnotically abusive relationships seek to annihilate controlling fantasy ideals. Yet, paradoxically, such annihilation of control fantasy may serve not to end the relationship. Embedded within is a redefinition of relating based on painful desperation and fear of loss. Sadomasochistic principles of relating are designed to maintain a relationship of viciousness and lost myth.

Attacking and discrediting one another serves to maintain a very powerful bond of negativity, hate, and blame as each is cast as the cause of all problems. There is a pyrrhic victory involved. The partner who succeeds in destroying by fiery, assaultive commentary their own emotional value with the other feels safer and secure. They are less dependent on the other partner and, as a consequence, are less vulnerable. Ironically, just when partners are purged of toxic, entrancing feelings (cleared of dependency needs through fiery conflict) and free to be together, they turn away in disgust, having devalued the very character of their partner most treasured.

Partners know they cannot go back to that romantic, hypnotic origin, but they also fear going forward to healthier relationships (fear of lost self). The rapprochement stage, designed to end the relationship, terminating the nightmarish fantasy, entraps partners in a frozen-in-time loop. The rapprochement stage can be a period of severe fixation where the relationship is frozen in time for relatively long durations. Partners may go through countless loops of reprisals before breaking the impasse. This impasse can go on for months and perhaps even years being mired down in endless controversy and entanglements of how each partner should, must, or ought to be. Before each person realizes it, this hypnotically fixed point of repeated conflict, accusations, and agony has lasted for years.

Neither partner may consciously realize just how much time, energy, and resources of their lives have been invested. Attacking and accusing each other as the cause of their miseries, pointing to the other person's sickness and inadequacy only serves to deepen their bondage. Partners may give the appearance of trying to correct and create a healthy relationship. Yet these efforts only stimulate and reinforce the most pathological, frightening fears and terrors that lie hidden in one another. The irony is that such a "special and wonderful" person (which our ideal partner is supposed to be) is now perceived to embody everything that was ever dreaded (loss, abandonment, betrayal, humiliation, etc.) in a partner.

The rapprochement stage seems destined to challenge entranced partners to resolve an essential paradox. Can partners live happily ever after in ideal entrancement with such imperfect, nonideal mates? Fulfilling the fantasy ideal requires perfect, ideal partners. Rapprochement reveals massive defects in the person of the ideal partner. Partners sometimes try to maintain the fantasy ideal of entranced relating whether the other one cooperates or not. Partners may continue to profess deep and undying love for one another long after his complete character assassination of her. Such paradoxical situations become complex and intense in an endless loop, spiraling deeper and deeper into entrancement.

Partners cannot go back, but cannot go forward. In this sense, they become more compellingly addicted in this stage than ever before, sensing impending doom to their relationship. The more the relationship collapses, the more frantic the "mud" flies with slanderous attacks upon one another. Imagine stampeding buffalo, thundering hooves pounding furiously, racing feverishly toward the edge of a gigantic cliff. The closer they get to this edge, the faster the pace until they have flung themselves wildly over into the abyss below. These are elements of entrancement.

When partners critique each other they are indirectly attacking and seeking to eliminate their own ingenuine and unhealthy ways of relating. The challenge is to survive with the true self intact. It is the all-powerful illusions of partners' fantasy ideals that such onslaughts are designed to eradicate.

In the rapprochement stage, both individuals seek to free themselves through destructive implosive/explosive kinds of attacks and critiques, from such false and unhealthy ways of relating. The outcome of partners' perverse attacks on themselves by attacking their partner is to liberate their genuine character from the illusionary hypnotic trance. Partners have the most to learn about themselves not by what one partner says to the other, but by what they project onto to their partner.

There may be attempted periods of calm withdrawal; periods in which they break up; periods in which friends console and counsel them to end the relationship. Yet every time they attempt to end it and emerge, they encounter the "brutality" of everyday life. The effects of the awakening seem to be agonizing, as they must confront their own identities. The pain of confronting the character of who they are can be so excruciating that they need outside controls. They may need such an intolerable argument that the two of them have to spend weeks apart from one another. It becomes blatantly obvious that when they get together after the sex, the surge of emotional rage and potential physical abuse and danger comes to the fore. There can be upheavals with police. There can be upheavals or physical altercations with neighbors. There may be lost time on the job. There may be actual chemical abuse of alcohol and/or drugs.

What is happening is that every time they surface from the hypnotic trance, they are reawakening with side effects of what might be called the "bends" (the shock to the system of a deep-sea diver rising to the surface too quickly). The shock of upheaval creates an abrupt surfacing and awakening from entrancement. Pain and panic result as neither partner feels safe enough to learn from the disturbing experience. At this point, partners long for the pain-relieving effects of numbness through entrancement. They dive back into their fantasy ideal as if nothing has happened, which only serves to deepen their entrancement.

The hypnotic induction and deepening effects of reentry into entrancement eventually expose them to a lonely, isolated abandoned kind of reality which again shocks them to the surface. Something eventually disrupts the deepened entrancement. The painful effect is the sudden, shocking emergence of coming out of trance without having time to integrate a mindful identity and pull together a holistic sense of purpose and fulfillment in their lives. They suffer from the "bends" of their fantasy. They lack the "holding tank" of stable relationships to allow them to depressurize and decompress all those "gaseous" fantasy bubbles. Their beautiful bubbles, in which so many of their hopes and dreams are invested, are now bursting apart right before their eyes.

Without a sense of personal character in which to integrate those hypnotic changes (this is achieved by reframing how hypnotic changes help the person's character attain his or her higher purposes more effectively), going into trance becomes a frightening experience. Therapeutic trances utilize the resource of anchoring a safe place for the subject. Entrancing relationships cost partners the anchor of their own character without which there is no safe place. Going into that enmeshed submergence with another person is the only way partners may feel they have an identity, a reality, a purpose, or even existence. We all may have some doubts and uncertainties about who we are and what we are all about. However, the false premise and promise of alluring, enticing, and mesmerizing bonding with another creates deceptive solutions to per-

sonal needs of fulfillment. Even Ulysses knew how to respect the hypnotic power of entrancing relationships by having himself tied to the
mast of his ship as he sailed by the island of beautiful sirens. This allure
and power is not gender-specific, as of course women can be hypnotically "swept off their feet" by their knights in shining armor. Yet in this
entrancement they discover that their identity as healthy individuals has
been obliterated.

They can only go down before they can go up. They need outside
intervention (holding tanks) to realize the growing loss of control of
themselves and of their character. Each cannot be a whole person to
themselves, to their children if they have any, to their friends if they
have any left. Their children cannot look to them for help or encouragement. They are emotionally unavailable. Usually, individuals who are
prone to addictive, hypnotically induced relationships lack an outside,
social network or communal group where they can immerse or invest
themselves in a larger-than-self reality. Many times, these individuals
may not even have a spiritual focus or a neighborhood focus. They are
usually very emotionally alone even though they may have many
friends. However, they may not have very close or intimate friends in a
way that allows personal access to their individual sense of self. Many
times the popular, highly charismatic individual with many friends
(lonely in a crowd) may be most susceptible to entrancing relationships.

While certain conditions can make some individuals more vulnerable to entrancement than others, no one is immune. It is of critical importance to understand the all-consuming nature of these hypnotically
induced addictive relationships. Individuals, whose lives are devoid of
meaning and depth, purposeful goals, communal bonds, and the like,
lack anchors that can prevent being drawn into entrancement.

Mature love has a primary bond and an open relationship with the
world at large. Primary bonding is missing in entranced relationships.
Entranced bonds require one hundred percent commitment toward losing
oneself resulting in downward spirals as compensation for primary
bonding. Entrancement erodes mature love away if not mastered.

Entranced partners become fixated on the emotional, sexual, and
sensual stimuli to provide a substitute bonding and reality for their illusionary ego. By ego, I mean that limited consciousness where partners
define themselves in terms of their image or appearance. They are like
vampires that can only exist in the darkness. It is an illusionary ego existing only in the hypnotic trance state of a specialized one-to-one enmeshment. There is not a relationship with two individuals but rather of

two sources of emotionally sensual stimuli emerging from a hypnotic trance.

Partners do not realize the vast amounts of energy investment (thoughts, emotions, sexuality, loss of their spirituality) they are committing to a noncommittal-type bondage. When partners begin to discover that they have committed themselves to a noncommitting relationship, they paradoxically emerge from entrancement. They realize it takes one-tenth as much energy to invest in a healthy adult relationship by simply maintaining a committed focus on the character they genuinely are. In this way, they could discover their own sense of personal truth of what is right for them as individuals in a genuine relationship.

Learning to attend and focus on the character of self is the foundation for growth and emergence from entrancement. It will be discovered how partners can gradually resurface and reintegrate their self-identity. Partners need to discover how gradually letting go of the toxic fantasy (nitrogen bubbles) of the submergence can allow surrender and release of these illusions. It may take an act of faith in ourselves and our spiritual character.

The minute partners relinquish efforts to control and change each other, there is a releasing, reawakening. The irony is that when they have given up attempting to make it work, they begin to come out of the trance. Indeed, the marvelous possibilities of genuine reawakening will be presented in cases of how partners learn to trust their inner, artistic character which guides them. Therein lies a genuine kind of immersion into that personal, internal guidance system. The purposeful self is the internal, unique character structure that partners can access for guidance to establish an intimate bond of mature love. They learn to access this self-quality of purpose through the entrance of spirit and character. This doorway allows access to remarkable, purpose-of-life qualities that allow each partner's life to open and expand so that they can establish healthy relationships.

CHAPTER 8

AWAKENINGS

Hypnotic frameworks can be utilized as a way of providing healing contexts within which entranced partners can successfully awaken. Awakening involves utilizing hypnotic techniques that reemerge entranced partners whatever their stage (idealization, disillusionment, obsession, or rapprochement). Awakening may progress at varying rates. Healtheir partners emerge from entrancement with ease and speed, passing through some or all of these stages with little or no difficulty. More intensely entranced partners, either because of stressful life events and/or individual pathology, will experience greater severity and intensity with some or all stages. Their journey toward reemergence can be quite agonizing.

Entrancement can be redesigned for success in dealing with addictive relationships. Such a design transformation may involve a journey into the darkness of lost self and identity. Traversing such darkness involves the searching, recovery, and reemergence of one's own true, unique self. To reemerge, partners need to realize how enmeshed and buried they are in each others' lives and reality. Partners can be constantly thinking about, dwelling on, and attending to what each other says, thinks, does, believes, and feels. Even when isolated by time and limited contact, partners may well be absorbed and preoccupied with worries and fears concerning their entire experience with one another. Such absorption serves to deepen the hypnotic dream/fantasy, which can then turn into a nightmare. It is in the fantasy-turned-nightmare where partners feel they can never be free seeing themselves trapped in the "other's" cruelty and betrayal. The real trap is within as partners fixate their attention on fantasy/nightmare transgressions of each other.

Entrancement creates a split in conscious/unconscious awareness as partners fixate on one another's actions and nuances. Immersed in nightmarish scenarios of loss and humiliation, partners feel helplessly dissociated from themselves (because of entrancement) in feeling they can do anything about it. This is similar to the hypnotist's swinging pocket watch where the subject attributes closure of his or her eyes to the "power" of the watch (the "power" is coming from the intense, watchful eye of the subject's stare). Entrancement interferes with the perceptual capacity to embrace the unique, holistic character of each partner. Entrancement blocks the valuable quality of character which can assist partners in decompressing, detrancing and reemerging.

DECOMPRESSING, DETRANCING AND DEPROGRAMMING

Critical to awakening is the need for decompressing (lessening the intensity of the relationship), detrancing, and deprogramming. This means grasping the principle that entrancing relationships are rigid, stereotyped, cognitive (thinking and imaging) oriented operations. What interrupts the trance is expanding beyond and going outside this rigid, cognitive domain of fixated fantasy ideals. Such a move helps to decompress and lighten-up the mood and intensity of the couple's fused, ideal one-to-one focus. What achieves this is exposing such cognitive fantasy fixations to unpredictable, novel, and unique experiences. Partners are shocked and awakened by the realization that their fantasy ideal is draining the life out of their relationship. Shocked into an expanded awareness, feeling increasing loss, partners begin to decompress and release their intense pressure to fit into fantasy ideals. The fantasy ideal is cognitively rigid (a set idea), which can require interruptive techniques to dislodge.

The important point about interrupting, decompressing, and detrancing is that of expanding and relating fantasy ideals to increasingly diverse realities and outcomes. This involves senses, heartfelt emotions, and interpersonal realities. Partners encounter painful, diverse realities in pursuing their fantasy ideal. Partners' collapse of rapport in relating can leave them confused, shocked, and reevaluating the relationship. With the collapse and unraveling of the fantasy ideal, awakening is now possible. Partners are now open and responsive to efforts (either by themselves or with outside helpers such as therapists) to take real steps in emerging from entrancement. What allows partners to benefit from such windows of opportunity is the hypnotically induced (shock) perceptual shift in the partners' fixation from fantasy ideal content to one of process. Decompressing and detrancing shock partners' perceptual attention toward how they are structuring the fantasy ideal into a fixated form or gestalt. Hypnotic techniques loosen and turn such fixated forms into open-ended process experiences capable of transformation.

Utilizing hypnotic techniques to awaken involves understanding the fusion process of entrancement. Notice for a moment how perceptual illusions occur when multiple cartoon figures are rapidly flashed, creating a serial transformation of movement (motion pictures operate similarly). Additionally, the spinning of circular paper discs with a small openning cut out causes the entire disc to fade from view leaving only the scene behind it. Such illusions occur because of retinal lag (new pictures cannot register in the brain until the one-sixteenth of a second time period has been completed from one image to another). Similar perceptual illusions occur in entrancement, where selective filtering and fast-moving mind-body associations create blurring, fused movements of unfolding fantasy ideal scenarios. Our fused, cartoon fantasies of partners come to life on the wide screen of the movies of our mind. Awakening involves utilizing hypnotic techniques to shift and refocus attention on the still frame of cartoonlike images, interrupting and differentiating blurred animated movements that create fantasy and expanding perceptual filters to see and learn about such mechanisms in action.

Entranced partners are highly enmeshed at the cognitive, emotional, and neurohormonal levels (fusing fantasy ideals, mood swings, and the erotic, chemical rush all into an entranced state called "romantic love"). Hypnotic techniques are needed to access and operate on these fusions. What can assist them in their awakening process is coming to terms with their eroticism. The entranced, erotic response is essentially one that is hypnohormonal (altered, perceptual states excite and are excited by sexual hormones--e.g., testosterone, endorphins, etc.). The arousal potency of this mind-body connection is quite staggering. The powerful "rush" experienced by erotic partners is not simply physical. Enhancement of erotic experience and hormonal effects on pleasure centers occurs through the powerful intensification of hypnotic imagery.

Even when partners self-stimulate, their powerful, hypnotic imagery and fantasy continue to operate. What energizes the physical mechanics of sex is the "sizzle" and tantalizing edginess of wondrously heightened

and magnified fantasy images. The effects of the hypnotic magnification and excitation of sensory forms, scents, and touches cause partners
to passionately (mis)attribute highly inflated wonder and fantasy to each
other's presence. Partners then merge through hypnotic attending of the
senses, which is a literal, one-to-one blending and merging. Hypnotic
magnification of erotic senses and fantasy creates a larger-than-life illusion which is unattainable. Entranced couples never "get enough of
each other." Partners are being blinded to the reality of who this person
is in everyday life.

The erotic response bypasses heartfelt needs. Partners can experience intense conflict as they find themselves erotically attracted to people not meeting their heartfelt needs. Integrating these two dimensions
assists partners in destabilizing rigid entrancement focus and opening
perceptual shifts and alternatives in the fantasy ideal's process and form.
New, loving transformations can now occur in the relationship (unconditional love).

Paradoxically, erotic responses are indifferent and detached from
genuine, unconditional loving. Partners can be in the throes of passion
at one point, then discover apathy and boredom with each other when
surfacing. Men can have sex without being in love and have a tendency
to feel possessive and territorial (she belongs to me). Women may have
to feel love before having sex and want to be held. Entrancement is enmeshment and no guarantee of genuine, unconditional love.

Partners compartmentalize feelings and behaviors, moving from one
partner to another. Having multiple entranced partners, either serially or
simultaneously, is not uncommon. It is this misattribution of unconditional loving to erotica that entranced partners need to come to grips
with and work through.

Partners can come out of their entrancement when they take back
their fantasy ideals that they have placed onto each other. As partners
acknowledge the roles, fantasies, and behavioral expectations they have
placed onto each other, they take responsibility for what they want from
each other and themselves. The process of taking back and accepting or
owning what fantasy ideals each partner has is involved in awakening.
It is what entranced partners need to do to come out of trance.

Coming out of trance is usually not complicated or difficult in formal hypnosis. The hypnotist will say, "As I count from one to five, you
will emerge out of your trance." Usually, the message is that the subject
will feel refreshed, relaxed, and reawakened; fully integrated in terms of
time, place, and event; feeling like a powerful, healthier, new, integrated

person. Unfortunately, in an addictive relationship, it is not that easy because the individual is quite immersed into this nightmare. Partners fear that if they separate, lose each other, and have no other contact together, they will cease to exist.

The question, "How can I exist without him or her?" needs to be experienced as what we might call a self-negation, a self-suggestion. When partners wonder how they will survive without the other, such thinking acts like a self-hypnotic suggestion whereupon partners self-induce a state of false neediness for each other.

Partners set themselves up to feel that they will not exist without each other when, in reality, they do not exist when they are lost together in entrancement. Yet such an illusion of nonexistence and nonidentity without the other creates neediness, dependency, and increased enmeshment. This ultimately leads to the inductive suggestion that "only by being with my partner will I exist and have purpose in my life." Partners become overly attached (anchored) to the idea or association of feeling comfortable and secure only in their presence together, reinforcing the illusion that life is meaningless without each other. So much of the partner is identified in the other that they feel fused or joined at the hip.

The illusion, therefore, is sustained when they fear or avoid exposing themselves to daily life without their partner. They think, feel, and imagine in a dancelike oneness of trance. Whether they are in conflict or in sync with one another, they act and react according to their hypnotic program. They do not exist because they have disconnected and disassociated from who they are as unique characters. They have done this without knowing it as a way of submerging themselves in the hypnotic enmeshment of the addictive other. Awakening involves using hypnotic techniques of selective attending to the self-suggestive qualities of entrancing self-talk. Healthier, inductive self-talk can now be suggested and installed (I exist independent of my partner).

In articulating self-talk, it is important to realize that intense conflict and refighting past battles is part of what needs to be detranced. Partners lose themselves dwelling either on their own or the other's needs and issues of who is right or wrong. At the core, partners may believe they have no value or identity without the other

Many couple's arguments at this point are unwittingly designed to create personal space. Partners need time and experience to discover how to be and exist without the entranced other. The association of nonexistence with the entranced other's absence induces a powerful deepening in entrancement. Leaving can mean death without realizing that it ultimately is each partner's liberation. This issue of existence needs to be confronted. Utilizing hypnotic techniques of imagery and visualization, to assist partners experiencing what would happen to them with prolonged periods of abstinence from one another, would allow both to function as more self-initiating individuals.

As both begin to act on their own, partners experience growing discomfort. As time goes by, they feel more comfortable as they begin to surface from the depths of entrancement. Each can begin to dissolve such entrancing associations of lacking existence with the other's absence by beginning to experiment with times in which such pain also becomes a form of identifiable pleasure. Both need to accept the "pleasure" of their pain of independence. With assistance from hypnotic visualizations, partners may gradually "step out" of trance.

Partners begin to embrace their life as it takes entrancing unique form and shape. The pain of withdrawal and breaking bonds exposes both to the startling effects of an awakening individuality. As they learn to enjoy having their own independent activities, the startle effects (like splashing cold water on a morning face) wear off feeling more comfortable. Partners discover their own unique characters and self-validating existence in a commonsense reality.

Hypnotic techniques of induction and creating safe places help partners stay focused on the trauma of coming out of the trance. They experience a kind of cure through exposure to this fear in a safe, desensitizing, and releasing way. Realizing that what they have had to fear is simply the loss of their shadows lifts them out of entrancement. By no longer fighting with their darkest fears, they terminate the source of energy that fed the fear in the first place. They discover the only thing that was lost was the darkness of their dreamlike state. Inner calmness allows the clouds of darkness to settle, exposing their light-hearted joy of being themselves with others.

STEPS TO AWAKENING FROM ENTRANCEMENT

Awakening from entrancement can be facilitated with the eight steps outlined below. They are based on the premise that partners will discover their unique character motif in the light of detrancing. The heart of awakening is for partners to articulate the precise kind of relationship design that will support and enhance their unique character motif. It also needs to be the specific kind of relationship design to which their unique character motif can contribute and enhance in a mutual way. Above all else, it needs to be grounded in a realistic frame of reality.

To achieve detrancement and articulation of the precise kind of relationship design that supports and enhances each partner's unique character motif, the following summarizes these eight steps. Step one calls for partners to change their frame of reference from an entranced reality to a commonsense one. Step two involves accessing the degree and intensity of hypnotic qualities present in their entrancement. Step three requires each partner to articulate the exact nature of their inner self-talk related to entrancement. Step four involves determining the double message and confusion communicated between partners while entranced. Step five involves partners clarifying the mixed messages of what one partner is saying, doing, and wanting with the other. That is, partners are busy reacting to each other's provocations, needs, moods, and fantasies. In the process, they don't know what they want in their own, unique way of being as they are busy accommodating to the needs and feelings of their partner. Sorting out one partner's message from the other assists in disentangling entrancement. Step six involves each partner suspending time and involvement from the other to get a felt sense of who and what they are in their own right. Involved in this step is the sorting out from the other partner, what one's own fantasy and desires are and have been in the entranced bond. Step seven involves self-attending and self-discipline skills to overcome entrancement and be more attuned to and aware of each partner's unique character needs and desires. Step eight involves each partner emerging with his or her own unique design of the kind of relationship that their unique character can support and enhance.

A central theme throughout these eight steps to reemergence is that of entranced partners needing to take back their lost unique character. The central theme is that partners need to disidentify (know that this is not who they really are) with the role of entranced, perfect lover and reidentify with that inner quality of their unique character motif. As partners progress through these eight steps, they take back their fantasies placed on one another, release their roles as perfect lovers, and learn to reemerge as their own unique characters, able to give and receive healthy love.

Step One

As a first step, each partner needs to realize that the relationship has a hypnotic frame of operation, not a reality-based one. As a consequence, partners need to change their frame of reference from a hypnotic reality to a commonsense reality. They lack a fundamental contact with a reality-based orientation. Yet they do not know this. They genuinely believe their dream is real. It is this reality confusion that partners need to clarify and come to grips with. They need conscious awareness of and access to their distinct character identity and sense of unique self. Partners need to realize that, because of entrancement, their personal senses of self-boundaries are vague, diffuse, and vulnerable to situations that compromise their integrity. Partners need to realize that developing clear, well-defined self-boundaries assists them in the emergence of their distinct character. The more partners assert their uniqueness of character, the clearer their self-boundaries become. This reinforces greater assertiveness of character motif, which creates a healthy, self-generating process of refining self-boundaries and identity.

Such assertiveness may come in the form of challenges and questions about the nature of the relationship itself. Many of the conflicts and struggles between partners at this stage of awakening are exercises of character assertions. Knowing that the addictive relationship is hypnotic in nature allows partners to ask essential assertive questions, challenging the real purpose of their time and energy together. Challenging the premise or basis for what makes partners a couple becomes essential. They need to ask, "How is it possible for us to be together?" "What fantasy reality is operating that makes our entrancement possible?"

The futility and falsehood of the purposelessness of the addictive relationship will become apparent when partners begin to confront their reality through challenging the hypnotic dream. Such challenges to purpose may involve "How much quality time do we share." "How well are we able to be ourselves together?" "Are we proud of what we have created together so that we want to share our relationship with the world around us?" "Is there an identity of 'I,' 'you' and 'we-ness'? In the initial stages, it is important to consider the reality of the addictive relationship as hypnotic in quality.

Step Two

The second step toward awakening involves accessing the hypnotic quality of entrancement. Partners identify times in which their "reality" was very transient and fleeting. As a partner, do you find yourself fading out of the here and now reality of who you are with or what you are doing? Do you have a difficult time concentrating and listening to conversations with others in the present? Do you notice your mind wandering and wondering about how your partner is doing or acting to such an extent that it interferes with your present enjoyment and/or task fulfillment? These are indicators of being in and out of entrancement in your daily life situations. It helps to actually count the number of instances occurring throughout a 24-hour period. The frequency of such occurrences may not be clear. Entrancement can alter our mental and physical states of time and space. As a consequence, partners may not realize how they relive the past or project into the future, all the while being out of touch with here-and-now reality.

Partners actually also need to count how many times a day they are imaging each other in mistrusting situations that may never be happening. For example, do you worry about what your partner may be doing with other salespeople when he or she is shopping, buying a new car, or selling products? Is there a worry, suspicion, fear, or even paranoia? These are times when you are actually inducing and deepening your trancelike addictive concerns, wondering if you are losing your partner. "Is my partner flirting with someone else?" Is your partner having high-energy dialogues with other men/women and having fantasies (your nightmares) about being with this woman or man? Partners are entranced by obsessive worry and are therefore enmeshed in an altered reality that stretches beyond a healthy sense of purpose. Partners need to attend to what illusions they are operating under in their fantasy ideal. They can begin to notice how such illusions undermine each other's unique identity.

Partners need to get a baseline count of how often they are engaged in entrancing activities together. This is simply beginning to access the number, amount, and length of how often and under what circumstances you and your partner engage in entrancing experiences. Included in the category of entrancing experiences are obsessive thoughts, images, feelings, and hallucinated expectations. The actual time in which each partner spends ruminating about the pros and cons of the relationship are also important to note.

It is interesting that in many addictive relationships, individuals begin to discover that time distortion (lost mental time spent dwelling on worries, etc.) begins to take up so much of their reality that they become consumed by it. Getting a baseline count of the frequency, length, and duration of fantasy/nightmare thoughts, images, feelings, worries, and anticipations can be quite helpful.

Step Three

Partners can gain clarity and focus of how their entrancement works by articulating the exact nature of what they say to themselves in their own thoughts. For example, he may think, "She is with someone else." "I could lose her." She might say, "He is flirting with other people." "I am not important to him." By articulating the nature of those subtle, inductive, and deepening messages, partners can begin to confront the exact nature and structure of the cognitive component in the entrancing process. Realizing these articulations of self-talk allows partners to respect and release them. They learn to realize how this type of self-talk mentally induces emotional and physical states of worry, tension, and negativity which serve only to intensify and deepen entrancement. Realize that excluding all other realities of who our partner is, except our ideal image of them, is a symptom of entrancement. They need to articulate and challenge these entranced self-talk messages. This may be difficult, especially if partners fear they are "nothing."

Indeed, this is not a matter of cognitive challenging but one of detrancing and awakening, which allows recognition of the existence and presence of the irrationality of the messages. Partners need to detrance first or recognition is impaired. This is not so much to find more rational realms, but rather to find a broader realm in which such self-talk statements are no longer taking on a power all their own. They only have power when selective and isolated from larger perspectives and a more commonsense reality. Self-talk in entrancement can be shocking and traumatizing, which only deepens enmeshment further. Detrancing and awakening will be more likely to occur by inducing chaos into the present entrancement. When partners challenge, question self-talk, and engage in experimenting with new situations of relating to each other, they are stepping outside the restrictive limits of the fantasy ideal and inducing chaos by introducing new experiences. Such new experiences will not fit with the fantasy ideal and will, therefore, disrupt and detrance the fixated ideal. However, partners need to be anchored in a safe place as this could cause them to retreat further into rapprochement. Hypnotically induced safe places are created in partners as they go into trance and access times, places, and events that allow them to feel nurtured, protected, and powerful.

Step Four

This step involves determining the double message and confusion that keeps both entranced. This takes the form of saying I love you. Good-bye. It can mean, "I love you, but I ignore you," or "I love you, but I am too busy," "I love you, but I am interested in others." It sets up a situation in which individual partners never feel on solid ground with one another. Many times this "I will always love you, good-bye" kind of scenario is a double message and a confusion technique which keeps partners disoriented, disconnected, and deepened into the hypnotic enmeshment of trying to figure out what the relationship is all about.

Remember, confusion is a powerful technique which keeps people disoriented and distracted from general reality orientation. Fixation occurs when attempting to find clarity and resolution in endless confusion (how many angels fit on the tip of a pin?). The more they pursue those double messages, the deeper they go into the confused state of trance. Confusion, indeed, is a powerful induction and both partners keep one another in a state of disorientation and imbalance.

There is a need to learn how to penetrate through the confusion and distractions which maintain ambivalent, unclear messages between partners. Self-attending can be used here by shifting the focus from the head to the heart. Partners can utilize a shift in strategy, moving from a cognitive (thinking and imaging) way of operating toward what may be termed heartfelt focus. Such a focus is defined as allowing inconsistencies in communication to be there without trying to solve them. One partner was asked to allow the chaos of his thoughts to be present without trying to "solve" the puzzle. Instead, he focused on his heartfelt sense of what he truly wanted and let that guide him through his confusion. This focus helped break the entrancement of head fixation. He achieved this focus by getting into a relaxed, self-observing position (relaxation of muscles, breathing, and visualizing calm scenes). He then asked and reflected upon pertinent questions and confusions regarding the relationship. He self-attended to which images, ideas, feelings, or inner words that spontaneously emerged. After that point, he allowed these spontaneous sensory experiences to come together in a way meaningful to his situation. This allowed him new information regarding ways he could deal with his entrancement. Such a soul-searching type of process provides partners an introspective resource in their inner search for answers.

It is important for partners to take a look at and challenge the ideas, illusions, and fantasies of loving. What does it, in the reality of every-day life, mean to say "I love you" without being able to show love? Meaningful love is being able to demonstrate love to one another in some behavioral or manifest form, enhancing rapport between two unique individuals.

Step Five

This step requires partners to clarify the mixed messages they are sending to and receiving from each other. Partners need to ask them-selves whether messages sent are something with which they can iden-tify and believe in as valid. If one partner says he really believes the other should quit her job and spend her time traveling the world with him, she needs to ask herself which part of such a message is right and real for her. Acting like a perfect entranced lover, she confuses what she hears from her partner as being her own desires.

It is necessary to clear out this confusion and chaotic induction. It is very important that both partners learn to communicate in terms of what they each, in fact, desire in their hearts. What does it mean to them to manifest what's in their hearts for each other? What is it they each indi-vidually think? What do they each individually want? Partners need to own their inner messages and revelations as they are filtered through what is real in their heartfelt experiences. They can then begin identi-fying with and attributing their own unique characters to the ideas, goals, activities, feelings, and behaviors exchanged between each other.

The criteria for this are as follows: Is this behavior, idea, feeling, and/or attitude something that will in some way serve to assert and ex-press my unique characteristic way of loving in this relationship? In-stead of saying, "I will always love you, good-bye," it might be more valid to say "unfortunately, because of the way we are treating one an-other, we will never really be able to bring our full experience of loving each other to life. Could we continue to enjoy what's particularly unique about us and leave till death do us part fantasies-and-longings alone?"

In cutting through this Gordian knot, it may be useful to utilize Sir Lancelot's approach. Instead of getting lost in the confusion of trying to "untie" it and "solve" it, it may simply help to cut through it. By staying heart-focused on the unique sense of character of who you are, you acknowledge the chaotic, mixed messages in your relationship as you express, in your own way, love and honest feelings to your partner. You can "cut through" this confusion in your head by trusting what's in your heart and risk who you are being loving to your partner in your own unique way.

Step Six

This step involves the need for partners to suspend time and activity from each other. Detrancement and reemergence require partners to take a temporary (or permanent, if necessary) time out to rediscover themselves as individuals. The particular need in this step is to, in an honest, self-encountering way, disidentify from the fantasy ideal.

Fantasy ideals are absorbing mind-body fusions capturing illusionary distortions. Such distortions are only a slice or cross-section (creating perceptual illusions) of character structure known as caricatures. To reemerge, partners need personal time alone and away from each other to reverse this process. Disidentifying from and releasing skewed, illusionary versions of our partner requires safe places to reflect. Hypnotic induction of safe places assists partners' reflection and review of the fantasy ideal. With practice, partners can, in the quiet of their safe space and time, reflect and attend to the contrasts and challenges that emerge regarding skewed illusions of each other. Partners can reflect and meditate on one another's unique person and character. As the unique reality of each partner emerges in reflection and meditation, the fantasy illusion begins to dissolve and fade. It's as if a morning fog is being burned away by the heat of the rising sun. As skewed illusions of fantasy ideals begin to fade, partners begin to rediscover and reemerge their unique character.

Of particular use in releasing fantasy ideals is a technique called participant/observer. Just as an individual can try on and take off a pair of new shoes to see if they fit, so partners can deliberately try to take on the fantasy ideal of being that perfect lover. If that particular descriptive role fits in a genuine, natural way, wonderful. Most likely, such perfect lover roles will not fit and need to be discarded. Partners could deliberately attempt to visualize and imagine themselves as the perfect lover, experiencing the discomfort of trying to fit into such role descriptions. Such conscious efforts at creating skewed fantasy ideals are quite helpful in bringing to light the absurd role expectations.

Another useful technique is for partners to practice the art of forgetting one's self. This may seem odd to do, because partners have already lost part of themselves. Yet entranced partners can be quite vigilant of how they are supposed to act as perfect lovers. While unconscious as to how entranced they are as perfect lovers, they are alerted when stepping out of role character. During their time out period from each other, they may discover how much more they each can relax and be their natural selves. The technique works like this. Partners need to suspend judgment and decision-making about what to do with their relationship. They next need to live totally in the here and now. That is, to focus on their feelings and needs of the moment and be fully aware of the sights, sounds, and activities in their surroundings. Partners can learn to leave their relationship alone by not trying to know and solve all its problems. Partners can now forget how they are supposed to be as perfect lovers and rediscover and reemerge what is unique and natural to their character. Being involved in an activity completely unrelated to one's partner can help enormously (painting, music, etc.).

As partners follow these techniques, they can begin to discover what's unique and individualistic about their own characters. Such discoveries signal emergence from entrancement. Partners discover they are in more than just an illusionary fantasy state. They no longer identify with a skewed illusionary fantasy ideal of a perfect lover. Instead, partners can reorganize their sense of self as persons with unique sets of qualities and characteristics all their own. Such uniqueness of character transcends fantasy states of romantic times and places. Such unique character has an inherent design structural motif all its own.

Step Seven

This step involves utilization and development of self-discipline and self-attending skills, which are essential to reemerging from entrancement. Self-attending involves the use of reflecting and meditating on inner feeling states. It also is a skill that involves knowing what the individual needs and how to take care of those needs. Self-discipline skills are those that enable individuals to stay goal directed and follow through on tasks needed to attain those goals.

In order to help dissolve absorbing states of entrancement, partners need to develop self-discipline skills of self-attending. For example, when analytical questions about the relationship emerge ("Can I trust her?" "Is he sleeping with someone else?"), it is essential that partners translate and get a feeling sense or image inside themselves of what that is like. Being noncognitive at this point is critical to avoid any further enmeshment. Partners need to allow internal representations of self-talk messages to move outside their sense of self-boundary. In such a safe place, they can ask about the meaning and/or structure of mistrusting images relevant to relationship needs. Detrancement from illusions begins when one asks, "How would I be if I absolutely knew this was all illusion?"

Partners need to ask with a heartfelt sense of their needs. Accepting the way images form in answer to self-queries is enlightening. Entranced partners want what they want "now!" Self-discipline skills allowing messages and answers to come in various mediums in their own time (dreams, drawings, inner movements) are critical. Attending to intuitive senses assists in knowing what is caring and valid in the relationship. Receptivity to body-mind-spirit connections allows answers to come on their own. Detrancing from one's illusions means being able to access what they are, exploring and examining them in light of what's healthy and caring for both partners. It takes self-discipline to attend to one's inner wisdom and a sense of direction in knowing what is caring.

Facilitating receptivity involves accessing the clarity and flow of sensory motifs. Motifs are the heart of our character and require a labor of love, and self-discipline to bring them to life. Accessing motif is precisely what entranced partners need in creating safe, healing spaces for meaningful answers and awakening truth. More detailed information on motif utilization will be presented in the last chapter.

Step Eight

This step involves designing the unique kind of relationship that each partner's character can support and enhance. As many partners lament that their relationship does not allow them to be themselves, it is critical that each partner takes responsibility for detailing and articulating what is absolutely required. All too often, partners are involved in repetitive entrancing relationships to which they could never make a genuine commitment. Partners seem to spend more time lamenting what is so wrong about their relationship rather than taking responsible time out to define what they in fact want.

Partners need to first describe what their picture of a perfect partner is. This is a trap, as there is no such thing as a perfect partner. This is how they got into trouble with entrancement in the first place. Yet it is

important for partners to describe in detail the exact attributes and qualities desired in their perfect partner (gender, size, weight, hair color, race,
age, IQ, career, and even shoe size, if necessary). What this does is put
partners on notice as to what their perfect fantasy partner is all about.

The next phase of this process is for partners to describe the realistic
picture of that particular person to whom they could commit and spend
the rest of their lives together. One partner, for example, may have a
perfect ideal partner who is five feet, two inches tall, blonde, blue-eyed,
and full of fun and joy. Yet in his realistic description he describes
someone who is brunette, five feet, ten inches tall, and has been a
teacher for ten years and is working on her master's degree. Getting
contrasting descriptions between a perfect and a realistic partner can be
an eye-opening experience.

Next, partners need to define their idea of a perfect relationship. For
example, how much time spent together, what activities will be shared,
will there be children and how many, will one or both work, and what
kind of passion (emotional and sexual) is desired are only a few of the
multitude of relationship questions to be answered. Again, this is another trap. What is a realistic description of the kind of relationship
design to which each partner can make a lifelong commitment? Partners
need to be clearly specific as to the exact kind of realistic relationship
design that is possible, desirable, and committable.

Notice that similar kinds of questions can be asked of a realistic
relationship design as compared to a perfect relationship design. The
essential difference is that a realistic relationship design is grounded in
the everyday, tried and tested reality of each partner's life. This is
where time commitment and genuine loving can emerge. It is in the
light of everyday reality, of the here and now, that partners can learn
about each other (the good, the bad, and the ugly). They can see the real
character of the partner's person, not some made-up fantasy ideal that
crumbles in the face of trial and tribulation. In the realistic description
of the partner and the relationship design, each partner can decide and
commit to a loving, long-term bond that enriches the uniqueness of both.

HOLD THAT THOUGHT--I'LL BE RIGHT BACK

Reemergence from entrancement involves the self-discipline skills
to stay focused on recovering tasks. This means partners need to learn
how to redirect their mental and emotional energies away from the dif-
fused absorption of entrancement to the sharpened focus of reemer-

gence. The following technique can help partners develop the self-discipline skills of learning how to redirect their personal energies. Entrancement takes energy as the absorbing bond is a constant drain and dissipation of each partner's efforts and investments in the relationship. Fantasy ideal notwithstanding, it takes energy to maintain illusions of entrancement (even Disneyland requires maintenance).

As partners are seeking to detrance and awaken, it can be helpful to learn how to deal with the tremendous energy expenditure involved with obsessive thoughts and anxieties that keep them absorbed and entranced. Realizing that energy is required to maintain entranced thinking (absorbed in obsessive thoughts and negative self-talk), learning a technique called "Hold that thought--I'll be right back" can be quite helpful. It is a simple, yet powerful strategy. When partners start to engage in obsessive worrying, negative self-talk and/or recall of painful episodes of the relationship, first identify through making a list of such chronic ruminations. Second, identify a sensation, word, or image that comes into awareness. Self-attending skills are utilized to identify inner activity and sensations. Review the written list of chronic, internal ruminations. Upon review, ask what ideas, feelings, sensations, and the like are happening now. Assuming a quiet, reflective posture assists in attuning attention to inner activity.

Being patient and opening to what enters awareness allows identification of inner sense experience occurring in response to list review. Inner sense awareness identifies chronic worry or obsession, serving to alert partners about obsessiveness. Entranced partners may not realize they are recalling or obsessing.

As a self-observer, partners can put painful memories and/or obsessive self-talk on hold. Instead of allowing negative, painful scenarios or dialogues to run their usual ruminating course, they can be cut short, shifting attention and preempting their being completely played out. One can now consciously decide simply to leave the memory or negative self-talk alone, no longer wasting the time or energy on it. What allows one to do this is using inner cues of sensation (for example, queasiness) to alert one to what's happening and to "come out of it" or awaken. With practice, this means reducing and ultimately eliminating such mental ruminations that direct energy into entranced thinking.

To accomplish energy reduction, partners need to redirect mental focus away from obsessive trauma or memory.[1] Redirecting mental energy means shifting focus to a more absorbing and captivating experience. What could be more absorbing to entranced partners but utilization of inner capacities and tendencies for intense mind-body fusions. Utilizing abilities to become keen observers of the ever-unfolding flowing sensations and images of the here and now is empowering.

Such experiences may be cars going by a window, a woman typing on a computer, a man eating a sandwich, the sound of traffic, the jumbled voices of people talking in the background. Observing kaleidoscopic, unstructured flow experiences absorbs and redirects mental energy into here-and-now, mind-body interactions with the external world. Notice that it's the unstructured nature of the experience that brings one out of a rigid, entrance-absorbing world. The absorbing world of entrancement seems to be one that is free-spirited and open-ended. Yet there is a hidden, structured agenda of the fantasy ideal from which partners need release and recovery. As partners continue with keen observation, not judging or analyzing such activities, they are now more free and open as they are brought into present time. Partners accelerate redirection by utilizing a here-and-now focus on a flowing activity which accesses unique interests and valued fascination (architecture of a city skyline, the structure of a piece of classical music, etc.). Utilizing an individualized focus of attention to heighten the speed and intensity of experience redirects energies into here-and-now time frames.

Through such utilization, partners discover an inner freedom unfolding. Attentiveness to the here and now forms a healthy way of projecting partners in relating (contrast this with entrancement where projection leads to fixation and lost self).

Partners now find they have more mental and physical energy (they are less depressed) and are freer in mind and body. Unstructured observing releases rigid, obsessive thinking and memory recall. Focusing on the energy of the unstructured, unfolding moment-to-moment flow allows partners to become what's observed (healthy projecting and regaining a unique self). Now more open and creative, partners are able to gain healthier perspectives on flowing events in the relationship. Partners can place illusions "on hold," viewing them in uniquely different, detranced perspectives. Such a process and technique takes time and some practice. With patient and nonjudgmental attitudes, an energized, here-and-now self emerges.

The way and type of observations partners have is a direct expression of their inner sense of uniqueness. Attending and being alert to the here-and-now flow of the world around and within inadvertently reveals one's unique qualities and perceptions, which are remarkable manifestations of character. Form follows function, as the architects would say.

When it comes to the unique self of each partner, the function of the way he or she attends to the here-and-now moment follows the unique form of each partner's unique self. What partners see may well be what they get in their relationship. If partners learn to perceive the uniqueness surrounding them, they will learn to perceive their inherent, formative uniqueness supporting them within.

THE TWILIGHT ZONE TECHNIQUE

Self-discipline skills are also involved in sorting out fact from fiction scenarios. Entranced couples absorb one another into fantasy and nightmare scenarios from their everyday events. Partners communicate provacative, suggestive images to one another with vague implications of infidelity and loss. Multiple meanings implied in messages induce multiple realities to race through the mind. Confusion is created as to what is valid. Partners can feel like they've entered the Twilight Zone of the real merging with the unreal of fantasy/nightmare possibilities. Hypnotic minds cannot separate fact from imaginary reality.

The Twilight Zone Technique invokes the split of fact from fiction. Detrancing from catastrophic, obsessive associating, partners need to invoke the self-discipline skills of detaching and differentiating. The Twilight Zone Technique does just that through mental practice and discipline. The first step is for partners to identify when they are being led into the gray area where the boundary between fact and fantasy blurs (known as the Twilight Zone). Each partner identifies the point where observation has faded into vague interpretations. Cues to when this point has been reached are confusion, anxiety, and difficulty defining the precise nature of the problem in the relationship.

Second is exercising the mental self-discipline needed to restrain the initial desire to make sense of the issue. A key phrase here is to just leave issues alone for awhile, as putting such confusion on hold is quite empowering. Immediately release all efforts to discover meanings, associations, and/or interpretations. Go into your own unique, sensory experience, clearing out all distractions in thought and physical sensation. Do this by remembering and associating with the unique states and senses of what it feels like to just be by and with yourself. Suspend judgment of possibilities.

Third, completely release thinking and analysis, sorting through what feels like unique experiences of doing "one's thing" (play the piano, watch a sunset, etc.).

Fourth, energize experiences through intense repetition and elaboration of sensory detail until they become the predominant mode of reality and experience. At this point, one may actually forget to remember what was so confusing. In this clear, healthier state of self, go back and explore the validity of possible concerns. Mentally discipline yourself to clarify the Twilight Zone of fact and fantasy. Realize that one can be manipulated, paced, and led down the path of mental and physical associations of loss, worry, and infidelity.

At first, this procedure may seem quite difficult as the taunting and tempting seductiveness of fact and fiction interfacing may be too close for conscious comfort to stabilize. Partners may temporarily have to eliminate the beneficial qualities along with the destructive ones, releasing preoccupation with provacative messages to get clear of toxic intrusiveness. This involves releasing any cognitive effort to rationally deal with such messages. Continued practice and mental self-discipline begin to play a huge role in learning to trust one's intuitive resources. Self-attending and clearing facilitates access of validating self-experiences. Finding suggestive fact/fantasy mergers continuing and intensifying, one must realize that for one's own survival, complete release and letting go of the relationship may be required. Letting go occurs by shifting focus from trying to solve relationship problems toward one of release.

This shift may surprise partners in that it disrupts the endless loops of trying to solve entrancement problems. Such a shift in focus releases partners from these endless loops. Partners can be their unique selves leaving the "what ifs" alone. The more partners discipline themselves to be attentive and true to their own unique experience together, the healthier their relationship.

Partners may have never allowed love to be manifest in addictive relating. The "lost-in-love" hypnosis prevents expression of an individual's unique, loving character. Romantic entrancement lacks the capacity of commitment that can be provided only by heartfelt character. Healthy partners mean what they say, standing by commitments. Because of constant confusion and compromise required to maintain illusionary roles, partners are pressured into identical, carbon copies of each other's fantasy. Romantic words are abundant but rarely supported in the give-and-take reality of relating. It takes uniqueness of character, the stuff courage is made of, to reach out and lovingly expose one's unique imperfections (meaning it doesn't perfectly fit ideal love roles). Being committed with heartfelt character in a loving way means cher-

ishing one's own and one's partner's unique "imperfections" as perfectly unique. Awakening involves partners having unique, external
expressions for their internal loving experience. Externalizing shape or
form of uniquely personal manifestations of love allows partners to back
up romantic love talk with genuine action. Partners awaken from internalized, fantasized euphoria of "I love you" experiences and are challenged to translate them into real-world behaviors. They discover that
particular manifestation that most uniquely matches the heartfelt sense
of love.

Partners become entranced with being in love with love. This becomes an end in itself if left in "heady" entrancement, remaining disconnected from uniqueness of heart. Drifting from one to another occurs, constantly soothing one entranced lost love with yet another. Each
repeated "emptiness" of the "last-lost-love" exposes partners to ever-
increased states of isolation, never feeling whole, but rather part of some
missing half. Fulfillment comes with yet another mystical entranced
relationship. It's as if the hypnotist lost his or her subject and now needs
a new one to induce into trance.

Challenging the validity of love through the behavioral manifestation of acting lovingly to one another interrupts the illusion of this reality. Notice that what is detrancing is moving outside the "heady-
sensory" loop of "sleep," striking the unique chords of putting one's
heart into relationship. Letting the heart speak its own uniqueness
breaks the loop.

The fifth part of the Twilight Zone Technique is to learn how self-
suggestions work and how to alter them in ways to dehypnotize, detrance, and utilize them in awakening. One partner perceives the other
ignoring, mistreating, or withdrawing, interpreting the experienced suggestion, "My existence is threatened if my will is not followed by my
partner." The suggestion is that love will hurt. Translation: "I'm not
getting the perfect love I want and I will have it my way no matter how
much it hurts. The more I want love, the more I will perfect love, the
more it will hurt." The entranced suggestion invokes qualities of love,
will, and hurt in that order. When one partner withdraws, the other's
anchored to respond on cue to the love will hurt suggestion and feel
pain.

Hurting and feeling desperate means "the more I 'will' (will to
power or force love) always love you, the more I will have only loss and
hurt to show for it." This type of self-suggestion results from the contrast effects of willing perfect love colliding with deviations from what

"should be." Partners perceive this discrepancy as signs of love fading. Because of intense enmeshment and entrancement, self-suggesting loss and abandonment to deviations from perfect love becomes automatic. Unique, heartfelt loving manifestations are obliterated.

Obliteration of "self" occurs as a natural consequence of enmeshment into a preoccupation with that fantastical, significant other. Learning about catastrophic, self-suggestion provides partners a format to resuggest affirmative autonomy (I am much more in charge of my life without this distraction and fusion). Accessing inherent, character motif, through the senses of the heart, provides resources for self-affirmations and reintegration.

Accessing motifs provides stable anchors as partners retrace trance steps out of enmeshment. Each self-suggestion is a kind of formula equating one event with a particular meaning. Learning to decipher these equations unique to each partner brings them closer to awakening's surface.

Sixth, it is important to explore from the perspective of uniqueness what's in each partner's heartfelt sense of love. In such a light, partners ask, "What am I trying to achieve beyond the short run of this enchanting relationship?" " Do I even know who this person is in the light of day?" "What is the real purpose of being with him or her?" Review painful realities continuously challenging the fantasy. "Knowing it will always be this way, what are my choices?" "Have I ever been in love with this person?" "Is there any genuine dialogue operating in the relationship?" "Is there a feeling of being empty after intense, sexual encounters?" "Is there a sense of tension and preoccupation with uncertainty and self-consciousness when engaged in activities with my partner?" "Is there a sense that neither one of us is never able to be ourselves in the relationship?" The focus here is to come to terms with what is the reality of whether or not there is a genuine quality in the relationship.

Seventh, partners need to access and get a sense of their own unique characters. The following questions can be explored by partners to access their uniqueness: Do I emerge as my own character? Is my unique character, as checked and referenced through my heartfelt sense, truly congruent in its manifestations? What sense of purpose or power, love, passion, or meaning do I seem to stray away from and lose when I am with him/her? What emerges as my purpose and passion that's lost with my partner? The emphasis is on articulating whether I can be my unique self with my partner. What really prevents this from happening with my partner?

Eighth, partners need to explore how to expand their uniqueness. The following questions can be used for that purpose: What do I love about the people I feel myself with? Is there attention, warmth, a sense of completeness, a sense of goodwill toward one another? What character or nature do I truly enjoy about being myself in an open, fully available, accessing way? What in the relationship allows me to express unique facets of my ideas, feelings, or interests? Notice in this step there is a sense of discovery and wonder at the way we expand and proliferate our own unique sense of character structure and design. The focus here is on how one's unique sense of identity needs to be able to flower and expand with one's partner. In addictive relationships, the flowers will wilt on the vines of strangulation or neglect.

Ninth, partners need to feel a sense of life purpose. In answering the following questions, partners can access this purpose. What is the structure of my purposeful self or motif? To answer this requires commitment to sensing what makes one so special, so unique. For example: Do quirks, idiosyncrasies, or unique character traits seem to typify who I am? How do I do "me" when being myself? What ways of acting, speaking, imaging, or moving are unique traits of mine? Do I enjoy expansive, three dimensional, open-ended places or scenarios? Do I enjoy colorful formats, interesting designs, and/or various shapes of sculptures and architecture? In what ways do I want to get my body, mind, and emotions in shape that I feel are healthy, streamlined, and efficient? What kind of relationships do I want to have? Do I want them to be warm, attentive, filled with dialogue and a sense of humor and compassion as a core focus? Would I enjoy a feeling of mastery and playfulness in the ways I express my ideas if I were in the most desirable of relationships?

Do I enjoy how my ideas, emotions, or behaviors seem to relate and ripple outward to people as if a pebble was dropped into a pond, sending out waves of expansive effects through people in my life? Do I want to express ideas that are stimulating and enjoyable in their unique effects of others? What unique sense of character, in my heart of hearts, gives purpose to my life? How does my character manifest my unique motifs or artistically structured ways of expressing my talents? Unique character manifestations of each partner are accessed through such self-reflection. Partners begin to reawaken from "lost self" entrancement with the revelation of unique, sensory motifs creatively emerging from real depths within. Partners discover what they like and care about through keen observation of unique experiences and situations to which they are repetitively drawn.

Tenth, the reawakening process calls upon a sense of courage to emerge from the trance, trusting in a genuine reality of personal ownership and uniqueness. There is trust in the self-validating acts of individual initiative originating from the inner self. Partners begin to rediscover courage and enlightenment flowing in the natural trance of self-awareness. Notice how each partner begins to reawaken into their own character. They begin to find experiences into which they can put their hearts. Partners discover a sense of their unique, inner fulfillment in the flow of their own motif.

Motif or structure has its own quality of transformation. Partners rediscover intricate and complex order in the sensory and cognitive interplay of their motifs. Access of previously ignored facets of their character structure now open to them. The transforming quality of motif enriches their lives. Partners become more aware of their likes and loves, being alert to what creates meaningfully intense moments in their life.

Each learns to courageously trust their inner motif and characteristic evolution. This is why loving requires a brave heart with open and awake eyes to see the truth of their love in the reality light of day. They learn to give time and energy to their own unique, creative expression of self. It is essential for each partner to establish and to emerge with his or her own sense of purpose and character. Sensory motif (structure or pattern of sensory experience) is their metaphor both literally and figuratively for growth. The more time and attention given to their motifs, the more refined they become to reemerge as their own person. As with any muscle, the more exercised, the more powerful it becomes. For some partners, this will be more of an emergence. That is, they may not even be aware of the presence of their own motif. Indeed, lacking a clear sense of self in terms of one's unique motif may well contribute to susceptibility to entrancement.

Partners can be assisted in their personal relationships by learning to discover what their unique sense of passion and purpose is. It's essential for partners to be clear to themselves who they are so that they can then be genuine in their relations with others. The courageous, heartfelt first steps identifying and accessing these motifs liberate that unique character and artistry. They are naturally trance-forming and healing. Acting on self-validating passions and purposeful motifs assists partners in generating the courage to free themselves from entrancement.

To initiate expression of motifs, partners need to take inventory of what their real dreams are and what it would be like if they were living them now. Partners need to notice their unique ways of attending and creating the here-and-now reality. Shifts from mind-body entrancement to heartfelt transformations begin to manifest themselves in achieving real-life dreams.

The courage to act is always embedded in the larger-than-self reality. Partners can discover that their unique character has an intricacy and artistry so well designed as to suggest that there is so much more to them than meets the superficial eye. Partners need to take time and patience to truly appreciate the miracle they are. In taking steps to realize and be self-aware of what's unique and intricately special, there can be a sense of doubt, disbelief, and questioning. The heartfelt quality is our rootedness. Here, I am a free and willing participant in my core self, not some detached ego in conflict with a helplessly fused, mindless body.

There may be feelings of emptiness or even death of having to accept the fantasy ideal as an illusion, not a reality. This can be felt as a real loss. In shedding old images, external notions of "who I am," "what's important," "what I'm striving for" now surface. There can be a subtle (or not so subtle) shift from externally to internally driven beliefs, acts, and goals originating from this core motif of self. Instead of depending on outside approval, partners can begin to have faith in their own inner beliefs and decisions. Faith becomes more internalized as partners act more and more on their own self-beliefs, trusting this core motif within them as real. In this way each is born of one's own character, allowing us to learn how to function on our own recognizance. The larger-than-self reality is the spiritual field in which our unique characteristic motif is embedded and from where it emerges in its own rite of passage. Our motif has an organizing intelligence of its own and reflects higher levels of social and spiritual organizing qualities (character values, art).

Accessing and discovering this unique motif and character is not a selfish or self-absorbing obsession. It is the lack of accessing character which leads to obsession and addiction in the first place. The motif has a self-revealing way of expressing each partner's unique character. Partners are engaged in their motifs when they are absorbed in flowing, attentive states involving some unique interest (music, swimming, etc.). The uniqueness of each partner's expression in the relationship resonates with each individual's internal structure. Partners need to articulate the unique character structure that allows them to establish confidence and faith in their core self. Partners can learn to nurture and give manifestation to their unique motif and design.

Partners need to give rise to and bring to life unique ways they organize, create, and express their inner and outer worlds, resonating to their own true selves. By attending, nurturing, and taking individual action to be themselves and enhance their sense of uniqueness, partners give birth to the character or soul of who they are. Giving birth to soul is essential to life's wake-up call.

Life-giving processes of putting the soul into one's life and relationship involves a coming-out process. Healthy, newborn infants are already imbued with their own unique characters and motifs. Indeed, in many ways they are already fully formed in temperament and motif. Giving birth to what's already in that infant now forms the next "nine-month" pregnancy that can last for 90 years, the next death and rebirth cycle. Resolving hypnotically entranced relationships involves understanding what perpetuates them and how this perpetuation may be a preparation for future birth (or rebirth). Resolution can be found by partners shifting attention and effort from entrancing images and toward absorbing, core self-motifs.

Partners respond only to those exchanges that enhance or threaten illusions of entranced fantasy. Partners are "boxed in" to a very tight, rigid frame of reference. Entrancement's fantasy ideal acts as a selective, perceptual filter distorting partners' intimate communications.

The irony of entranced relationships is that they become obsessed and fixated at a set point that is designed to fix the degree of allowed intimacy at a certain level. They rarely get to fantasy. Partners spend more time in the struggle and/or conflict (journey to them) of getting there. Partners wouldn't know what to do with each other if they could enjoy a loving, shared evening out together without something to fight or feel hurt about. Because they respond to their internal fantasies and not who their partner is, they engage in magical thinking that they can control and change each other.

The key point here is that the relationship is designed, structured, and perpetuated to abort and fall short of any continuous gesture that suggests genuine intimacy and/or honest pursuit of heart-to-heart contact or growth. This set-point interruption prevents the birth of their character or soul. The progressive deterioration of the relationship and its partners is the consequential collapse of trying to maintain illusions of fantastical love in the face of an ever-mounting body of behaviors that challenges its validity.

What are powerful mechanisms maintaining such try-and-fail patterns which interrupt intimate gesture after intimate gesture, but the hypnotic pull of entrancement? In trying to make it better, they make it worse. The ultimate illusion is in constantly trying to make it better. The illusion of trying to make something work that is already geared for failure is fostered by thinking, "If only he or she were to change, then we'd have this wondrous, beautiful, eternal bond." A variation on this can be, "If I go into therapy, I can learn how to fix my fantasy relationship." When this fails, the therapist is usually blamed. It sets up the next series of interruptions to demolish all hope until the next go-round. This may also be true in entranced relationships at another level within each partner. Partners react to what is inside themselves (internal unmet needs), feeling that the other person is responsible for a breach of love and good faith. Partners find they also self-interrupt their own needs for love and closeness. Each tries to justify the unhealthy ways personal needs are met by trying to manipulate and control the other into taking responsibility and blame for his or her own infidelities.

The challenge and intervention is to break open this contained, boxed-in frame of reference. To get out of any box or frame requires a creative, courageous leap. What prevents partners from doing this is the belief that terrible things will happen (abandonment, emptiness, or brutal annihilation). After all, wasn't there once the belief that if we sailed too far out into the horizon, we would fall off the face of a flat world? Entranced partners keep each other so intimidated that otherwise healthy behavioral steps are, in fact, setups for failure.

DEFRAMING

Deframing involves short-circuiting or jamming this pattern the couple has of interrupting intimacy gestures and efforts. Deframing involves an honest, specific leveling. Instead of John trying to be sweet, loving, and caring after a huge brawl, he might be encouraged to honestly assert the genuine loving truth. Truth at this point is, "I feel very frustrated that we do not allow ourselves to love each other any more than we do." He confronts the hidden agenda limits that both have colluded to accept but were unable to acknowledge while entranced. He dares to step out of the boxed-in frame of entrancement.

Deframing can be a naturally occurring experience that awakens us from this fused, entranced pattern. Honest commentary between partners reveals the true nature and feelings each partner has but that they may feel too guilty to acknowledge. Focusing on what is implicit or subtly hidden in the entrancement brings partners out of endless communication loops. Honest, intense, focused commentary on hidden agendas in entranced relationships assists deframing. Such leaps involve hypnotic techniques of intense focusing critical to stepping out of boxed-in frames. Selective attention on fantasy ideal deviations creates a hypnotic collapse of entrancement and destabilizes the structure of entrancement. Creativity and openness to incongruities in fantasy ideals can energize partners' efforts. Seeing the human being of your partner requires suspension of self-absorbed needs. Perceive from the outside frame (detranced) your partner's individuality.

Detrancing will only lead to relapse and regression if partners do not learn to create larger, character-oriented frames of reference to move toward. Asking what is needed from a caring point of view allows uniqueness of heartfelt responses. Honesty of character is being accessed when thoughts and feelings give way to the priority of our unique values. What makes loving so enticing and entrancing initially is discovering an artificial vehicle that brings out what we want in ourselves, acted out and manifested in our partner. Our uniqueness of character can be highlighted and gratified by basking in the artificial light as our partner mirrors back reflections of our hidden desires and disguised qualities. Psychoanalysts would call this a form of narcissism. We envy what the other has, which is the best part of what we already have present in ourselves without realizing it.

Begin to take back the projected self through honest acknowledging of envy. In accessing our unique character, partners release artificial props and mirrors. What could be more exhilarating than complete confidence and comfort in being uniquely who and what we are? Accessing artistic motif extracts partners from boxed-in entrancement. Access to motifs occurs when partners feel motivated to be open, creative, and fully living in the present here-and-now moment. They are now connecting not to some artificial image reflected in the other, but to a real sense of their artistic structure and design. Partners can now begin discovering and aligning with an inner sense of beauty, and an inner confidence of wholeness. Accessing inner motif empowers partners to share out of feelings of abundance, not neediness.

S.T.A.T.E.

Critical to the awakening process is a more unified and comprehensive program called S.T.A.T.E., which facilitates deframing and character development of sensory, artistic motifs. S.T.A.T.E. is an acronym that stands for *Self focus, Time focus, Access focus, Trance focus* and *Emergence of self-in-relationship focus*. These five types of foci reflect ways in which this fixation, this "stale sense of now" commonly known as "stuck in time," operates on five different levels that when fully functioning free and liberate enmeshed partners. This involves more than resonation with what is inside each of us. It involves the revelation of unique characteristic motifs present and operating in the here and now. The eight steps previously presented serve and support the development and enhancement of these foci.

The *Emergence of self* focus is more commonly known as differentiation of self in the relationship. It has a special meaning in the entranced relationship where the "self" is coming out of an absorbed state. This involves learning how to distinguish or identify the unique characteristics of one self from another while still intimately involved. The remarkable feature about these five types of foci is that as individuals learn to progressively develop each focus, they find themselves developing a clearer identity with each focus achieved. Partners in hypnotically addictive relationships discover that moving through these five levels supports them in surfacing and reemerging from their entrancement. Each focus progressively surfaces partners more and more to an awakened rebirth, bringing up with them buried treasures of the soul waiting to be discovered.

Each of these five foci progressively allows partners to break entrancement, discovering a variety of multiple realities, points of view, and ideas. They begin to defluff (move from vagueness to specificity) or demystify the hypnotic illusions, generalized statements, and vague realities that keep partners lost in an enmeshed wonderland.

Self focus encourages each individual to practice how they put themselves in a trance with the other one. For example, as was mentioned earlier, partners create internal self-statements of "I cannot live without her." "What will happen to me if she is with other men?" "Who is he with?" "He is out on a business trip and now what if he meets someone?" "I have to call him." "I have not heard from him." We encourage people to begin to be aware of these types of self-talk and even practice inducing themselves. The focusing is not on the content of the other person, but rather on the process of self-talking and self-inducing. Focusing is now on how one goes into a trance itself. A special feature is on how their worries and questions reflect that they have somehow lost their "best self" to the other and are envious of what their partner really has. This is again part of the unique "out of the loop" heart focus that helps to detrance partners. It thereby opens many future doors to recovery.

Partners consciously focus on how they self-induce and self-talk themselves into trance. Focusing is on how one partner serves as a misdirection of attention for the other to go into trance. One partner can recreate an imagined scenario of how he or she may question the other's activities while simultaneously attending to the projected worries and terrors of entranced abandonment. In this way, partners learn how they self-induce entrancement, which can be utilized to dehypnotize. Practice assists partners in learning that they use each other to misdirect their attention away from their own inner needs and feelings. Misdirection distracts partners from volitional control of cause/effect actions, leaving them sensitized to autonomic, self-induction of sensory impressions. The more misdirected partners' attention is displaced from their internal suggestions, the greater the intensity of projection and entrancement. Misdirected attention is more probable when ambiguity and confusion exist between partners.

Self-focusing reverses this process. It encourages partners to establish internal awareness of their own, unique orientation. Taking one's attention back from absorbed misdirection involves learning how to direct focused attending. Self-focusing involves partners getting a clear sense or descriptive picture of their self-inductive process. The entrancement process becomes more conscious, self-focused, somewhat less hypnotic, and lighter.

Partners begin to develop a sense of control through reconstructing entrancement. Partners learn through visualization how they allow fantasy ideals leading to entrancement to emerge and at first draw them into absorbing experiences. Visualized fantasy ideals being reconstructed are allowed to deteriorate into the disillusionment, obsession, and rapprochement stages, vicariously working through regressive entrancement. Finally, partners visualize and reconstruct how they are awakening from deteriorated, collapsed fantasy ideals to a healthy sense of their own unique motif. At this point, release and deframing of the fantasy-ideal is worked through. What was once an intense, powerful, absorbed entrancement has been dissolved and diluted into the thin air of re-freshed awakening.

In the release and awakening from entrancement, partners some-times wonder how they could have ever made such a big deal about the encounter in the first place. They now see the illusionary nature of the fantasy ideal as having the constitution of cotton candy. Such a reframe of the fantasy ideal reveals the genuine character of the individual as constituting the real, unique strength in their lives. An important caveat to note is that such an awakening and release process requires that part-ners go all the way through the stages to expose the fantasy ideal for what it is (which may not be easy for them to do).

The second step in self-focusing is learning how to identify states in which partners are partially or completely fixated. They learn how to interrupt those thoughts and begin to shift to self-inducing a healthy trance. Engaging in flow states involving unique motifs (experiences in which we joyfully become absorbed and move or flow unself-consciously--that is, forgetting to think about ourself while doing it) can be a prime way partners interrupt destructive thoughts and affirm self and relationship. Partners begin to discover activities and interests that are preoccupying, absorbing, and have value in and of themselves. Such activities embody flowlike states that have their own hypnotic quality (music, dance, socializing). Any activity that focuses the partner's at-tention in an absorbing way has such a hypnotic quality. However, this time it becomes self-focused instead of other-focused. Partners can use the self-affirming flow states of hypnotic experience to break the en-trancing, hypnotic experience. Shifting focus from the significant other back to the self is a powerful paradigm change. Trance is utilized to deal with and work through entrancement.

In referring to *time focus*, partners are stuck in time. Partners appear to live in the present, yet present experience involves countless repeti-tions of the same old pattern of conversation, conflict, and contact. Re-peating cycles of acting and reacting occur such that partners' here and now is the dead-air stillness of a stagnant swamp.

Partners are encouraged to focus on their stuckness and learn to shift their focus point to create movement and a real sense of change in their time together. They can learn to move their relationship into the future, visualizing outcome scenarios and consequences to staying stuck. An exercise to assist is to look at one's finger in front of one's face, then look at a point an inch beyond that finger, then look at a point three inches beyond that finger, then look through the wall, then look through the building, then look through the trees. Eventually, partners image looking through time to see their future, resourceful selves. The self as perceived in a future time line embodies the heart of what partners want to be and achieve in time.

As partners utilize such a process, they see themselves in the future beyond the encapsulated, self-enclosed bubble of entrancing scenarios. Partners can burst through by looking through the bubble, looking through time to how they want to be in that future self. This is another way to awaken from trance. Time is altered in trance. Partners learn to consciously move forward, backward, and return to the present, integrating commonsense reality with entrancement. Partners continue awakening, bringing new discoveries of self resources with them.

Access focus encourages partners to access resources of characteristic uniqueness. Accessing artistic motifs and communal groups assists awakening. When detrancement occurs, partners are able to access multiple realities, roles, talents, and possibilities. Fixation is broken when multiple realities (enjoying many ways of being themselves) integrate into an expanded awareness of their reality. Such an integration suggests partners experience many facets of their character motif, increasing diversity in their lives. Such diversity involves discovering a unique variety of resources relating to partners' artistry, interests, fascinations, and absorbing activities enjoyed for their own sake (be it chess, tennis, dancing, or watching a sunset). The diversity of so many absorbing realities prevents fixation into any one. The resulting contrast of each partner's encounter with his or her own varieties of experience challenges each partner to get to the heart of what matters.

Partners need to develop variety in themselves by accessing resources that offer a variety of their own characteristic self. Multiple ranges are needed for partners to discover self-expansiveness. Integrated wholeness permeates diversity, creating a sense within and between partners of uniqueness. Resulting mosaic patterns weaving through varieties of experience are unique to partners' motifs. For now, suffice it to say that motifs manifest themselves in diverse experiences echoing similar themes with multiple variations (one's signature).

Entranced partners touch on themes of their motifs but rarely follow through in manifestation. In the access state, partners are encouraged to follow through (take piano lessons, practice their talents, etc.). Such manifest activities are not about losing oneself in a smorgasbord of affairs, but of discovering and tuning into one's inner sense of what nurtures that unique, core self. Experimenting and exploring with how

these core inclinations begin to break us out of that hypnotically encapsulated small world marks the road to reemergence. What's important
here is getting a clear inner sense of what are one's unique core themes
that need expression and not to get lost in multiple activities.

Trance focus is what the issue has been all along. It is a focus where
both partners are taught how to go in and out of a trance. They also develop skills to be transconscious. This means to be conscious of how
and when one is being absorbed, preoccupied, or lost in thought, which
is a part of entrancement. This is to be distinguished from healthy daydreaming. It's important to learn the signs of being in and out of trance.
Being able to be objective, to judge, to think about things in a reality-
testing way are important out-of-trance behaviors. Knowing which
"state" you're in is as important as knowing what city you're in.

Emergence of self-in-relationship focus involves a critical dimension
of awakening. Individuals in addictive relationships feel they can be
themselves only when they are outside the relationship. Individuals may
feel safe to be themselves only when away from one another, or when
they are doing things that do not seem to involve the relationship and
contact with the hypnotic fantasy. Partners may feel they can be themselves only outside of any close contact. Entranced partners do not
know how to be themselves with each other because when they go into
trance, there is no self to share. There is simply the absorption of each
partner into a fused bubble of euphoric fantasized experience. It is as if
you just dump everything into a junk box or stuff it all into a closet.
This is what happens in an addictive relationship. Everything is
"jammed in there." The merged-self of each partner has lost its unique
integrity. The idea of the emergent self is learning how to discover and
differentiate uniqueness in oneself while in relationship. The goal is to
be able to do this without having to feel the need to break out of the
relationship in order to be yourself. The lack of an emerging self in
relationship prevents healing and any detrance work. Partners need to
learn how to be their unique selves with the other partner present. What
good is being yourself only when alone in your room? Partners need to
open up their true, unique characters to each other to experience real
intimacy together.

Emergence of self in relationship is a powerful focus in addictive
relationships. A key to healthy relationships (assisting detrancement) is
to understand rapport. Rapport develops as partners pace and move
together in dancelike rhythm. Yet entranced partners step on each
other's toes and/or struggle for the lead. Boundaries between self and

other become blurred. Rapport is eroded, collapsing under the weight of fused boundaries. Healthy partners release their personal boundaries as appropriate yet know how to recover them. Entranced partners lose sight of their individual identity, preventing recovery. Rapport dissolves into internal/external fusion. Each partner seems to become one with the other at the expense of character. Rapport in its meaningful sense is never attained, only compliance or fusion. Rapport presupposes two unique partners being present experiencing harmony in their engagement. Entrancing relationships have lost the uniqueness of each partner that makes relationships possible in the first place.

It is rare that healthy relationships have the exact, identical partners. They may be similar, but never identical. Perfect love's fatal mistake is striving for identical twins. Fitting into fantasy ideals requires sameness of mind-set feeding into the illusion of total harmony. If this identical function ever did happen, the entire relationship would collapse anyway. Relating requires some contrast. Exact sameness obliterates relationship. Partners are not exact or the same and don't need to try to be. Partners are composed of unique individuals that may fear their differences might keep them apart. Yet individuality is okay because we have harmony and rapport in our shared uniqueness. We may or may not move exactly together. How we complement and add a sense of completeness (to what's already there in each partner) by our differences creates the rapport. It is what the yin and yang concepts of the East suggest as complements of the whole. We can be whole individuals simultaneously, completing a greater union at a higher level. This does not mean that we are incomplete as individuals. It means that in a relationship, we find a greater fulfillment of who we are as human beings without losing our uniqueness. We will have learned how to be ourselves in a holistic and healthy relationship.

Do not try to be the same or different. Just appreciate similarities and differences. Avoid an emphasis on being all or none, focusing on differentiation. Appreciating the differing yet similar kinds of realities, talents, roles, interests, and values that each partner has to share is essential to relating.

The self, time, access, trance, and emerging self-in-relationship foci are fundamental in releasing the unique character of self. Reflect on the acronym S.T.A.T.E. Notice an intriguing idea. The key to recovery and emergence of a healthy self in healthy, intimate relationships is to appreciate the S.T.A.T.E. of our own consciousness and our experience with ourselves involved with the other person. The idea of healthy self-change in S.T.A.T.E.-dependent learning and growth entails a magnificent shift in consciousness. It involves shifting both focus and sense of purpose from the other back to self. It is a focus of "what am I doing, what am I creating, what realities am I generating in this relationship?"

One point I want to mention about S.T.A.T.E. is that all five types of foci refer to changing fixation. Fixation is characteristic of what it means to be in a trance. Trance is a fixation. Take a look at the word "fix". Hypnotically induced relationships have fixation as partners get a fix on the other, go into trance, and become absorbed into fantasy. They see each other only through the filter of hypnotic trance or fixation. Changing and breaking the trance involves changing the fix or focal point of attention. Breaking addictive bonding necessitates focus shifts for real change.

Therefore, these five types of foci are extremely important. The shift onto self (what is congruent for my true self) breaks fixation from the illusion or fantasy of the other. It interrupts self-absorption into the dreamlike quality, challenging and "popping" the bubble of that dream by challenging, "How is my lack of being congruent to my true self encouraging so much pain and agony?" "How am I creating fleeting euphoria that drains the characteristic energy of my being?" These questions get to the heart of the matter exposing the heart felt holistic sense of our true caring.

Focal point shifts challenge the reality of the dream, testing what is real by "sticking one's hand through the mist of illusion." Testing reality changes the fantasy focal point. In this way, partners no longer fabricate what the other is all about but rather identify the fabric of their own tapestry. The illusion begins to open and disappear. There is the realization that the fabric of entrancement is made of fluff and can evaporate into thin air.

Changing the focal point from absorption with the other to a focus of "what I am doing to create this?" immediately restructures the relationship. It is important to understand that it is the shift in the focal point where real change and emergence of self begins. The shift is not what the other one is doing to me, not "Why isn't this fantasy working out for me?" but rather the focus becomes, "How do I structure my own experience?" One can create this trance as one can create mirror images of self through reflecting lights from a movie projector onto a screen. Partners realize they have the source to change and restructure scenarios of their life within them. Partners realize they can create those scenes and can also recreate them.

Shifting focus for change by coming from within begins to challenge the validity of how permanent, concrete, and valid these entrancing fantasies are. Focus coming from the inside out allows an empowered sense to create any kind of image partners want. Perhaps what each partner is creating is not as real as he or she thought it was. Partners know it is creatable. The same is true about time. Partners are shifting out the frozen-in-time, stale present (which means the stuck present) to a moving "now" that's future focused on the kind of self they want to be (expanded, vivacious, energetic, and outgoing). Each sees their desired self emerging.

The idea of accessing resources is powerful in terms of creating possibilities of multiple realities, multiple roles, multiple communal groups, multiple activities in which one can follow through and develop. Getting the heartfelt sense of themes and patterns of each partner's motif through this multiplicity of activity gives shape and form to their motif. Partners can reach this point by working through (either on their own or with the assistance of a therapist) the five foci of S.T.A.T.E.

The idea of being trance-focused increases one's awareness and helps partners develop the idea of focal point. It changes the fixation of entrancement to the presence of trance. When do partners go into trance (or call it entrance) or when is the trance ending? When are partners in or out of trance? Being in trance is fine as long as partners know and have choices.

It is critically important to develop an awareness of trance focus. The fixation shifts not into a static point (gridlock of boxed-in entrancement) but into a point of movement, which is healthy in relationship. Such movement through time of healthy change and growth suggests an ability or competency of knowing how to use trance. This shifts the idea of time focus not into the lost self of entranced limbo, but rather into the discovered self of purposeful time.

The final focus of S.T.A.T.E. is the issue of emergence of self-in-relationship. There is a need to learn how to focus (which implies moving through the here-and-now point in time without fixating) on how the self grows in a relationship. The opportunity to learn how to grow and be one's unique self in the context of an intimate relationship emerges through this type of focused movement through time. As that unique growth begins to occur in the field of an intimate relationship, one's unfolding purpose is revealed. It is revealed in the joy and pleasure of each partner's personal absorption into their own flow activity shared together. The vitality and richness of each partner's artistic motif in conjunction with the other unfolds into beautiful, maturing character.

Partners emerge into the flow of their own characteristic activity or motif, moving closer together, discovering how to express, create, and be themselves in the field of relating to the other's presence. Each can enjoy and encourage one another in unique, manifest ways of being themselves, complementing and enhancing their sense of relationship. There is room and space for both of them to enjoy unique oneness together. Both valued and respected each other's abilities in how unique and talented they were. They shared and enjoyed with each other how much pleasure they received from these activities. In such sharing, they experienced a flowing state of rapport and pleasure at being able to express their uniqueness to each other. They found that the character of their unique motif expressed in their activities was also being manifested in the ways they communicated, planned their time together, solved problems, and made decisions. They had accessed their motifs and realized how enhanced this made their relationship together.

When partners access the depth of their unique activity (which is more their unique artform or motif), they are open to their inner, unique characters. It is this opening and accessing of the core self that is now receptive to mutual sharing as both lovers and valued human beings.

Partners who have experienced that they have grown apart in their differences are those who have not shared their unique motif in the relationship. Entrancing relationships interfere with partners sharing unique activities and characteristics because of rigid, perfect love roles required.

Entrancement involves the mind's imagination, the body's hormones, and a sensory, erotic connection that bypasses heartfelt sensing. Fusion of mind and body into a misdirected fantasy occurs where partners begin to fall in love with one another's attributes, parts, qualities, or fantasies. As a way of extricating and liberating mind-body fusion, it is important to understand that freeing experiences occur through releasing fixation on inflated, misconstrued fantasies. Reconnection requires spontaneous, nonrigid experiences of heartfelt sensing.

Challenging fixation-based fusion, a curious question was asked by a therapist to partners years ago. The question was, "Do you come by this (voice pause) honestly?" The question implies that such fixation is something that partners may have come by (have pleasure in believing) without being honest with themselves. Do you get to this mind-body loop with an open-hearted honesty? Do you come to this point in your relationship through façade and self-deception? Dishonesty happens in fixation as does denial and disconnection from reality.

Distortion and selective filtering of partners' uniqueness satisfies entrancement as inner needs fuse with external demands. Entrancement selectively amplifies and exaggerates universal, human vulnerabilities. As such, it can expose them and provide a healthy challenge for growth. Entrancement distorts character defects as much energy is wasted chasing the red herring of fatal flaws. As partners become healthier, they discover their point of fusion-triggering entrancement.

This point of fusion involves a hypnotic logic-association-action-strategy of a powerful, imaginative dynamic. Such a dynamic symbolizes the senses into a fantasized reality that now appears real. The irony of this fantasized symbolism is that it is made of complete mind-body stuff that is a total bypass of the heartfelt motif of a real person with real care. This is intellectual fantasy posing as romantic reality. That is why accessing the heartfelt senses creates such a disorganizing and detrancing effect of reawakening.

Indeed, the creator of a dynamic change process called psychocybernetics, Maxwell Maltz (1964), indicated that the mind cannot distinguish what is real and what is imagined when the vivid imagery has the richness of the sensory, auditory, kinesthetic, and visual qualities. To awaken is to sort out a commonsense reality that is based on being our unique selves from fantasy ideals based on illusions. Awakening out of entrancement involves piercing the veil of illusion through penetrating honesty in one's relationship.

NOTE

1. There are times, however, that direct and deliberate focusing on being consciously obsessive and dwelling on anxieties can short-circuit them. This is a form of paradoxical effort of deliberately encouraging the unconscious, entranced thinking to interrupt and abort it. Such an approach may not always be helpful in working through the trauma.

CHAPTER 9

TRANCE MASTERY

INS AND OUTS OF ENTRANCEMENT

Delineating when and how entranced partners can move in and out of trance will be presented. With skill and practice, partners can begin to master specific conditions and situations that, in the past, would have helplessly enmeshed them in entrancement, but now having mastered trance, they can skillfully resurface and emerge through the masterful utilization of the following methods and strategies.

Trance mastery presupposes partners' personal responsibility and creativity (relating is creating) for the quality of their encounters. Being willing to acknowledge that at some level of consciousness (continuum of conscious to unconscious) partners can cocreate even the most illogical and absurd of relationship encounters is critical to trance mastery.

One approach to mastery utilizes the "as if" game, where partners act as if whatever the relationship's desirable or undesirable conditions both have somehow created. Such acts of creation can be initiated by either partner at some level of conscious and/or unconscious pattern(s) of response. It is the ultimate responsibility of each partner to identify and master whatever hidden and distracted (disguised) triggers of response each has created and manifests in perpetuating entrancement. Partners can seek to answer questions such as "How do I create my fantasy/nightmare with my partner?" If partners had to show or teach someone how to create this, what would be the very first thing they would need to imagine, feel, say and/or do to begin the enmeshment? Would he have to imagine the way she smiles or the wonderful lilt in her voice? What would be the very next thing to do to continue and deepen the enmeshment? What are the hidden fantasy triggers initiating reactions (sights, sounds, feelings, images, etc.).

After the entire mechanism is clearly elaborated, each partner could learn how to take his or her fantasy/nightmare process to such an extreme that it collapses under its own absurdity. There is some irony in depicting such absurd extremes because the actual perversity of entranced relationships can indeed culminate into such bizarreness. Exaggerating caricatures resurfaces from entrancement and empowers utilizing more meaningful, reality-oriented values to serve as criteria for relating to unique character.

In light of the preceding framework for trance mastery, Figure 9.1 details the "ins" and "outs" of entrancement and how to intervene. Mastery of these interventions can greatly enhance each partner's ability to generate meaningful and purposeful choices of when and how to move in and out of entrancement. With such mastery, partners will be able to establish healthier, longer lasting, and loving relationships together. Remember that entrancement can be created by any verbal and/or non-verbal stimulation that fixates absorbing attention or invokes mental imagery and/or body sensations within the person. This may involve surprise, shock, and sudden changes in attitude/behaviors which are repetitive. In reviewing Figure 9.1, the reader will take note that some of the "outs" interventions will break the "old" entrancement. At the same time, they can initiate healthier, alternative, self-induced, self-directed trance experiences.

Figure 9.1
Trance Mastery Chart

Ins		Outs
I.	Matching partners' responses, ideas, feelings, and/or behaviors	Mismatching responses.
II.	Fluff language: vague, general statements of ideas, feelings, desires, etc.	Translate vague words into concrete, specific language.
III.	Repetitious experiences: same old arguments, same old routines, same old rituals.	Novelty of behavior/attitude, agree instead of disagree, put a limit on endless arguments using time-outs if needed, breaking routines. Change love-making rituals (positions, who initiates, where, when, etc.).

IV.	Shock and/or surprise that keeps partner(s) off balance in the relationship (broken promises, mental and/or physical abuse, threats, etc.).	Create a safe place for shock effects to wear off, allowing partners recovery time of full range of thoughts, feelings, and senses.
V.	No-talk rule; unspoken agreement not to openly identify problems and/or dissatisfactions; hypnotic negative hallucinating.	Create safe atmosphere to risk breaking established, hypnotic norms allowing for open communication.
VI.	Absorbing, romantic memories and interludes activating entrancement.	Freeze the movement of the memory, shifting to nonromantic contexts.
VII.	High intensity and maintenance of fantasy fixation (must always be perfect with the other partner).	Interspersed fantasy allowing time to learn to love the "deviance" of each partner's uniqueness.
VIII.	Obsessive thoughts and compulsive acts (ruminating about loss, abandonment, insecurities, jealousies, etc.).	Thought-stopping, identifying periods of repetition by yelling "stop." Redirection to artist endeavors (motif).
IX.	Rageful rapprochement, hating, blaming, revenge-seeking related to damaged or impaired romantic ideals.	Stay focused on external here-and-now reality, enhancing sensory motif involvement, reality checks and testing.
X.	Absorbing tendencies with mind-body fantasy-sensory body/ part fusion.	Practice capturing the full range of each partner's characteristic profile getting a realistic picture of all his or her traits as one whole person.
XI.	Feeling a need to control, direct, and/or judge what is said or done and with whom.	Awakened, mature feelings of freedom and trust in the loving character and nature of each other's commitment to the relationship.
XII.	Demanding beliefs about the relationship: The relationship must work!	Utilizing healthy self-statements of what each partner prefers: life will continue on into the future with or without the other.
XIII.	Long, intense dialogues and reflective interchanges resulting in fatigue and unresolved conflicts.	Time-limited exchanges between partners distilling essential problem themes and resolutions.

(continued)

XIV. Fixation on details and tangents, losing sight of the real problem.	Maintain a sense of perspective keeping a practical and pragmatic attitude on reality-based, here-and-now issues and resolutions.
XV. Persistent, intense confrontations exaggerating everyday issues into major traumas and disasters.	Appropriate, nonsarcastic humor and positive metaphors to lighten the impact of issues that have been blown out of proportion.
XVI. Partners feel adversely affected by some magnetic quality in the other, becoming intolerant to imperfection.	Identify the source of "magnetic" pulls as coming from somewhere inside one's own self-constructing fantasy of the partner.
XVII. Overcomplicating issues that overwhelm and keep partners entranced in a helpless enmeshment.	Keep it simple is the rule for such controversies. Simplify issues into brief, descriptive form focusing on conscious, solution-oriented tasks.
XVIII. Neediness and dependency become so intense that partners feel miserable, helpless, and lost as to how to preserve their relationship.	Develop a practical, here-and-now conscious set of choices as to how each partner can responsibly assert their needs, bypassing fantasy ideals.
XIX. Partners absorbed by interspersed hidden innuendoes, presuppositions, and images embedded into their communication.	Partners observe, define, and nonjudgmentally stay with the here-and-now experience, allowing the entrancing action to surface the provoking suggestion.
XX. Partners caught in the passion paradox, entrenching and entrancing them deeper.	Raise the intimacy set-point by asserting and sharing unique individuality and sensory motif.
XXI. Feel somehow split off or separated from one's conscious choice and controlled by the other partner's presence.	Reown and reconnect with disowned parts of themselves through reassociating with the larger self of motif.
XXII. Taking or splitting off some aspect of the other partner and incorporating it into his or her own projected distortions of the other (distorts vivaciousness as immaturity).	Each partner releases distorted, entranced parts, reincorporating multiple aspects of their own character in meaningfully valid designs (accepts vivaciousness in other and value in self).

AWAKENING TRANCE AFFIRMATIONS

An additional tool to assist partners in trance mastery is utilization of a Trance-Script which is a self-verbalization of an affirmation for awakening. To construct such a Trance-Script, utilize each of the twenty-two interventions in Figure 9.1 and create a word or phrase from each to fill in the twenty-two blanks below. Examples of words/phrases are given as aids, though you are encouraged to create and develop your own.

I. I can awaken my mind and body whenever I choose to enhance a loving relationship with my partner. I will mismatch my partner's responses by *(increasing voice tempo, become task oriented)* when it assists me in being lovingly assertive.

II. I can be more effective in my loving expressions by being more specific about *(sharing with my partner what I behaviorally like about him/her)*.

III. I can enhance the quality of my loving relationship by increasing the novelty of how I am when I *(create variations in our love making)*.

IV. At times of shock and surprise, I will help myself and my partner create safe places by *(taking a time out)*.

V. I will encourage honest and open communication with my partner by *(self-disclosing what I feel frustrated about even though he/she may not like what's said)*.

VI. When my partner and I get stuck in dwelling on the dead, lost past, I encourage each of us to freeze that memory into a past moment and let it be laid to rest. I will encourage both of us to share how much we have grown and developed to be who we are today. I can see my growth as *(feeling more confident in what we have created)*.

VII. When there is a need to enjoy more space and uniqueness between my partner and me, I will remind myself how important this is by *(telling myself how valuable and refreshing breaks can be)*.

VIII. I will use the word "stop" to interrupt times of obsessive thoughts and redirect compulsive activity by focusing on my unique, artistic motif of *(expansion and variation in playing the piano)*. In this way, I can shift my attention and energies to healthy and realistic efforts.

IX. At times of intense negativity and ragefulness, I realize how important it is to lovingly protect both of us and take a healthy time-out to get a reality check of what's happening by *(learning how to ask for helpful intervention)*.

X. While I realize that having fantasy illusions about my partner may be temporarily exciting, I can remember to take the time and energy to appreciate his/her uniqueness as a real person by *(asking myself what do I respect in him/her as a person)*. In this way, I will continue to capture the character of my partner and enjoy more balance in my relationship.

XI. I can realize that consciously choosing to support my partner's and my needs for mature freedom and awakening will be enhanced as I challenge and honestly dispute the following insecure, fear-based, irrational beliefs of *(he/she always has to be perfect and loving)*.

XII. I can enjoy the many beneficial qualities and resources experienced in my relationship while following healthy self-statements of how I create quality in my own life with or without him/her such as *(I love my music whether I am sharing this with my partner or not)*.

XIII. As my partner and I encounter problems in our relationship, I make efforts to assure that what I say and do serves the purpose of healthy resolutions rather than mindless blaming and hurting by *(remembering to focus on healing words that have been helpful and how hard it is to undo the damage of destructive attacks)*.

XIV. If my partner and I lose sight of the real issue that disturbs our relationship, instead of attacking each other over false issues, I can make efforts to maintain a sense of perspective regarding our conflicting beliefs by *(stating my overall intention and desired purpose)*.

XV. If my partner and I begin to complicate everyday tasks and problems with extreme negativity, I can discover positive, simple, and even humorous ways of lightening and enjoying our daily challenges by *(stating how far we have progressed, using tactful humor such as "if these 'pot holes' in our relationship don't kill us they will certainly make us stronger in our resolve to go around them in the future")*.

XVI. Even if I feel overwhelmed by some "magnetic" quality of my experience with my partner, I can realize how my own fantasy projected onto my partner has created such an experience. I will remind myself of how I am creating such experiences by *(asking myself what fantasy ideals may be occurring)*.

XVII. If I find myself overcomplicating and dwelling on problems in the relationship, I will call attention to how we are at present treating each other and direct my energies to the consciousness of identifying existing, realistic solutions by *(stopping in the middle of unrewarding exchanges and simply ask what here-and-now steps one or both of us can take toward a solution we may have overlooked)*.

XVIII. If I begin to feel needy and dependent on having to be with my partner to feel life has meaning, I can realize and affirm my own conscious choices and attitudes, asserting what I need in my life with or without my partner by *(taking responsibility for my real need for caring attentiveness by getting a massage)*.

XIX. When I feel drawn into a vague, uncomfortable, absorbing state of suggestion by my partner, I can realize how this may be a cue for entrancement. I will consciously identify such vague discomforts, be patient, and just attend and observe my experience. I will then specifically redirect my attention to some here-and-now activity. I will choose to focus on some specific, external sight, sound, or movement such as *(commenting on how much time has passed, how we need to put things on hold for awhile or go take out the garbage)*.

XX. When I feel limited in not being able to have more intimacy with my partner, I can realize the need for asserting and sharing more of what is unique and individualistic about myself. I will share more of my uniqueness by *(showing, telling, or asking my partner to participate in some unique, personal activity of mine such as listening to poetry and/or music)*.

XXI. If I feel part of my emotions and/or conscious ideas and perceptions are unduly influenced or controlled by my relationship to my partner, I can realize how to re-own and take responsibility for these parts of myself by emphasizing my own unique contrasting experience with that of my partner. I can emphasize my unique contrast experiences with those of my partner by *(creating a safe atmosphere by being nonjudgmental where I can be tactfully honest, focusing on how I experience the same situation as my partner but in a highly individualistic motif)*. One partner may emphasize to another that he enjoys networking with other people to feel a sense of vitality and connection. She may contrast her experience with her partner's, which is a sense of uncertainty and worry that her activities might weaken her relationship to him in the process. At this contrast point, healthy dialogue and clarification of desires and motives can occur by both partners.

XXII. If I feel that part of what I communicate and express is absorbed or incorporated (redefined into a new meaning) by my partner in such a way that disrupts my desired goals, I can realize how important it is to reclaim the meaning and quality of what I've asserted by *(reframing what I expressed as having my own unique, intended meaning and purpose)*. One partner may get angry when the other appears passive and uninterested in initiating intimate contact. He had expressed his need to wait for her to show some sign of interest (that special look in her eye and/or subtle, physical gesture) that would let him know she was in the mood. She wanted him to be a caveman and take charge. She tried to entrance him into her fantasy. He reclaimed his need to wait for a sign of interest on her part because he wanted to be assured that he was not imposing himself on her, who had previously complained of being enslaved and dominated by previous partners. His reclaiming of his own communication allowed her to see him as being strong and assertive in a way that was healthy for the relationship. Both partners were now at a point in their relationship where they could work through how to enjoy various fantasies together without losing their identities in such role-playing. To thine own self be true and one can not be false to any partner.

An important feature regarding how to move in and out of entrancement is the dimension of attunement. Attunement is where partners are communicating and relating at the same level of energy and understanding. For example, partners may be initially attuned and therefore sensitive to each other's needs and feelings at the very beginning of their relationship. As the relationship deteriorates, they have to mutually lower their level of intimacy to stay attuned to the negative feelings and pain. When one partner feels lonely and rejected, the other maintaining corresponding attunement also feels similar feelings. Both partners can drag each other down into destructive experiences.

Learning how to break off negative attunements and initiate healthy, loving attunement is a key objective in dealing with entrancing relationships. A couple who had just returned to Chicago from a vacation in Florida commented how good their mood was before they encountered numerous, negative, unhappy people on their return trip, which infected them with toxic resentments and hostilities. This couple needed to shift their attunement away from such negative people by changing and shifting the frequency of their energy level and attentiveness given to the negativity of others. Learning to refocus one's attentive energies toward one's own positive outcomes, releasing the tendency to get caught up in a partner's or any other's pessimism and negativity involves utilizing the aforementioned interventions.

Another way of understanding this shifting of a positive focus away from a negative one is the concept of ownership. If one partner refused to allow his or her sensory experience to be joined or mixed-in with that of the more negative partner, then the partner can break free of the other's negativity. For example, one partner, upon hearing the other shout and critique her behavior with men, realizes her body is beginning to feel tighter and tighter (as her feelings mix with his words). She now chooses to refocus her attention on slow breathing from her diaphragm and separates out her behavior away from his framework by affirming to herself her own meaning and purpose of her activities. Such a shifting allows her to suspend attending to her partner's provoking words, gently disengages her body feelings from his abusive sounds, and reconnects to her own body's sensory experiences.

Refusing to be taken into the trap of feeling responsible for other people's moods and feelings requires staying awake and out of absorbed attentiveness to their neediness. Partners can realize that getting drawn and absorbed into intense negative people, places, and things (including each other) creates an entrancement that pulls them in like a sponge. Learning to "squeeze" out the absorbed energy by utilizing the trance mastery interventions presented can assist in creating and maintaining healthy and loving attunements with each other and those whom we may encounter. While the preceding list of interventions is not meant to be an all-encompassing one, it can provide couples with a strong start in the detrancing process. They can learn how to discriminate and choose when each will go in or out of entrancement. The essential point is to learn how to identify and master the opportunity to make healthy choices of when partners can and need to move from one state to another to support the growth and development of a healthy, long-term relationship.

ORGANIZATIONAL STRUCTURE OF CONSCIOUSNESS

Awakening the consciousness of each partner's unique, self-character involves mastering trance states at various levels of conscious and unconscious awareness. Depicted in Figure 9.2 is a graphic illustration of the organizational structure of consciousness. A simplified structural map of the brain is marked off in terms of right- and left-brain functions.

The organizing structural design is one symbolized by the pyramid. The vertical movement from top to bottom is indicative of a shift in awareness from an objective, rational, goal-oriented approach in everyday reality (known as left-brain functioning) toward one that is intuitive, subjective, and process-oriented (focus on the sensory experiences of how things are happening without regard to consequences). This latter level of awareness is known as right-brain functioning. The upper levels of awareness are directed toward objective, cognitive understandings and interpretations of specific events, people, places, things, and such. For example, the common, everyday experience of having a cup of coffee may be interpreted as taking a stress break or enjoying social time. As deeper levels of awareness are reached, the experience of having a cup of coffee can take on sensory, symbolic meanings such as soothing and warming associations of early childhood nurturance. The activity of drinking coffee itself could be experienced as a sensory trigger for playful mixing, movements, and daydreaming. Have you ever noticed anyone swirling their coffee, staring out a window with that dazed look in their eyes?

The pyramid design of consciousness reveals a limited range of self-awareness at its uppermost peak and progressively broader, expansive ranges of self-awareness at deeper levels. It is at the deepest levels of awareness that access to vast, unconscious domains of each partner are

Figure 9.2
Organizational Structure of Consciousness in Self-Awareness

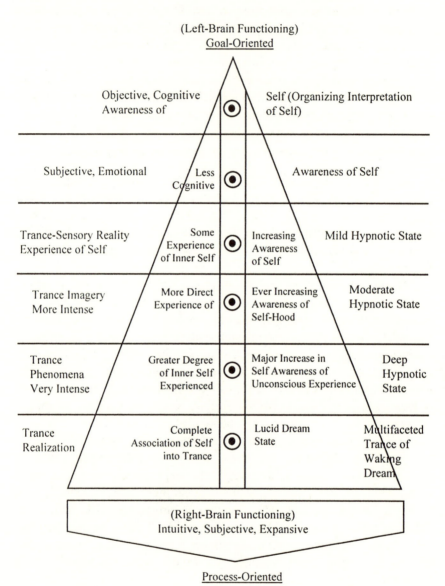

available. As partners are able to move or trance-port their conscious to various levels of self-awareness, they demonstrate trance mastery.

Sometimes one partner is stuck at one level of self-awareness and the other partner is stuck at another. Imagine a building of six floors with two elevators. One elevator works only on the top three floors and the other works only on the bottom three floors. If you needed to go from the bottom floor to the top floor, you would have to take the elevator that worked on the lower floors up as high as it would go and then transfer to the other elevator to go up the rest of the way. If the floors each of the elevators served did not overlap, you would be stuck at the floor limit of the elevator you were on.

Such a predicament happens to entranced partners. One partner's elevator does not go all the way down deep enough to develop self-awareness; and the other partner's elevator does not go all the way up to deal with everyday reality. Trance mastery is developing the ability to trance-port one's elevator to the required level of self-awareness as is deemed necessary to maintain and enhance healthy relating. If either partner is lost in his or her own fantasy/daydream at one level, not dealing with reality consequences in certain areas of relating or limited in their depth of accessing and learning about themselves in other areas, the relationship becomes fixated at such an impasse and remains entranced. Awakening through trance mastery penetrates and clears the impasse, allowing free-flowing intimacy and mutual growth.

The organizational structure of everyday consciousness (left-brain), is the inverted pyramid as depicted in Figure 9.3. It functions in contrast to deeper levels of consciousness in organizational self-awareness (right-brain functioning).

Notice in Figure 9.3 that the upper levels of external reality consciousness are broad and expansive, yet involve minimal levels of self-awareness. At the lower levels, self-awareness is greatly enhanced but at the expense of a very narrow range of reality orientation.

When the design for consciousness of self is paired with the consciousness for reality orientation, a balanced, structured design that is mutually supportive emerges (Figure 9.4). It is this inter- and intraactive balance of self and reality that provides couples with a sense of stability and balance in their relatedness. Imbalance of awareness for both self and reality orientation is the consequential state of affairs in entranced relationships. As partners learn how to awaken and master trance, their reality orientation becomes a natural and normalizing experience. Partners become mature and comfortable with realistic limits and are more responsible in their decisions about how to handle relationship issues.

Figure 9.3
Organizational Structure of Consciousness in
Everyday Reality

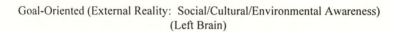
Goal-Oriented (External Reality: Social/Cultural/Environmental Awareness)
(Left Brain)

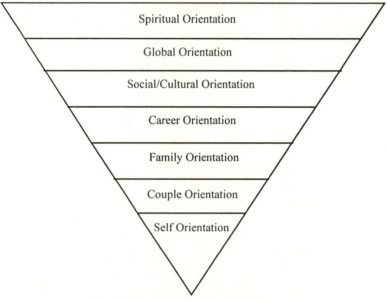

(Right-Brain) Process-Oriented (Self-Awareness)

The structural designs in Figure 9.4 depict the contrasting balance between both types of consciousness. The greater the ability of partners to master the movement from one form of consciousness to another, the greater balance and alignment of resources are available for healthy, long-term, intimate relationships.

Entranced relationships are unbalanced. Partners are fixated at deep levels of internal fantasy ideals. They lack self-awareness of how absorbed each is into fantasy illusions. Figure 9.5 depicts this fixation where partners are blocked from the full range of consciousness. Self-awareness is prevented with such fixation as partners are lost in fantasy.

Entranced relationships are also fixated in external areas of family, social, and other levels of functioning. Partners may lose part or all of their sense of closeness in external areas (family, friends, etc.) of functioning. One set of partners encountered difficulty in maintaining the

Figure 9.4
Contrasting Interactive Planes of Internal
and External Consciousness

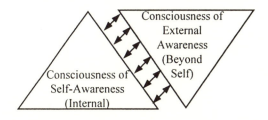

Goal-Orientation of External Awareness (Left Brain)

Process Orientation of Self-Awareness (Right-Brain)

illusion and fantasy ideal of romantic oneness when faced with the reality of family and social challenges for full participation in community activities together. Partners may either maintain a social façade or split off from being together in order to participate in the broader social context. One or both may feel smothered or abandoned in such settings and split off (separate from each other and their sense of fantasy ideal). Jealousy, insecurity, and/or feelings of betrayal may emerge. Such splitting off from the fantasy ideal is called entranced isolation. Figure 9.6 depicts such a condition.

Trance mastery removes these blocks to the free-flowing movement of awareness. Partners have mastered the "ins and outs" of self and other consciousness process. Healthy, balanced, nurturing contrasts of inner self and outer reality awareness and functioning in the relationship are now established. The intimacy and mutuality are now available whether couples are alone together on a fantasy vacation or in the middle of a huge family reunion. With the full ranges of internal and external consciousness having now been made available to both partners, there is an expansion to higher levels of spiritual relationship consciousness between them. Integration of inner and outer consciousness (left- and right-brain functioning in harmony) tends to create a refined and articulated consciousness of each partner's shared, sensory motif. Trance mastery assists partner's integration of a sharper, more refined image of each other's unique qualities and motifs, which crystallized and heightened the consciousness of their relatedness.

Figure 9.5
Fixation at Deep Levels of Inner Absorption

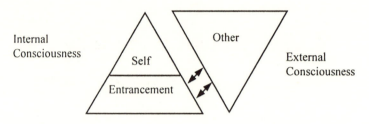

Figure 9.6
Fixation at High, External Levels of Isolation

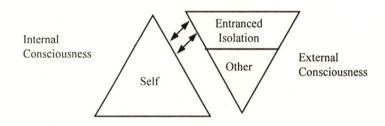

At balanced and integrated levels of consciousness, couples experience a euphoric, flowing sense of oneness or rapture.[1] Such rapture is not romantic in origin (though may be infused with romance). Their motifs have found a genuine, flowing manifestation in the growing reality of the couple's relationship. Witness such rapture in the beautiful, articulate love of an elderly couple. They know the genuine character of one another and how to behave, communicate, and "dance" with one another in such elegant, flowing ways. At such levels of rapture and spiritual relatedness, true romance may indeed exist. Figure 9.7 depicts the structural consciousness of such a relationship before and after trance mastery has been developed. Note in the "after" design (Figure 9.8) how each partner's sensory motif expands, overlaps, and becomes a shared, flow experience for both. By developing trance mastery in their sensory motifs, partners can have the best of both worlds (able to be their unique selves while enjoying the intimate flow experience of relatedness).

Figure 9.7
Nonspiritual Relationship Consciousness

Before Trance Mastery:
Partners' Separate Sensory Motifs

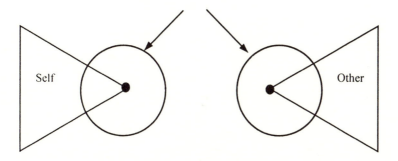

Sensory motifs serve as an additional resource in learning to master trance. This master anchor of motif serves as a powerful resource to sustain the transition from a state of entrancement toward one of awakening our core motif of character essential for relationship growth.

NOTE

1. The limbic system located in the mid-brain serves as an emotional/sensory gatekeeper to altered and expanded states of consciousness. When stimulated by unique, sensory motifs of partners engaged in flow states together, the limbic system initiates access to expanded relationship consciousness experienced as rapture in the higher brain centers of the right and left hemispheres. The limbic system is directly connected to the heart feeling centers and guides unique sensations of emotion from the heart into higher consciousness.

Figure 9.8
Expansive Spiritual Relationship Consciousness:
The Rapture of Partners Being Their Unique Selves Together

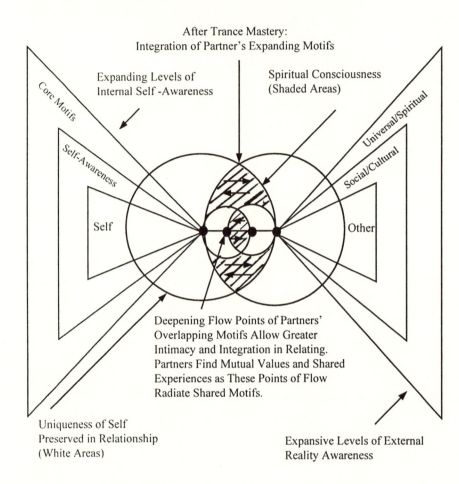

After Trance Mastery:
Integration of Partner's Expanding Motifs

Expanding Levels of
Internal Self-Awareness

Spiritual Consciousness
(Shaded Areas)

Core Motifs

Self-Awareness

Universal/Spiritual

Social/Cultural

Self

Other

Deepening Flow Points of Partners'
Overlapping Motifs Allow Greater
Intimacy and Integration in Relating.
Partners Find Mutual Values and Shared
Experiences as These Points of Flow
Radiate Shared Motifs.

Uniqueness of Self
Preserved in Relationship
(White Areas)

Expansive Levels of External
Reality Awareness

CHAPTER 10

A-RISE AND SHINE
THE ARTIST WITHIN

ARTISTIC MOTIF, BIRTH OF UNIQUENESS

We now move to an articulation of sensory motifs and their utilization by partners in recovering and reawaking from entrancing relationships. It is important to present what happens to partners as the invigorating, self-induced alignment of their sensory motif occurs. The sense of inner congruence resulting from the self-aligning effects of one's motif allows partners to discover their own intrinsic, organizing qualities of purpose and prosperity in their lives.

Remarkable empowering and reorganizing effects occur through aligning with motif. Sensory motifs can operate to supplant and replace the addictive relationship. Accessing the sensory motif generates new relationships with one's self and others. Such a relationship is abundant in the unfolding creativity that is within each person's unique, artistic self. There is a rising and shining of the artist within as partners align with their emerging motifs. In order to demonstrate the empowering, self-aligning effects of motifs, it is necessary to illustrate the supportive roles motifs play in working through entrancement.

THE HYPNOTIC SHIELD

Entranced couples are by definition absorbed in a hypnotic, trance-like experience and not readily amenable to reality confrontations. Such an impervious quality insulates entrancement's fused logic from scrutiny, operating as a filtering process of selective attention (only those experiences consistent with fantasy ideals of relating are recognized and incorporated). Filtered selectivity prevents discrepant or challenging realities from altering fused states. Liberation of self in relationship from fused, fantasy ideals means working through selective attention's impasse.

Working through this impasse's bottleneck can be an inside and/or outside job as personal and/or reality factors create disruptive shocks, motivating expansion of perceptual filters. Partners exert massive energy bending themselves in and out of various, accommodating shapes in entrancement's high maintenance. It is only a matter of time until meltdown. Some couples simply are so abused for being in the relationship that it no longer sustains any entranced fantasy even to lose. They reason that because they have been through so much together, how could they ever leave each other?

The absolute insanity of his kind of "logic" is fully explained by trance logic. Because of the distortions of reality in entranced relationships, partners magnify events hurtful to them, and, paradoxically, ignore the sequence and context in which they are created. Living in a world of non sequiturs (the expected sequence of cause-and-effect events does not follow one another) keeps partners confused (entranced) and selectively attending. The effect of partners' efforts causes unexpected and shocking outcomes of increasing pain in the relationship. Repeated shock effects numb or obliterate cruelty inflicted on and by partners (in the name of love, of course). Sadomasochistic features can be so intense and agonizing as to increase selective attention's impasse.

MOTIF-ATING ONE'S SELF IN RESOURCEFULNESS AND RECOVERY

One can fight insane imagery with absurd imagery. There is a difference as one leads to psychosis and the other, reality. Partners are directed (either by themselves and/or a therapist) to return to the past initial point of fusion fixation (where they were first entranced). This can be done using a time-line technique (that visualized line of events in time linking past, present and future experiences together). Partners get into a relaxed, comfortable mental and physical state (relaxation, slow breathing techniques, calming images, etc.). They imagine and experience themselves going back to that past time of initial fantasy fusion. To do this, they imagine themselves floating up out of their bodies in the present, here-and-now moment. As they are floating up, they need to rise high, above their own heads so that they can look down and see the tops of their heads below them. As this point, they are to imagine themselves and experience what it would be like to float all the way back to the very moment (or range of moments) that the fantasy fixation began (where they encountered their partner). They are now in a good position to learn about and heal the experience.

They can now begin to observe what was happening and talk about what the fantasy was. What was the story line? What were the series of associations? What were the themes, the scenarios? What drama, dreams, and eventual nightmares were conjured up? What were the fantasies of achievement and grandiosity? What is the narcissistic quality of grandiosity as amplified in each other's fantasied images, constructions, and strategized associations that give energy to one another's fantasy?

Second, while still floating back in time to that fixating moment, they can begin to articulate what those features were, what the fantasies are. Partners can begin to discover what I call the embedded structure of that fantasy, which embodies features of the unique self. They need to discover how the themes of that structure are a kind of "skeletal" support system of themselves, the "I" beams, if you will, of that building. It's the "I" beams of the relationship that support the "I" of each partner.

These "I" beams are also the "eye" of the hurricane of their stormy relationship. Partners are encouraged to review their motif or sensory-select architecture as it is embodied in the shape and form of their partner. Such sensory-selective-attention serves as the "I" beams upon which partners build their hallucinations of who the other is. Such hallucinations projected onto the other are based upon the actual unique, internal structures already present within partners but left unrecognized and unattended.

Partners reexperience how they create their hallucinated story line in their own lives as well. By floating forward or backward in time, partners use visualization and imagery, identifying similar experiences. Partners can explore how the story line or structure has operated in other facets of their lives (projected hallucinations onto friends, family, and colleagues at work).

There is a strong fixation of one partner perceiving the other as embodying or symbolizing his or her unique, sensory motif, represented in disguised fashion. Fixation is a projected distortion of partners' own, unique motif. This is, in part, what both fascinates and frightens them. Intriguing, emerging structures of fantasy themes, qualities, and attributes regarding our partner embody our disowned motif. Partners need to rediscover the "that could never be me" quality projected. Recognition is needed to recover our "best self" (which is our core) previously lost when we gave away in entrancement our heartfelt sense of who we uniquely are.

In the third stage, partners are encouraged to describe themes, structures, emerged attractions, designs, and images of admired or despised projected qualities. While still floating back in time to the moment(s) of fixation, they integrate the whole scenario. Floating fifteen minutes back in time before the moment of initial fixation, partners can act like a director of a movie and review how they have been operating in many areas of their lives long before they ever met one another. The idea is to begin to expand that skeletal, architectural type of structure or design of each partner's uniqueness back to themselves.

Partners begin to internalize their schematic scenario of motif. To accomplish this, while still floating back in time before the initial fixation, partners can see these structures in their time line and step into them as if these motifs were like new shoes that fit like they'd been there forever. Partners can see how, even as a child, their motif has been manifest in multivaried experiences. There is a shifting out of the hypnotic fixation, out of the "hypnotic other," as they begin to discover structures, themes, patterns, and attributes in the genuine vision of their own lives. It is important to discover this "expanded sense of self" in order to move out of the "me" in narcissism to the "I" of the individualized, unique, creative self.

In the fourth stage, partners continue to be encouraged to expand by discovering how those "dramas" are their own projected motifs in distorted form. There is the expanding discovery of their own motifs in their family life, social life, and work arenas. Partners can float forward on their time line, stepping into more and more experiences along the way that reaffirm expressions of their motifs. They can get richer and clearer elaborations on how their aspirations are inspired by their motifs.

Partners are encouraged to continue to play out those dramas while moving through their time line, highlighting the structure of these scenarios of their distorted motifs. The goal is to sort out the distorted drama of entrancement (which distorts motifs) from the genuine motif of their own unique character.

The technique of exaggeration is used by taking distortions of partner's motifs to extreme, absurd limits thereby extinguishing them. Partners can decide to intensify and create in visualizations and imagery what would happen if they exaggerated caricatures of one another's attributes. One partner visualized the other as sleek as a beanpole, drenched in red paint. The consequence was amusement at these exaggerated distortions and discovery of lessened attachment.

As the partner continued in one imagery session after another, thirty to forty-five minutes each, day after day for twenty-one days, he played out the scenario of what would happen if he maintained his compulsive pursuit of his partner and her attributes. He realized that it was not his partner he was after, but the qualities he so admired and secretly envied. He shifted the focus of his fixation from his partner to the attributed qualities he had conferred upon her in his initial fantasy fixation. In so doing, he slowly crystallized how much he identified with being sleek, fast, and colorful. From the use of time-line work, partners can discover that many admired qualities are inherently embedded in their own life experiences. Release from fixation on the other partner is replaced by embellishing such attributes in one's own future life aspirations.

THE DRAMA OF ENTRANCEMENT

Partners are encouraged not to only play out attributes and scenarios of each other, but to begin to make the drama larger than the relationship. Exaggeration highlights and focuses their attention on how overinflated their relationship has been. After doing these exercises, partners realize they have made problems out of events in their relationship bigger than necessary. It is important for each partner to discover that the excitement of their dramatically distorted motifs is what the draw or attraction is in entrancement. It is not necessarily the partner. Partners are simply the precipitating point upon which to project the dramatic and theatrical antics of one's own unique play. As partners reintegrate their disowned uniqueness, the relationship reveals its truly unique character.

To grow healthy, beautifully designed vines requires the necessary structural support of a lattice. To grow healthy, beautiful relationships necessitates the structural support of each partner's latticelike character. Growth of entranced partners becomes less important than the drama of entrancement. As a consequence, the guiding, structural lattice of motif is distorted and warped as entrancement's heat deforms the integrity of its uniqueness. This distorts the manifestation of partners' healthy growth on the "vine" of relationship. Entrancing relationships warp and distort the vision and perception of guiding motifs. As entangled, heavy, overgrown vines may bend and warp the very lattice that supports them, so entranced, overinflated, dramatic relationships weigh heavily on a partner's motif.   The consequential pressures prevent partners from feeling they can be themselves while together.

Fusion of entranced relationship with partners' guiding motifs restricts the very growth it was consciously intended to foster. Instead of partners enjoying the fruits of their labors from the vine of relationship, they feel stilted and stuck. They have let the tail wag the dog rather than allow the uniqueness of their whole being to motif-ate them toward a healthy direction. The heat of drama interferes with the natural, free-flowing interplay of guiding motifs designed to structurally support the vine of relationships. The drama of relationship can be a cancerous growth entangling and entrancing partners in distorted structural motifs.

The therapeutic intervention involves giving the drama action, color, and energy, making it larger than the relationship. Partners find the intensity of the drama peaks and then subsides as cresting and falling waves onto a beach, harmlessly dissipating. Partners need to see the drama for what it is, to extricate themselves from trance, to release and reawaken. Partners visualize and image entrancement caricaturized into a movie or play. The procedure is for partners to get into a relaxed, comfortable, self-reflective time and place. After relaxing and releasing physical and mental anxieties and tensions (utilizing muscle relaxation procedures of tightening and releasing, calming breathing, and pleasant imagery scenes), partners visualize and verbalize their own version of fantasy ideals each has about the other. Partners visualize and describe to themselves how they view each other as ideal, long-term mates, always there for each other at any cost.

As both partners continue to elaborate on their entrancement with each other, they can embellish and create caricatures of themes, roles, and patterns of expected behavior. One individual caricaturized his entrancement with his partner visualizing a scene having dinner together. The waiter comes up to take their order and starts flirting with his partner. In his fantasy, she is supposed to be polite but remarkably unimpressed and essentially unresponsive. In his caricaturization, he has her becoming irritated and offended that the waiter is making overtures to her. She turns to him with a look that says, "How could you let him do that to me?" This person's caricaturization has him rise to the occasion and, as a Knight of the Round Table, protect his fair maiden's honor. He visualized himself verbally dueling with the waiter, who has now been cast as the Black Knight.

While such caricatures may seem outlandish, many real-life conflict situations that occur in entranced relationships have these distortions. Partners discover that the way they caricaturize their entrancement refers to scenes that have, to some degree, already happened. Visualizations are verbalized to themselves (verbalizing or talking out loud to one's self emphasizes and helps to define the visualization) and they loosen and release entrancement's restrictive hold on the way partners relate.

Techniques can be utilized to amplify or reduce imagined scenarios and dramas for the purpose of giving clarity to entrancement. Through visualization and caricaturization, partners change the structure of particularly difficult or powerful experiences, such that they can detrance and exercise healthy choices. Through alteration of timing and sequence of behavior, partners are encouraged to pursue unique outcomes offering more genuine intimacy.

These techniques and interventions allow partners to have conscious choices as to their participation in various roles, qualities, or images of the drama. Partners begin to sort out their unique motifs without getting entrapped and entranced with them. By comparing and contrasting the caricaturizations of entrancement's rigid role requirements with the unique motif of self-expression of each partner, a clearer sense of who both partners are as individuals outside the entranced relationship emerges.

Individuals who have had previous entrancements together can be capable of seeing their former partner as a human being in his or her own right as contrasted with being how that person was seen as a lover. Partners may attempt to articulate what makes each other unique and special as people. A technique for doing this is for partners to visualize and verbalize how each would be perceived as individuals if, instead of having met, they only observed one another in a variety of settings. Articulation of unique, special attributes perceived would occur. Through contrast and comparison, partners get a clearer sense of what makes each one unique and special. Transcendence of rigid role boundaries trapping partners is now possible.

TAKING IMAGES BACK: THE MIRROR OF
ENTRANCEMENT

As partners reconnect with their disowned attributes, they can identify with such qualities in themselves. Partners step into such qualities
and no longer fear losing the other as they have regained themselves.
This type of reassociating imparts a sense of ownership and integration
within each partner.

A curious feature is that partners beginning to reestablish self-
identity boundaries, becoming angry and defensive about "going back to
the other partner." At this point, one partner may step up efforts to pull
the other's "identity" back into the bond. The anger is indicative of the
"self" of one partner striving to emerge. The need of these dynamics
requires raising the set-point to a higher level of differentiation. The
techniques on visualization and verbalization can be utilized at this
point. Allowing greater space and time for each partner's unique expressions of self creates a safe place for being one's self in relationship
together.

Each discovers within themselves that kind of "crazy," dreamlike
logic empowered and embedded in their fantasy ideal that they had previously projected onto one another. Being encouraged to act out and
take on those fantasy ideals and own these projected qualities and attributes leads to discovering an expanding sense of uniqueness and character. Such discovery empowers partners to function at a more integrated
level of mental and physical conditioning. When entranced drama is
released, genuine motifs of character are revealed. This is a time-
consuming process and does not happen overnight. The birth pains of
partners' emerging motifs is a labor of love and involves many "con-
tractions and dilations."

Through these processes, each of them could realize that the hypnotic quality of the relationship was beginning to shrink. Entranced
partners need to learn these processes of how to shrink entrancement in
their relationship. The hypnotic quality of their own structures and fascinations had supported the drama they had built around each other. It
had become more powerful than the players. Becoming more alert and
consciously accessing the relationship's drama helped them to disconnect it from entrancing the relationship itself. What begins to happen is
that each partner now becomes fantasized, not with the other as a hypnotic ideal symbol, but rather with the quality of being "high" on fulfilling their own life character in the shared uniqueness of togetherness.

It is at this juncture that the intriguing and unique nature of their inter-action reveals the real character of what they can now have together. However, some partners may find that once they discover their own unique character, they want to go their own separate ways. If this were so, is it not better to know such truth rather than waste time in a genuine, unloving relationship? This can be the price of preserving the fantasy. To suffer one's relationship death and be reborn is not easy, but it is truly awakening and awe-inspiring. Such rebirthing involves recovering the lost attributes of our motifs.

This recovering of lost qualities and attributes of our unique char-acter can take many forms. Each partner may begin to act out different facets of these attributes and qualities until there might even be a role reversal. Recovery of attributes may be a deliberate effort by each part-ner or it might be done naturally, without conscious awareness. For example, each partner can first identify that quality (or set of qualities) he or she most admires and desires in each other. Each partner can then visualize and image what it would be like to have that quality and/or attribute as part of their behavioral repertoire. As each partner begins to take on attributes and qualities from the other, he or she needs to refine and adjust the degree and intensity of these features, individualizing how it may work.

The recovering process may also be more natural and already hap-pening by each partner. In this process, partners find themselves taking on and acting more and more like the other without realizing what they are doing. As partners go through different positions of one another's perspectives and characteristics, each begins to realize that, in a sense, they are actually playing out a version of themselves.

What begins to emerge through this type of structuring and restruc-turing is that each person begins to recapture the different types of fla-vors and images they superimposed on their partner. A remarkable shift then begins to happen. They begin to discover that each of them has a unique kind of self, a unique artistry, a unique set of talents and inter-ests.

Through this kind of emergence and vast range of expansive discov-eries, the kinds of conscious attitudes and qualities they can take on (assertiveness, strength, intense emotions like anger, rage, tenderness, joy) seem infinite. One could be the victim one minute, hero the next, and persecutor the third. They begin to discover through these different kinds of strategic postionings in the relationship that, indeed, their lives are very rich and very full. They never realized the capacities that were available to them.

Even though it may have been initiated in this hypnotically bounded relationship, the types of opportunities and multifaceted personality attributes that were opening became quite enhancing. They enhanced their ability to understand the realities they were creating. They both began to grasp and appreciate their own capacity for imagination and symbolism. Such appreciation and awareness are the result of a ceaseless effort to structure and restructure the various attributes and qualities each admired and eventually adopted into their own unique version. The irony is that such qualities were inherently a part of each partner's inherent motif in the first place. This is what partners mean when they say they carry a part of the other within. That is why partners have to reown their unique version of that part. With such awareness, each partner discovers how their sense of time and space can bend and change. They learn that images can emerge like evolving pots of clay that can be molded and shaped at the will of the imaginative mind and creative capacities of one's own fantasied associations and logical symbols. Partners learn to appreciate the logic of their own symbolisms. Such logic involves their own memories and how those memories began to take shape and form.

THE WHOLE OF TRANCE IS GREATER THAN THE SUM OF ITS ENTRANCED PARTS

The whole (Gestalt) of the relationship is greater than the sum of its individuals or parts. Each couple forms a uniquely constructed fantasy that embodies a hidden, unfolding vision or motif. The fantasy ideal involves a fusion and interweaving of romantic illusions (eternal love, passion, 'til death do us part) and unique, core motifs interlaced throughout (towering, sleek, and powerful structures). The particular nuances of that uniquely constructed scenario frames and outlines the quality, degree, and intensity of such dimensions as control, surrender, closeness, separation, creativity, conventionality, conflict, stability, and so on.

Partners seek to increase the quality and duration of peak intimacy between them. To increase the frequency of peak moments, there needs to be movement away from the fused structure of the hypnotic fantasy. For more intimacy to occur, energy needs to focus more on motifs and less on fantasy. An important key to change is to grow the fantasy up in mature form. The structure of fantasy changes through its evolutionary development into differentiating, multifaceted ways of operating. The set-point of intimacy will be raised to allow more sharing in the experience, as higher levels of differentiation is self-allowed. Set-point alterations occur as evolution of the absorbing fantasy grows into a healthy, differentiating form.

Partners have a logical system unique to themselves. It does not give way to commonsense logic. As partners begin to appreciate their capacity for exploring one another's unique frames of reference, they develop differential ways of increasing the quality of their intimacy. One partner may look for a foundation and a sense of depth, a sense of rich, powerful grounded-ness. The other seeks a higher life purpose. Each partner, in a sense, may go in an opposite direction and yet begin to move toward a complimentary edifice and structure of building a relationship in which both could live and feel alive.

The structure of their absorbing fantasy is evolving and differentiating into that towering skyscraper founded on a wonderful, rock-solid depth. It is developing the kind of roots-to-China foundation. With this foundation of depth, the relationship can now solidly reach for the moon. This discovering process of both themselves and their relationship is fueled by an impassioned absorption that had been in conflict with its own reality. Such is the paradox and power of entrancement. If utilized within a criteria for health, what a wonderful force for compelling change and evolution of the self and the relationship.

It is remarkable how, in their collision with one another, they begin to collude in a sense to assist one another, without realizing, in discovering the different facets and uniqueness of each other's capacities. This is a classic example of the seeds of a solution being embedded in a problem. It allows them to take on different qualities of one another (strong, emotional, independent, feeling like a towering giant, able to be clinging, dependent). Instead of being one stereotype or another, they appreciate the multiplicity of themselves, individually and together. Doing so, they begin to develop a respect for the person's characteristics and character that served as a foundation in the other. Indeed, they become more fascinated with their own capacities and how the two of them could develop a kind of friendship, if you will, and a kind of journey, not only inward, but also outward. They become companions in these discoveries.

They gain a facility of power and choice over their dramas, their scenarios, and, therefore, their relationship. The "addictiveness" begins to be eliminated when they learn not how to totally stay out of a hypnotic bond, but how to bond with and without it. They develop the ability to move in and out of trance together and apart. Yet they learn to feel and sense their evolving connection. They begin to utilize their recovering skills as a capacity to discover their full range of human qualities.

In so doing, the fixation of the addictive relationship no longer becomes a quick fix. Rather, the fixation of entrancement takes on a fascination of how different positions and fixations can create different scenarios. Partners may notice how one minute they could be panic-stricken, horrified, and worried. The next minute be calm, cool, appreciating how they can go in and out of this trance at will. Partners can use the perspective of seeing contrasts in the relationship (absorbing images versus objective assessment) to lighten up entrancement. Partners discover their capacity to frighten, fantasize, be on alert, or to just enjoy being themselves in different ways. When one partner left on one of her many week-long trips, the other discovered how his panic of abandonment could now quickly flip to the peace and quiet of abundance in self.

Partners learn that through visualization of recovering attributes, they can focus their attention, their images, and their scenarios. Partners learn how to focus their attention by visualizing themselves with admired attributes. They discover how their developed, perceptual field can serve as a context for interpreting their images, scenes, or whatever emerges between them. They can create a perceived field of harmony and safety or of fear and danger.

Partners are elated to see how the context or atmosphere they emphasize powerfully affects the meaning of what they express to one another. It becomes clear to them how the context they create also affects nuances of words they use to capture a slant or angle of fascination. These capacities come by beginning to appreciate how the focus of their attention can be fixated or not fixated at will. They realize they do not have to be in bondage.

Partners may have felt trapped with the horrible pain of betrayal and abandonment. Prior to recovery of lost attributes, partners would feel hurt and fight. Partners realize they can focus their attention and energies onto a healthier perceptual field of meaningfulness in themselves and therefore in their relationship. Recovering their lost attributes involves rediscovering their uniqueness, which sets them free to be loving instead of fearing.

To enhance this recovering process of one's unique attributes (motif), there is a specialized technique designed for this purpose. Partners can benefit by utilizing the following directions:

First, focus on a wide variety of scenarios to which each possible relationship situation could lead. Now, select the most desired scenario. Recall at least five past situations where that desired scene proved valid. Identify common components between past and present situations (what you saw, heard, felt as observer and/or participant). Fully see and feel a part of these connections. It is interesting how couples are able to engage and disengage in different places and exchanges in their relationship together. The realization emerged that they both not only can survive, but they can thrive in that capacity to move in and out, above and below, constructing new experiences at will. The scenarios that they find supporting desirable outcomes tend to embody structural attributes of their unique motifs.

They can see positions not only from the other's point of view, but also from the observer's view and observers of observer's points of views. There are multiple perceptual positions that each could begin to take. Yet, whatever the vantage point, they are accessing various facets of their unique motifs. What I am describing here, what I really am alluding to, is that both partners discover their own unique artistry, their own motif of themselves in relating to each other. Their motif has a kind of flow, a kind of intense absorption, a kind of fascinating interaction of how partners choose to perceive "reality" from their own uniqueness. That flow allows partners an expanding field of vision, taking in and integrating multiple related experiences. Whether it is playing tennis, painting a sunset, engaged in a chess game, or mindfully trying to one-up their partner, each partner's uniqueness serves to construct its own specially designed frame of reference and point of view. It is this intact uniqueness and point of view that allows partners flexibility and makes them able to cope with differences and contrasts. In effect, they become adept at problem-solving when accessing their unique motif. Accessing their own scenario, design, or motif construction unique to each is essential. Methods for accessing motifs will be presented later in this chapter.

They find that "one-upmanship" need not be malicious as it could be a stimulating, challenging banter that is arousing to each. They find their creative abilities stimulated to construct, reconstruct, destruct, and instruct with one another. Many couples fight and challenge for the purpose of this type of stimulation and intimacy. This kind of creative, bantering, brainstorming expands and opens both of them. This need not be in a perverse, abusive way, but in a way that allows them to discover an all-pervasive multiplicity both in themselves and each other. They could choose and articulate many capacities, various ways of combining what happens between them in healthier frames of reference. One partner realized the other was trying to protect him when she was "acting" flirtatious to keep other men from thinking they were too close and thus getting competitive. It was enlightening to see how such a frame of reference could occur.

UNIQUE CHARACTERS: EMERGING THE MIND-BODY CONNECTION

An essential quality in dealing with hypnotically addicted relationships is to be able to appreciate many different positions, points of view, and a variety of realities. The constant theme of fixation of attention prevents multiplicity of varied, unique points of view from emerging. In a sense, one might view relationships through the eyes of an insect. The lenses of insects have multiple cells and images. Perhaps the one that "bugs" us the most has the most to teach us.

Imagine walking into a disco and seeing not one television but sixteen different television sets, sometimes showing the same picture, sometimes showing different pictures. Yet you know that there were many parts that could interact to create many different wholes, many different roles. Just like there are many different actors creating different scenes from different scripts, one can appreciate that reality has a certain relativity and creativity. This multiplicity allows both partners to begin to get a sense of how unique each of them could be in their choices and selections. To facilitate this, entranced couples may have to "hit the wall," painfully surrendering that their way no longer works. As they go through the stages of entrancement and utilize the techniques presented, they discover in their scenario of "death of a relationship" a rebirth of their character and tenacious will to live. They have survived and thrived in their trials by fire. Their mettle has been tested and like hot irons in the fire, the impurities are burned away leaving the true self-revealed.

It is helpful to describe the steps and the procedure.

- The first, of course, is to get into a relaxed, receptive state. Some people call this the relaxation response; others call it a form of self-induced hypnosis. Allow your mind to become open and clear and enjoy a certain kind of safety and comfort in that space.
- Second, allow yourself to meditate and simply connect with your sense of the relationship by asking, "How is my relationship now?" "How do I feel about this type of involvement?" Allow whatever happens to come to be there. You may simply reflect and sense in a kind of receptive state, on a strong feeling, mood, emotion, body sense, and/or image. Attend in that relaxed and safe place on whatever you feel is not functioning or is dysfunctional. Focus upon something that is not comfortable or pleasant for you in that relationship, such that if it were resolved would allow you and your partner to fully enjoy, even now, the fruits of your relationship.

    Allow whatever sense or reality that comes to emerge. Whatever image, whatever sound, whatever feeling about your relationship, let it express itself in any kind of mind-body communication. That communication can be both a sense of your body reacting to the dysfunctional condition and the way you become aware of it. Whatever seems to come, just respect it.
- Third, let yourself attend. Attend to it with a sense of respect for its uniqueness. If, for example, you get a strong tingling sensation on your skin, respect it as simply that. Allow yourself to nurture that, intensify that, and let it evolve. It may be anything from a kind of creepy, crawly feeling to a tense, nervous feeling or a sense of gloom and doom associated with it. Whatever evolves, just let yourself notice without any kind of interpretation what comes.
- Fourth, as you are attending and focusing, ask yourself the following questions: "What is that experience all about?" "What are the qualities, the attributes that seem to stand out the most?" "What is it about that experience, sense, or image that seems to be very impactful for me?" "What does it seem to want to tell me?" "What does it seem to be doing?" "Where does it seem to want to go?" It is not necessary to ask, "Why is it there?" Just ask, "What does it is seem to be about?" "Where does it seem to pull me?" If that tingling sense seems to get more intense by sweating, or you feel heat, when you think of your relationship, let it begin to surface. Let yourself begin to discover your own body and mind response to it. This allows the heartfelt sense to emerge stronger and more defined.
- Fifth, ask "What about this tingling sense, this heated sense, is so important when it comes to my relationship?" "How does me being in this relationship seem to create that kind of response?" "What is it about that tingling, heated, sweating kind of response?" "What is it about it that seems to be such a strong part of how I am when I am in this relationship." "Am I fearful?" "Am I nervous?" "Am I excited?" "What does it tell me?"

- Sixth, just let it respond to you. Then, let yourself begin to relate. Begin to feel a sense of connection, a sense of rapport with what comes. Let yourself notice whatever kind of gift or value or whatever kind of metaphor it wants to emerge into. Let yourself begin to enjoy a kind of flowing detachment of the evolving experience. For example, let yourself notice what it would be like if you were an observer watching yourself as if you were a friend or if you were watching a friend going through the same sensations you were. Let yourself attend to how you saw the expression on this person's face. What thoughts do you image that person to have? What needs, what goals, what purposes seem to be there? Let ourselves also ask, "What does this need from me?" "What does it seem to want?" You may even want to become that experience for awhile. Become the tingling. Let it become you. Let the heat begin to spread.
- Seventh, then begin to ask, "What about this condition is it that I feel so overheated?" If it begins to open up to you, it will begin to give you information. It will begin to give you ideas about the condition you have. Begin to ask yourself, "What type of images, scenes, or dramas would I or could I play from this kind of tingling sense?" "Would it be a spine-tingling thriller?" "Would it be a horror movie?" "Would it be an exciting adventure?" "Would it be the gentle, loving tingle of one partner touching another?" Ask yourself what kind of play or character or role this might suggest.
- Finally, becoming quite creative and inventive, explore the healing value of the information received. Let yourself begin to create and identify healing scenes or images from those sensations that you get. Select those scenarios that embody healthy manifestations of your unique motif as the ones you use to heal troubled areas in your relationship.

Going through these procedures can allow you to have access to the scenarios, qualities, attributes, and unique characterizations of what the dysfunctional issues and resolutions are. Be careful to not let yourself become so engrossed into it that you lose the overall purpose of this exercise. Remember that you can move in and out of those evolving scenes with the goal of resolving the irrational conditions operating the relationship. You could move in and out of many different scenes. You can be different characters in that scene. Be sure to pay attention to the way in which you are perceiving and relating to what is troubling you. This can be a source of disturbance and also healing resolution to your relationship. You may want to seek out the assistance of a trained professional helper to work with you in this endeavor.

So let this kind of mind-body sensory experience become a trigger or anchor for you to create healthier stories and action adventures that can serve as guiding metaphors in your relationship. For example, what kind of spine-tingling thriller would begin to emerge from that sensory experience? Focus on that creepy, crawly kind of thing. Do you feel this way when you are around your spouse? Or, do you feel kind of excited and tingling that you are in the presence of some kind of God? Are you at the altar of some kind of powerful being, or are you simply altering the course of a small spring? Let yourself kind of unfold in this story line.

Let yourself discover the kind of relationship you are in through reflecting and imagining stories, themes, and dreams that may capture salient features. These are some of the many ways you can access the metaphorical myths with which you might be playing. Remember, there is one thing about a myth. It usually myths (misses) the point (pardon my pun) of what the reality of the relationship really is. That is, the illusion of the myth can hide the genuine quality and character of a loving relationship.

It can "myth" the point in the sense that every myth is just that. It is just a myth, but it touches on an important aspect of our character. As a result, we tend to take it for real, yet it is a real myth like a real dream. It captures only a narrow picture in the vast panoramic view of relating. It is there to give us information and knowledge. Myths embody a hidden kind of wisdom about qualities that we need to have, to act, and to embellish in our lives. However, the question always becomes, "Are we becoming fixated by this kind of mythical quality?" "Is it capable of being utilized to help us?" We need to discover multiple, creative ways where we can clear our fixated, entranced relationship. We can do this through the realization that embedded within our myths are our unique motifs. These are the guiding qualities that bring wisdom to metaphors. Discovering the exciting and invigorating ideas of what we are all about (our motifs) and how we can respect that, both in our identity and the identity of others, is a big step in the right direction. This kind of exercise can be helpful in any type of relationship that may be entrancing (friends, colleagues, family members, etc.).

While we have focused on a singular kind of relationship that is romantic in quality, there may be entrancing, addictive components in many other aspects of our lives. Partners may find that kind of enmeshed overinvolvement with many different family members, many different friends, even with their own kind of preoccupation with that "me" inside. They may find feelings of suffocation and crowding even with relationships very genuine and rich in character. This can be experienced with many people for whom they love and care. Yet they may not have found the breathing room and expansion to let creativity and variety prosper. This may be because of entranced features at various points in their relationships where character wears thin. So, follow these exercises and the steps and let your creative imagination free to discover who you can be.

ENTRANCEMENT CHARACTERISTICS

Up to this point, the focus has been on accessing and healing the entranced relationship. The emphasis will now shift to characteristics present in these partners. First, let me say that anyone can be entranced in these types of relationships. Healthier people come out quicker than unhealthy ones. Individuals who are more vulnerable are those who are probably isolated, feeling unloved, and extremely needy, either situationally and/or chronically. They are vulnerable to distractions and scintillations. They look for a certain flash and sensory diversion. They may be extremely alone or at least lonely and empty in certain features of their lives and intimacies. One frustrated, entranced patient in therapy exclaimed, "I drive a hundred-thousand-dollar sports car but have a 'Volkswagen' for a relationship."

Part of the recovery involves enrichment, encouragement, and empowerment of both partners discovering the broad range of attributes of who they are. Characteristics of entranced partners tend to be narcissistic, possessing a grandiose quality. Extreme levels of emotional sensitivity are present, making them vulnerable to the slightest rejection and prone to rageful revenges. One partner may be a narcissistic extension of the other partner's grandiose needs. The success of one partner mirrors the other's hidden, grandiose need for recognition and power. In reality, narcissistic qualities are very self-focused and self-centered. When one partner is narcissistic, the other can become very needy and other-focused. This sets up the push-pull theory of "wanting what you can't have." Usually narcissism involves an emotional aloofness and appears insensitive, very hard, very rigid, and very stereotyped. The narcissist is literally looking for love in all the wrong places. He or she is looking to find positive reflections of him- or herself to glorify and glamorize an otherwise empty and shallow sense of self in the relationship. This false imaging is produced by fantasized ideals and role playing evolving from entrancement in the relationship.

The absorbing and enmeshing, self-involving quality of how the other person is affecting "me, me, me" is prominent in entranced, hypnotic relationships. Partners can never see the "other individual" in the relationship when they are so lost in their narcissistic "me." They are lost in themselves. That is why expanding this narrow, rigid sense of what it is to be "me" is so important in creating an openness to the rich variety couples actually can have, but are ignoring.

In the recovery aspects of these relationships, understanding this narcissistic quality of self-involvement is invaluable. There is a constant preoccupation of one's self-evaluation, one's comparisons to others or some rigid ideal. This can be in terms of talent, brains, beauty, status, power image, if you will.

Narcissistic reflection creates an enormous amount of anxiety when it involves comparisons with others. Partners are constantly wondering, worrying, and prone to anxiety attacks over how they measure up. One may meet someone in his or her day-to-day experiences who seems to challenge his or her sense of self-confidence. There is obsessive worrying that someone might be quicker, faster, more beautiful, more intelligent, more cool, more classy, more whatever. The problem with the narcissistic focus is that each partner begins to value and evaluate themselves based on a comparative fixation of other individual's assets, resources, looks, attributes, or behaviors. In doing so, they lose their own identity. The valuing of their own inherent humanity and qualities as an individual, as a person, becomes undermined. This is the consequence of the narcissist's fixating on other people's reflection of his or her self-image as a main source of self-esteem.

Because of these narcissistic, self-centered dynamics, it is important to realize the need to develop a center of evaluation and self-esteem that genuinely resides within the person. As entrancing relationships can precipitate narcissism in partners, it predisposes them to constant worry and anxiety about either losing each other or being controlled and suffocated by their partner. The core anxiety is that of ultimately losing self.

The paradox of narcissism and self-absorption seems rather ironic. Partners' narcissistic qualities are quite absorbed in themselves. With all this self-preoccupation, narcissists lack true self-confidence and turns to their partners for evaluation and affirmation of themselves. They live through the eyes, ears, and feelings of others, constantly comparing if their attributes measure up to a standard of perfection. They tend to make the fatal mistake of fixating on external, overinflated features, values, and validation by others, ignoring their own innate beauty and charm.

They tend to inflate other people's self-image, resources, beauty, and talents around them. They undermine their own narcissism (diminish their own self-value) by abandoning their core quality of beauty and unique artistry, which is the source of their inner worth. They have a difficult time accepting the inherent beauty, structure, and genius within themselves. As a consequence, there is a heightened tendency for emptiness, depression, and anxiety during times of uncertainty and change in the relationship and within themselves.

Let me emphasize that these mistakes and fixations can grow out of the entrancement itself, not necessarily from character defects of partners. Entrancement magnifies the imperfections in everyone involved. If entrancement serves any real purpose, it may be that its induced turbulence is an amazing motif-ating force for change and personal growth. Of course, what partners have to contribute to the relationship from the very beginning can enhance or diminish entrancement effects. Partners who function in a genuine and mature manner still have to deal with entrancement affects in order to bring out the best in each other's core quality.

What such an assessment of narcissism adds up to is a very important quality of recovery. In seeking to separate from unhealthy entrancement with each other, partners may go through periods in which they lapse into states of anxiety, hypnotic regression, self-absorption, self-negation, and entrancement with other people. They may fixate on the other partner's beauty, talents, youthfulness, status, power, or whatever.

Narcissism is not the only characteristic of entranced partners. Related to narcissism is an insatiable need for attention and personal gratification (partners never seem to get enough sex, love, compliments, understanding, etc.). Additional characteristics of entranced partners are mood swings (from euphoria--as in all the world is in perfect harmony, to depression--as in the world is a disaster and nothing seems to be right), hypervigilance (always watching to make sure things are okay), and psychosomatic illness (the stress of entrancement can create many physical dysfunctions such as hypertension, ulcers, impaired immune system, colds, flu, headaches, etc.). These characteristics tend to decrease in intensity (or even disappear) as partners emerge from entrancement. It is not uncommon that partners are warned by friends and/or family to get out of these types of bonds lest they die of a broken heart. Research has shown that depression causes internal stressors to adversely affect the heart. The statistics indicate that 50 percent of heart attack victims suffered from depression.

The final characteristic that permeates partners almost from the beginning is anxiety. Anxiety marks entrancement as an experience in uncertainty. Partners are nervous and fearful as they feel out of control and helpless while in the throes of entranced bonding. They feel that way not because they are defective or neurotic but because they are, in fact, out of conscious control while entranced. Such characteristics of entrancement need to be addressed in the recovery and healing process.

PATHWAYS OUT OF ENTRANCEMENT

Recovery does not always take a straight line. It is a process of learning to manage the anxiety and to accept that there will be periods in which one falls back into the "bond of their mirrored image" of the other. Partners may start making comparisons of each other's physical, emotional, social, and even spiritual attributes. There is a tendency to lose one's center of balance or internal reference point, shifting it to the outside. When that happens, it is important to note that one has entered into an entranced absorption of a smaller version with other people, places, or idols. By being able to learn the signs of entrancement, partners will be able to identify when they are entrancing one another. This recognition and heartfelt honesty will allow each person to regain his or her center of balance, center of self, center of illness, by realizing and understanding what has been given away. Each can now begin to take back lost qualities. Instead of seeing valuable pieces of themselves in their partners, they learn to recognize the unique qualities within and get a whole new sense of their own inner glow.

It is important to understand that this anxiety component of losing self may begin to surface in future entrancements with other people we may meet. We may become jealous or envious of other people's personal qualities, possessions, or their image as we lose our sense of self. This vulnerability is what happens when we "give ourselves away" (ignore and/or discount our own unique qualities and values) in the projected admiration of others. What we "give away" (give way and not stand our ground for our own sense of value) and expose is the real doubt we have of ourself. We fall entranced into a fixated longing for what someone else "seems" to have that we, in our self-doubt, have overlooked in ourselves.

The incessant demands of narcissism are a breeding ground for the emptiness of feeling that more is never enough. Remember that entrancement fosters the emergence of narcissistic neediness. Being at the center of a narcissistic universe costs us the center of our balance and the center of evaluation. Such is the price we pay for entrancing with devilish images of illusionary, fantasy ideals. Children have great fun building sandcastles by the sea. Yet even children know that castles are for temporary fun, soon to be washed away by the sea's waves. Entranced partners try to move into their fantasy ideal sandcastles only to discover that, in so doing, they risk authority and ownership for their lives being washed away.

Developing an internal focus of authority and sense of our own unique character means to accept, unconditionally, that one never has to make an evaluation or comparison of self-worth except to who we are within. This requires partners to be alert to the signs of when an entrancement is beginning. Overidealizing and self-absorption are key indicators.

Entrancement raises anxiety to very high levels. Partners may have feelings of loss and/or suffocation. We are not talking about impairment in the capacity for intimate relationships, as analysts would describe. Rather, the focus is upon the powerful effects of entrancement on anyone in these types of bonds. This happens to most, if not all, of us at one point or another in the course of our lives and to various extremes. Who has not fallen prey, at least once in their lives, to idolizing and/or worshipping some person, place, or thing? Such extreme relationships typify the focus of evaluation and essential resources as being outside ourselves.

Entrancement creates preoccupation not with what we do have, but rather with what we fantasize will happen or is supposed to happen to our lives by having that person, place, or thing ("having money will make my life perfect"). Externalizing our source of evaluation exerts an unstable and powerful force on our life. An external source of evaluation leads to narcissism. In recovery, this narcissistic quality of anxiety and being vulnerable to unfavorable comparisons with others needs to be worked through by internalizing the focus of evaluation. This creates feelings of potency and self-esteem. Entrancements can drag partners back into the hypnotic absorption and nightmarish fantasy of a life-and-death struggle. To prevent regressing back into entrancement, partners need to continuously support and encourage an internal focus of evaluation. In addition, both partners need to enjoy who they are, discover their own beauty, appreciate their own radiance, and appreciate their own ability to connect and relate to others.

Without denying other people their talents, it is important not to deny ourselves our own interests, intrigue, and unique wonder. Indeed, the interpersonal aspects of intimate relationships need to instill a quality of unconditional acceptance for self and for others. In an age of image, performance, and seeking a niche for one's self, it is essential to learn to stand in our own light without feeling shadowed or overshadowed by others' lights and beauties.

Learning how to share the spotlight becomes a critical issue for those who are in the narcissistic stage. It is important to realize that the recovery may involve going to support or self-help groups dealing with addictive relationships. It may involve individual, couple, or family therapy. Medication may be needed to help people overcome the intense anxiety and sense of trauma that addictive, hypnotic absorptions of "lost weekends" can arouse.

It is important that partners realize the daily effort required in expressing and asserting their own unique artistic way of being themselves. It is of equal importance that we encourage our partners to do likewise. We each have something to contribute. We need to be alert to the proneness to sink back into those anxious comparisons and obsessive worries of hypnotically entranced relationships.

When we focus on our uniqueness and remarkable diversity, we can reveal the miracle of our own artwork. There has never been one quite like you before, nor will there ever be another quite like you again. Of course, from the point of view of a frustrated partner, one of us may be quite enough. We each are a very special one of a kind. We need to do more than just give lip service to these ideas. Our strength comes in careful attention and articulation of that inherently special sensory motif that is innate to our character.

THE MANY FACETS OF CHARACTER

In an automotive stamping plant, what gives strength to the extremely thin sheets of steel are the unique shapes and angles of the tool and die design pressed onto that metal. As the angles and shapes are stamped into the thin metal, it develops a unique, structural shape or form with its own character and strength. When we are true to that unique design or motif, inherently structured to create our character from conception and made manifest through healthy challenge and growth, we can maintain the most resilient stamina to be ourselves in the most intense of intimate relationships.

FUZZY BOUNDARIES, FUZZY CHARACTERS

It is not just about control that we lose in these hypnotic pulls. It is about blurring or fogging the unique artistry of our character development. When we trust our personal truth and intuitive flow of what makes us a miracle and wonder of creation, we are immune to these extraneous pulls in relations. We are unyielding, even while we may be firmly flexible. Indeed, we might even have some fun in them. The unique shape, peculiarities, and wondrous nature of our personal realities give us the very strength and power far beyond a narcissistic ego trying to "muscle" or control life events. Making evaluations of ourselves through the ego of others will only cost us our center. We become focused on emptiness.

Ironically, to recover our own center of balance means reawakening and recovering our unique motif. In this way, we can release our narcissistic preoccupations of who other people are and how we may feel pressured to mirror them. We can discover, instead, how and who we are. Learning to grow happens while struggling with problem-solving issues and relating and empathizing with ourselves and those around us. We can do this by learning how we no longer have to over- or underevaluate ourselves or others.

Such attention to each partner's unique motif could be construed as somewhat self-centered. Yet this type of self-centeredness or narcissistic component can be very enhancing. It can be grasped as a need to establish one's expanded sense of self. It is an expanded sense of balance within partners themselves to reach out and enjoy healthy bonding with one another. Entrancing relationships engender narcissism. To break the trance is to break the fixation in the bubble of what narcissism is.

The myth of Narcissus is that he looked into the pond and saw a beautiful image. Not believing it was him, he leaned over, tried to kiss it, fell in, and drowned. This is an interesting metaphor. When partners view one another as the ideal vision of beauty they have to possess, they lose control and identity. They do not realize the image they have fallen in love with is a hidden reflection of themselves.

The entrancing aspects of narcissism (like hypnosis) involve the art of misdirection. Partners do not realize that they are projecting all their hidden qualities onto each other. Such projection blurs their unique artistry within. Awakened partners discover an expanded, multiple, open-ended, new sense of identity of who they are in each other. Such partners release the "me"-ness of narcissism and embrace the "I"-ness of identity. This sometimes may be experienced as a form of betrayal by the other, as taking back one's attributes leaves the other feeling like an empty vessel that was used. There was a unique quality about the softening, expanding, and multiple realities of each partner discovering their unique sense of self in the other. The quality was that each realizes that the thing that was so entrancing about the other person was something owned already. Partners were too afraid to let go, surrender, and allow the other person to be themselves for fear of losing what they believed they could never have in themselves. This is experienced as fear of losing a sense of themselves that they may feel only exists through the presence of their partner. Much to their surprise, when the mirror breaks, the real truth of their personhood can finally emerge. They discover that the part of themselves that they admired in their partner was already within, seeking its own unique expression.

Perhaps this has to do with accessing our unique self. It is interesting that in releasing the other person from the hypnotic bond, we are releasing our own self from hypnotic sleep. This is rather like Sleeping Beauty in the one hundred years' sleep. All it takes is a certain kiss from our own beautiful self, our own kind of Prince or Princess Charming. Within our own, wild unconsciousness, our partner may temporarily serve this purpose. If we do not learn how to awaken ourselves, we will return to sleep.

This is the power of our unique motif. Addictive relationships serve a powerful purpose. They help us in their own perversity to discover what we are meant for and always had. The motif of our own unique beauty and artistic quality, talent, grace, charm, and form are truly inherent. If only we knew what we already had, we would attend more to what we could abundantly share with our partner rather than what we should get from him or her.

In recapping the ideas presented thus far, we have discussed how addictive relationships are hypnotically induced. They tend to parallel hypnotic stages of pretalk, hypnotic induction, deepening dream work, and utilization of posthypnotic suggestions. Entrancement proceeds with a seductive sensory awareness and a self-talk, inductive fixation on the illusions and fantasies of being with another person. There is the fixation of obsession in the deepening hypnotic dream and nightmare.

Steps for detrancing and accessing one's unique motif have been described (identifying signs of entrancement, baseline data, self-attending
skills, recovering lost attributes, and uniqueness of expression). Finally,
there is reemergence with learning for future change. It needs to be
noted that this process can recycle itself through a process called fractionation, where partners go in and out of entrancement.

We have also talked about how the reemergence operates in terms of
expanding our focus and awareness, shifting our focal point to our multiple selves and multiple roles. We have reviewed the need for lessening
the narcissistic tendencies of being self-absorbed in mirror images. This
involved learning to discover the center of our self-value in the unique
kind of beauty and art of our own motif. There is a liberating, a freeing,
not only of ourselves, but also of our partner.

STAGES OF GRIEF AND RECOVERY

It is important to stress that liberation can feel like a death with no
afterlife. The violence and destruction can increase when partners begin
the initial steps of differentiating from one another. The monitoring
resource of a third party such as a therapist, respected elder, or a self-
help group can provide support in the transitional stages of reawakening.
These stages parallel those of entrancement, but in reverse order. That
is, couples encounter the meaninglessness of rapprochement, accept that
obsessiveness means loss of control, grasp the contrast of disillusionment as ideals that clash with everyday reality, and rework their idealization of each other discovering the genuine motif of self within.

The recovery stages of entranced relationships involve the "death"
of the bond as it was initially defined. This can be as intense as any
physical death. Partners actually need to go through grief and loss
stages, mourning the death of their loved relationship. There is shock,
anger, and hurt. There is bargaining and holding onto the last breath,
pleading for one more chance at it. There is the ensuing depression and
melancholy.

Ultimately, there is integration and acceptance of learning from loss
as a fact and facet of life. The evolution and maturation process occurs
as partners are challenged to come to grips with and encounter what is
real for them in the relationship. The process of an honest, personal
encounter with what's real and what's illusionary about the relationship
is a challenging and maturing experience. The grieving process involves
the removal of protecting, blaming, and feeling unrequited in love. It is

the acquiring of empowering beliefs that each partner can decide what each, in fact, is willing or not willing to commit. Such an encounter with one's personal truth is a sobering and detrancing experience.

Such honest coming to terms with the illusionary nature of fantasy ideals in entrancement serves to remove them and is experienced as a real loss. Yet this loss is the clearing away of adolescent fantasizing and infatuations. It leaves behind in its wake and upheaval the residue of fertile ground and mature character. Partners mature and evolve into their unique character motif of self. This process is time-consuming, filled with regression and recycling.

These stages typify the grieving process. It goes without saying that having a support group, enduring friendships, therapy if needed, and strong anchors of security in one's own family system can be quite stabilizing. The grief and loss process involves a staggered pattern of recovery. Some days one will feel hopeful that life will go on. One can feel that everything will be okay and believe there is a "next," bigger and better person in your life. Other days, you might question all of the above, grab your gut, and stay in bed all day wondering, "Why and how is this happening to me?"

This two steps forward and one step backward can be experienced as quite normal and something to be expected. Facilitating the grief process is to let what comes, come, acknowledging what the experience is all about. Soul-searching and self-honesty about what you are all about in your entranced relationship can ease the pain (that is, if the bubble of entrancement is pricked with the truth of reality, it may sting a bit but it relieves the aching pain of external love lost). For example, "Was I being loving to my partner or playing out my own trauma and drama?" "Did I act out my life insecurities, blaming my partner for what I'm needing to deal with?" One might say, "It was a beautiful relationship, but was there a real sharing or was it sensation oriented?" "Could I and my partner ever be ourselves together?" "How consistent and reality-oriented was the commitment?" "Did all the nice words exchanged ever have consistent behaviors that backed up all the sweet talk?"

THE SAFE PLACE

In dealing with grief and loss of entrancement, there needs to be a sense of hope that the light at the end of the tunnel isn't just the headlight of a train coming at you. The idea of accessing secure anchors and safe places where you can safely heal is very important. Needless to say that the tendency to "hit the bars" or jump into another relationship is all too common, even when we know better. In the recovery process, it is important to have relationships that offer a safe place. Such safe places involve being with people we can talk with and feel safe in "borrowing" their reality long enough for us to regain our own. Remember, they are only there to provide a temporary safe place, not an "until death do we part" bond.

This also applies when we are resurfacing from entrancement and experiencing this loss as we go through the recovery stages in an on-going process. For example, in emerging out of rapprochement, there needs to be a safe place established where partners can rework their sadomasochistic tendencies. Partners are used to experiencing pain as a form of perverse pleasure, believing that this is all they can ever have in a "hopeless" relationship. Whenever partners just might have an enjoyable evening, one or both would pick a fight by reminding the other of how rare the good times are, blaming and attacking each other for this.

Recovery first involves helping partners identify and understand how their relationship has become a learned set-point or stuck-point between them. The establishing of a safe place allows partners the opportunity to feel safe, secure, and test out how they can enjoy parts of their relationship without expecting the nullifying sabotage that usually follows. It also sets boundaries for possible rage and violence.

With the establishment of a safe place, the power of entranced attractions begins to work for instead of against them. The drive for absorbed attraction between partners can begin to disengage and be available for their own personal self-discovery. Each partner could now have an absorbing excitement about who they are as individuals. This accelerates individualization.

REAWAKENING: A LONG AND WINDING ROAD

Reawakening can be impeded by regressive tendencies. Entranced partners may experience tendencies to renew conflicts and resentments. The loss issue is strong in entrancements. Couples learn that violence, both verbal and physical, is a suicidal form of annihilating what they, in error, have come to believe is unattainable in any form. Their fixation actually prevented them from attaining what they needed. This is typified to them when attempts at working out issues either fall short or are imperfect. Couples usually say something like, "This only goes to show it will never work." They are so conditioned in striving for what they believe is beyond their reach, that they project this sense of futility into everything they do with each other. Mastering this phase of recovery is a major step in couples reawakening from their entrancement.

As couples recover, they deal with issues of wanting to control the relationship and one another. As they encounter the obsessive stage, they once again struggle with worrying, fretting, thinking, and imaging in worse-case scenarios of loss. To counteract this, partners need to stay here-and-now focused and avoid going inside, seeking mental control of ruminating thoughts. To achieve this, couples are structured by themselves and/or a therapist to focus only on the situation at hand. Their focus is on working on realistic and achievable behaviors that reaffirm mutuality. They learn that thinking and projecting into the future can be a form of sabotage.

Partners need to learn to stay focused, each believing that his or her partner will genuinely seek to respond to this need in his or her own way. This design obviates the need for control and shifts the focus of energy toward relating as part of a trusting experience learning to be interdependent with one another. This is no small task. Partners struggle with trying to control and make things "better." This is reframed as causing each to feel more manipulated. They may have a difficult time following through on any creative, problem-solving steps. They need to release rigid expectations of each other. This is where they pay their dues to learn and earn the art of relating. Partners learn to value and enjoy what each has to offer at that point in time, not constantly demanding more and more. When partners learn this and have experienced the futility of past efforts to control, they take small "leaps of faith" to test this new releasing and trusting approach. As partners identify their own unique character and quirks, they are empowered to have more of their own intimacy to share. Control games are thereby diminished.

Finally, entranced couples emerge to their original level of idealization in the relationship. Here partners realize how their admiration of each other's attributes and qualities blinded them. They realize that, while it's fine to enjoy attractive features, learning to get to know the true self of their partner allows their own true self to emerge. The honest challenge and in-depth exploration to their idealization and overidentifying with their partners' attributes can go a long way in this process.

Remember that these changes are not achieved in single steps. What facilitates this process is the unfolding discovery and attending to each partner's unique character structure. It is only by discovering one's own true nature and uniqueness that one could love oneself and thus another human being. It is to this core function that much of this work is directed.

Entranced couples tend to internalize (take inside and personalize) what happens in their relationships. Recovery involves partners learning how to stay outside of themselves, avoiding overidentification and personalization of events while observing behavioral interactions. This is why the motif is so critical. It provides the core internal structure partners can go to instead of reliving the traumatic, old inner stuff.

MOTIF: THE CORE ANCHOR FOR MASTERY

Accessing core motifs provides structured anchors and safe places. Without it, partners are vulnerable to illusions. The problem with illusions is they have no flaws. Partners feel trapped in the hypnotic entrancement, enmeshed in the grandeur of ultimate love. They can feel controlled, compelled to bend to each other's will as the only way to maintain this long-sought-after type of "unconditionality."

This type of entrapment happens again and again in entrancing relationships. The first step in this process is the major premise that this relationship fulfills some long-sought-after type of universal need (human beings need unconditional love and acceptance). Partners sometimes try to fulfill such a need by turning to the other partner as the only one who could ever know or want them in this very unique way. Ironically, it is this very uniqueness that partners have ignored in themselves that they persist in misattributing to each other. Partners may perceive the other as what they have been waiting for their whole life. Partners may feel the other is able to give them what no one else can. They may think that the other can make them feel like the truly special, unique person that no one else really knows. The second step is that in order to maintain this so-called perfect love scenario, partners pressure one another to adapt and fit themselves into what they believe are the requirements for perfect love.

The third step is when the entranced relationship progressively deteriorates through the stages of disillusionship, obsession, and ultimate rapprochement of each other and the relationship itself. For couples to break free of this entranced entrapment, partners need to awaken from entrancement sufficiently to begin to question the whole situation. This is done by having them stay in the here and now. They are asked to describe their level of present pain in the relationship without trying to make sense out of it initially.

Partners may be tempted to deal with entrancing illusions of conflict, which threatens to resubmerge them into a lost identity of absorption. Partners can become lost in endless ruminations and images of what each could be doing. Entrancement feeds off of anxiety and ambiguity. When partners feel threatened and are unclear about what is a real threat or what is no big deal, they are drawn in even deeper into an absorbing, entranced bond.

Motif serves as the master anchor as it accesses unique, structural designs within each partner that, by their very nature of uniqueness, are immune to enmeshment. As parts of each individual may merge and entrance with another, when that part or aspect of the self is experienced as part of the larger whole of motif, reassociation as an integrated whole person is now possible. Partners entrance various aspects of their identities with one another, remaining grounded in their unique, sensory motif. Partners can associate to the entranced part dissociated in the relationship by the realization that that part is actually an extension of each partner's unique, greater wholeness and therefore can never be fully absorbed into the other.

LOSING ONE'S MIND, COMING TO ONE'S SENSES

Partners are more effective in their effort to emerge from entrancement if they temporarily suspend cognitive efforts of making sense out of it. This is achieved by simply focusing their attention on what feels and appears to be right and effective in the here and now to relieve their painful responses in the relationship. At first, the sense that comes about what would help, makes no sense at all. This may involve a time out (taking a break from being together) or suspension of dialogue. It may involve enjoying a simple laugh when they are supposed to feel miserable. Partners get entranced into their programmed dialogues and verbal conflict patterns, saying the same negative statements to each other without thinking. They need ways to disrupt and break these cycles.

After partners have established a safe place to begin to question why they are in so much pain in what's supposed to be their "ultimately perfect love," they discover just how absurd the design of the relationship is. They learn to realize the futility of trying to change and prove themselves to attain this unconditionally. Of course, every relationship requires mutual adjustment, but not to the extent that it is at the expense of the core self.

The next step is for partners to begin to access what universality (all-encompassing need or quality) they are in search of and learn to give that to themselves first. When they take initiative for this is when they begin to fully awaken from the entrancement. The accessing of sensory motifs is a powerful way in which partners can begin to give themselves this type of universal acceptance. Ways of accessing motifs will be presented later in this chapter.

Resurfacing couples need to get to know each other all over again in their alert, awakened consciousness of self. Such couples need to be quite gentle and patient with one another in the resurfacing process. Many vulnerabilities, sensitivities, and untested facets of each other's personality are being revealed. Time, acceptance, and a sense of respect for the emerging motifs within each partner are essential in supporting such new awakenings. A sense of openness and receptivity supported by unconditional acceptance and avoidance of rigid expectations are additional factors in the process.

Emerging out of entrancement frees both partners and their relationship to be what they were meant to be in the first place. Couples can have all the love, charm, and beauty they desire. Awakening to the call of their inner truth frees them to arise out of the ashes and manifest the true inner and outer beauty of the character they were meant to be.

MOTIF: UTILIZATION AND REALIZATION

Illuminating partners' artist motifs serves to illustrate how such self-knowledge and understanding can be a powerful resource in developing a healthy, intimate, long-term relationship. By learning how to access and identify with their own motifs, partners are in a healthy and empowered position to participate and contribute to a loving, passionate, and mature relationship. Establishing the unique ground of each partner's character enables both to be honest and loving in a growing and enriched bond. Motifs in partners are unique designs that can never fit (because of their essential uniqueness) into entrancement's fantasy ideal of role/image perfection. As motifs are inherent, organizing principles of character, they can be accessed and utilized by partners in times of stress, change, and transformation. Motifs provide resilience and empowerment when couples require the courage and stamina to weather the emotional storms of intimate relating. Such empowering designs in partners serve their need to work through another variable in entrancing relationships called hypnotic set-points. As motifs are inherent, organizing principles of character, they can be accessed and utilized by partners in times of stress, change, and transformation. Motifs provide resilience and empowerment when couples require the courage and stamina to weather the emotional storms of intimate relating.

ENTRANCING SET-POINTS

The hypnotically induced relationship, like all relationships, is governed by a set-point which determines the degree to which partners can uniquely be themselves in close, intimate relationships. The body's metabolism is governed by a set-point of how efficiently it will burn fat calories. Relationships have a similar set-point of how high and efficient partners' interactions can burn and heat up their intimacy such that they can come together as their true selves.

Individuals function differently as single people compared to being a partner in a relationship. In relationships, the whole is greater than the sum of the parts. If one partner wants to move closer or farther away, seeking to exert more or less influence and change into the relationship, the set-point, if being challenged, will require the other partner to exert an equal but opposite reaction to maintain stability and homeostasis. We see this in action when one partner seeks to become more affectionate and intimate than usual and the other partner pulls away, questioning the change.

Increasing this powerful regulator in relationships necessitates three structural changes: (1) mutually encouraging each partner to internalize a higher degree of personal authority and internal focus of self-control; (2) enhancing each partner's unique character and sensory motif and; (3) nurturing the fantasy vision into a real-life "dream come true." There needs to be an expanding, growing version of the fantasy vision each holds of the basis of the relationship mutually. This then needs to be evolved and developed.

This expanding version allows for higher integration and self-differention of unique motifs. At the same time, there is increased intimacy at higher levels of love, value, and spirituality without precluding lower levels of passion and romance. There is transcendence. This preserves the original romantic qualities in healthy, real-life situations. There becomes an expansion of themes and emotions that are not fixed to any rigid space, time, or form. There is a gradual enhancement of each partner's internal sense of authority, operating more from a felt sense of choice.

They have become increasingly unique and diverse in who they are, taking on characteristics of each other. They have more to share and invest because of their diversity. They feel grounded in their values and more expanded in their abilities to be and express themselves. The motif of the relationship can open up and incorporate the vast, unique universe of partners. It is the sense of being mutually incorporated in their growing bond with boundaries ever expanding yet inclusive of how they are as unique individuals. Their synergy of coming together has more facets to share. As long as the relationship is framed as encouraging and enhancing as much uniqueness as each partner chooses, relationships can and will expand to accommodate it.

The set-point increases to accommodate and stimulate two partners developing and expanding their motifs. The synergy of two individuals pursuing genuine, character-structuring motifs creates high-energy rapport, elevating set-points to new levels of connection. What prevents partners from growing apart and moves them together is that in accessing motifs they are openly accessing loving qualities. Not only do they love each other for who they are, they can now synergically be guided together by their loving motifs of one another.

Set-points can be raised by expanding the space and boundaries of each partner's internal frame of reference. This means that instead of partners having to constantly create new diversions to keep one another interested or go outside the marriage for new challenges, each partner continues to grow and differentiate according to their own unique motif. This allows both partners to evolve in themselves and each other. They learn how to be themselves with their partner in a shared and yet individually creative way.

Set-point determines the available degree of genuine intimacy defined as ability to maintain identity while feeling a sense of oneness with a partner. Accessing sensory motif enhances identity in relationship. It allows partners to release and give themselves to one another, having an inner guidance system to focus them while in the energy field of the relationship. Accessing their motif allows partners to discover balance, knowing who they are while relating with their lover. Neither partner needs to fear either being engulfed or abandoned as they have teamed to develop the confidence to truly be themselves with each other.

Accessing one's own motif also allows partners to deal more effectively with the issue of attainability. The paradox of relationships is that the more confident one partner is that the other partner belongs to him or her, the less desired the other partner will be. For a relationship to grow, it is important to recognize that full possession is impossible. The myth of possession is entrancing. Partners maintaining their motifs refuse to allow others to possess or fixate them. Motifs eliminate the paradox of possession.

A corollary to possession is attempting to keep the relationship stimulating. Trying to change various features in themselves and in their partners regarding dress, travel, enjoying a different hobby, and such may help. However, this type of change is of a basic, first-order level, simply altering the content of their activities and images. It may work for awhile, but eventually couples need to change the way they go about doing things to create a real change.

Even friends can get old at some level. What truly sets the stage for a real change is that variation in activity that in some way touches and challenges them at their core, sensory motif level. A wife may have a great career and loving husband. However, she may not be touched or challenged in terms of some core passion or inner dream that makes her come to life. She may well come to perceive things and people that she has attained as eventually boring and could lose interest over long periods of time. Many times, having children may be the only real adventure partners allow themselves. This pressures the children to continually come up with new and exciting ways in which to keep mom and dad on edge. Children may get entranced with parents (absorbed into a fixated enmeshment) based on challenging ideals espoused by the family. As any parent knows, children are quite wonderful at keeping us challenged to the max and beyond.

To take this pressure off our children and overcome the paradox of no longer wanting what we have attained, it is essential to grasp that we can never own or possess any living person. Partners need to have the courage and creativity to realize that typecasting each other into set roles is actually a reflection of the limits they have placed on themselves. When we get too comfortable with ourselves and our partners, we take for granted who we are and the miracle of our infinite uniqueness.

In healthy relationships, partners realize that they are continually growing and evolving in one form or another. Attainability makes sense only when you've climbed the top of a mountain and can go no higher. When we assume that we've peaked out with our partner and have nothing to learn about them or from them, we are usually in for the surprise of a lifetime. One fellow who believed this came home one day to find his wife had left, leaving him with four teenage boys. The odds are that we have set an artificial limit on who and what they and we are all about.

By passing paradoxical illusions of no longer wanting that person who has presumably been attained, it is essential to cultivate a clear, mutually nourishing frame of reference, encouraging partners to develop motifs within. The beauty of enhancing sensory motifs in couples is that they serve as a never-ending unfolding of who and what is so magnificent but hidden within each of us. Partners need to be willing to have the courage and mature love to seek to discover these wonderful motifs in themselves and their loved ones.

When we appreciate that every new stage of our relationship is the birth of a new identity, a new layer of self emerges that redefines the old self. We can never say we have attained another person. It has been said that we love what we are. To expand and raise the set-point of intimacy in a relationship, partners need to be willing to expand and explore each other's core natures, and sensory motifs. In this way, they can learn the art and skill of how to be their unique selves together.

In many couples, being together usually means "I go my way and you go yours and we'll meet up later if schedules permit." Of course, everyone needs some time on their own. Yet too many times this "being myself" is an excuse to avoid the challenge of how to truly share our unique self with another human being. As one young lady said on a Friday night when asked why she wasn't going out with her friends, "It's Friday night and I'm going home to my husband after work because he is my happy hour."

When partners take on the maturity and creativity to live their lives from the center of their own motifs, they now are living lives of purposefulness. Living a life on purpose through activating one's freedom to follow and be true to one's unique motif supports partners being true and faithful to one another. This is a classic case of "to thine own self be true and thou cannot be false to any man (or woman)." Partners can spend their whole life pursuing their purpose through aligning life tasks with motifs. As they are ever-expanding, motifs are not things ever totally attainable. As such they can be a tremendous source of wonder and stimuli for couples. Couples begin to realize that over long periods of time, just when they think they understand their partner completely, their partner does something completely unpredictable.

The power of the motif is that it keeps us alive and alert to the reality that we will never totally attain or understand another human being completely. With a healthy respect for that wonderful motif in all of us, these shocks and surprises can be the rejuvenating forces that enrich and inspire our relationships to ever-renewed heights. A relationship, unlike a mountain, never has an ultimate peak except the one we impose on it.

As is clearly apparent, knowing and accessing your sensory motif is critical in dealing with living and recovery aspects in entranced relationships. The following outline assists you in just that endeavor.

ACCESSING YOUR ARTISTIC MOTIF AND PURPOSE

1. What is it that you love to do in a way that seems to happen naturally and just flows? While it may involve real effort, it's what you "just find yourself doing or being" without having to think about it. Describe three personal experiences as you answer these questions.

2. Please be specific. What about these experiences attract you? Does it have something to do with the way it looks, feels, and/or sounds? Look at each experience and describe what appeals to you, what you get a kick out of. What are the qualities and/or attributes common to all three that you love?

For example, if you enjoy flying, roller skating, and team-leading a dynamic sales meeting, what common qualities, themes, and/or features do these three experiences have in common? What "figure" and/or design might emerge when you review all three experiences?

What is it that you like about these experiences? What about these experiences absorbs you in some special way? What words, images, sights, sounds, smell, dreams, scenarios emerge that seem to capture unique features about these experiences? Notice the themes that seem to echo and/or resonate throughout the experiences. What structural shapes and/or forms seem to lie within, without, or throughout the experiences? Allow nonverbal images, shapes, and forms to emerge as you reflect and relive these experiences. How does the architecture configuration of the experiences seem to pervade or move throughout the content of what you experience?

What repeated design motif seems to transform the experience into that which is most meaningful to you? One woman's imaged structure was a beaming bright ball of fire (the sun) emitting radiant energy and warmth. Make an effort to depict your imaged structure of motif in some rough or general way as a beginning step.

Remember, you are seeking to discover some nonverbal constructed image, shape, or even geometric design that may capture the way these experiences seem to structure themselves and/or move interactively through and with you. It may help to think and draw upon images, symbols, and various architectural structures and objects and/or natural phenomena in nature.

What is important here is to, in some way, grasp the uniquely synergistic combination of patterned events that, even in their variations, embody a repetitive design and structural integrity. Just as you could recognize a Picasso, can you recognize your own signature and your own flowing motif's structural pattern or design?

Remember you are alive, and in a unique way so are your motifs. Therefore, your representations could be reflective of a dynamically evolving structuring process. For example, trees are growing, not static. Even buildings are renovated. Your images, scenarios, and symbols need to be interactive with your participating in your flowing motif. This is not to say that "being" motifs (unfolding meditative patterns, mandalas, etc.) are not valid manifestations of your unique motifs. Self-interaction can be a quiet reflection of motif in itself.

The motif is a formative blueprint generating its varied uniqueness throughout your life tasks and experiences. You can get a clearer picture of your motif if you imagine it like a unique collage or vast array of your life experiences. What events stand out in areas of work, love, and friendship? Imagine how many ways you sign your name. Each signature has some variation from the other. Yet what is it about all your varied signatures that lets you identify them as coming from one and the same source? Your motif's structuring process or patterned movement creates an ever-emerging design that continues to manifest itself in ever-renewing variations.

3. What purpose is served by what you love to do in these three experiences? What do you find challenging about these situations? What do you sense you've accomplished in completing or even taking on this task/endeavor? What does it in some way touch or seem to answer in your inner questioning and/or your vision of that perfect picture of your life?

For example, a thirty-six-year-old female patient claimed she had no real friends, interests, or hobbies. When asked what she did for a living, the woman replied that she was a bill collector. She said that was all she enjoyed doing. When asked what the purpose served, she stated that there was a real love of how complete it felt in being able to get something out of nothing. When further explored, it was found that it was like making the desert bloom in actually having bad debtors come up with "flowing" revenue out of a pocket that was "dry and barren." This motif of making a desert bloom was actually a hidden sense of purpose that was like a secret oasis in her life. The woman could have taken this motif or design and applied that structural theme in various other life settings. Review your experience with this frame of reference in mind. Articulate what sense of completion and/or meaning it may have for you in terms of an inner feeling, question, and/or picture.

4. Identify times when you've been remarkably successful and times when you've been remarkably disturbed. Notice that the design patterns of your successes are inside out, reversed versions of the very same design patterns of when you are disturbed.

5. Formulation of essential qualities for meaningful prosperity and success can be depicted. One's unique sensory motif characteristics + external

sensory flow experiences (action-oriented artistic activity) + ability to access these two dimensions in psycho-social-vocational settings = meaningful prosperity and success. Such formulation is generative in that once it is in operation, it becomes self-perpetuating and self-emerging. For example, partners can utilize a sensory motif of being the pillars of strength such an artful design between partners supports a prosperous relationship.

6. How do you manifest and articulate your motif in terms of career, family, friends, and personal life endeavors. To what extent can or do you find your satisfaction? How would you structure or restructure your day-to-day experiences in these areas in terms of using your unique characteristics, sensory experiences, and ability to access these dimensions in the areas of career, family, friends?

7. What are the resistances that exist to doing what it is you love to do? What conflicts, disabling beliefs, and so on prevent you from doing what you love?

A. Do you feel guilty for pursuing your own endeavors and leaving others behind? Is there a sense of undeservedness (past acts of transgressions) that impairs self-esteem. As a consequence, artificial, but self-imposed limits can unwittingly be set that prevent growth past a certain point.

B. What do you fear about your success? Will you be hurting others in terms of making them look bad? Overwhelming others with powerful narcissistic demands from your successes? Overwhelming yourself with your achievements challenging your identity and boundaries of who you are and how you define yourself?

C. Are you lacking interpersonal skills in synergistically combining self-with-other and self-on-your-own in relating to both family and career/cultural/social systems? That is, do you know how to be yourself when in the company of others and, most important, when by yourself?

D. Are you lacking precision in applications of unique, personal characteristics? What are those unique contexts that most access alignment of your inherent sensory motif? Sometimes we overlook how our specialness can be applied.

E. Have you learned how to utilize past setbacks that tend to disconfirm future efforts? It's time to clean up the past.

What messages have you said to yourself and/or heard and seen from others that may have discouraged you to discount what your unique talents and artistic motifs are?

EXERCISE

The following alignment process utilizes the empowering, organizing, and integrating properties of your artistic motif. With this exercise,
you can begin to clean up these resistances and utilize them for
achievement.

Align yourself with your motif in verbal and nonverbal ways
(through those unique movements and/or sensory designs that echo your
motif). For example, focus upon the various forms of music, painting,
craft, or work that strengthen and reaffirm your structural design. Recall
the three experiences you love to do. Create a working symbol or design
that captures unique structural features of your motif. Now, temporarily
align yourself with those negative messages that are limiting you. Ask,
what they are trying to protect you from? Let yourself notice nonverbal
as well as verbal signs, memories, associations, events, past and present
dialogues with yourself and others that relate to these messages of unhealthy "protection." If you feel a sense of more or less discomfort, let
yourself stay with it long enough so you can give it a symbol, shape, or
name.

Now take the imaged structure of your motif and saturate it with the
uncomfortable symbol and/or shape of unhealthy, negative protection.
Notice the contrast between your motif of what you love to do and the
awkward and/or uncomfortable response you get from the negative symbol. As you notice this contrast or juxtaposition, embrace the paradoxical, conflicting nature in the context of feeling what you love to do as
contrasted with the injunctions that seem to prevent you from doing it.
Now, simply continue to focus on the symbols of the motif, the discomfort, and the juxtaposition of the contrast itself.

Instead of trying to force any change, just allow the unique design of
your sensory motif to guide you in aligning the symbols as they move
with each other in an increasingly coherent, unified whole. Let your
alignment with all symbols come to be guided by the intricate design of
your sensory motif itself. Take all the time you need to allow these
symbols to rearrange themselves in ways that most resonate with your
sensory motif. This is a synergistic process that will result in a sometimes subtle and sometimes not-so-subtle set of personal shifts. The
integration process that takes place is reflective of your core self and
innermost character. If there is a sense of "stuckness," then just allow
your focus to center on the structural design of the motif, letting the
unhealthy "protection" dissolve into the motif.

Like all change processes, this type of integration could occur in a stepwise fashion or in a single step where a sudden and dramatic total transformation results. Such changes can lead to a highly integrated, self-actualized state of being.

BIBLIOGRAPHY

Achterberg, Jeanne and Lawlis, G. Frank (1980). *Bridges of the Body Mind.* Champaign, IL: Institute for Personality and Ability Testing.

Andreas, Connirae and Andreas, Steve (1989). *Heart of the Mind.* Moab, UT: Real People Press.

Andreas, Connirae and Andreas, Tomara (1994). *Core Transformation.* Moab, UT: Real People Press.

Andrews, Frank (1991). *The Art and Practice of Loving.* New York: G.P. Putnam's Sons.

Barbach, Lonnie (1995). *Erotic Interludes.* New York: Plume/Penguin.

Barber, T.X. (1984). Changing unchangeable bodily processes by (hypnotic) suggestions: A new look at hypnosis, cognitions, imagining and the mind-body problem. *Advances,* 1(2), 7-40.

Beck, Aaron T. (1988). *Love Is Never Enough.* New York: Harper and Row.

Bernard, J. and Sontag, L. (1947). Fetal reactions to sound. *Journal of Genetic Psychology,* 70, 209-210.

Black, Jan and Enns, Greg (1997). *Better Boundaries: Owning and Treasuring Your Life.* Oakland, CA: New Harbinger Publications, Inc.

Borysenko, Joan (1987). *Minding the Body, Mending the Mind.* New York: Bantam Books.

Borysenko, Joan and Borysenko, Miroslav (1994). *The Power of the Mind to Heal.* Carson, CA: Hay House.

Braiker, Harriet B. (1992). *Lethal Lovers and Poisonous People.* New York: Simon and Schuster, Inc.

Brandon, Nathaniel (1990). *The Psychology of Romantic Love.* Los Angeles: J.P. Tarcher, Inc.

Briggs, J. (1988). *Fire in the Crucible.* Los Angeles: J.P. Tarcher, Inc.

Brody, S. and Axelrod, S. (1970). *Anxiety and Ego Formation in Infancy.* New York: International Universities Press.

Brown, Daniel P. and Fromm, Erika (1986). *Hypnotherapy and Hypnoanalysis.* Hillsdale, NJ: Lawrence Erlbaum Assoc., Inc.

Buber, Martin (1958). *I and Thou.* New York: Charles Scribner's Sons.

Butler, Katy (1997). The anatomy of resilience, *Family Networker,* March/April, pp. 22-38.

Carnes, Patrick (1992). *Don't Call It Love.* New York: Bantam Books.

Celani, David P. (1994). *The Illusions of Love.* New York: Columbia University Press.

Cheek, D. (1981). Awareness of meaningful sounds under general anesthesia: Considerations and a review of the literature, 1959-79. In *Theoretical and Clinical Aspects of Hypnosis.* Miami: Symposium Specialists.

Childre, Doc Lew (1994). *Freeze Frame.* Boulder Creek, CA: Planetary Publications.

Chomsky, N. (1967). Recent contributions to the theory of innate ideas. *Synthese,* 17.

Condon, W. and Sander, L. (1974). Neonate movement is synchronized with adult speech: International participation and language acquisition. *Science,* January 11, 99-101.

Covington, Stephanie and Beckett, Liana (1988). *Leaving the Enchanted Forest.* New York: HarperCollins.

Csikszentmihalyi, M. (1975). Play and intrinsic rewards. *Journal of Humanistic Psychology,* 15(3), 39-54.

Csikszentmihalyi, M. (1990). *Flow.* New York: Harper & Row.

Dabrowski, K. (1967). *Personality Shaping Through Positive Disintegration.* Boston: Little, Brown.

Dabrowski, K. (1970). Positive and accelerated development. In K. Dabrowski, A. Kawczak, and M. M. Piechowski (eds.), *Mental Growth Through Positive Disintegration* (pp. 27-61). London: Gryf.

Dabrowski, K., and Piechowski, M.M. (1977). *Theory of Levels of Emotional Development: Vol. 2. From Primary Integration to Self-actualization.* Oceanside, NY: Dabor Science Publications.

Delis, Dean C. and Philips, Cassandra, Philips (1990). *The Passion Paradox.* New York: Bantam Books.

Ebersole, P. and Quiring, G. (1991). Meaning in life depth: The MILD. *Journal of Humanistic Psychology,* 31(3), 113-124.

Erickson, M. (1980). Hypnotic investigation of psychosomatic phenomena: A controlled experimental use of hypnotic regression in the therapy of an acquired food intolerance. In E. Rossi (Ed.), *The Collected Papers of Milton H. Erickson on Hypnosis: II. Hypnotic Alteration of Sensory, Perceptual and Psychophysical Processes* (pp. 169-174). New York: Irvington. (Original publication 1943.)

Erickson, M., Rossi, E., and Rossi, S. (1976). *Hypnotic Realities.* New York: Irvington.

Erickson, M. and Rossi, E. (1980). Two-level communication and the microdynamics of trance and suggestion. In E. Rossi (ed.), *The Collected Papers of Milton H. Erickson on Hypnosis: I. The Nature of Hypnosis and Suggestion* (pp. 430-451). New York: Irvington. (Original publication 1976.)

Erikson, E.H. (1950). *Childhood and Society.* New York: W.W. Norton and Co.

Escher, M.C. (1989). *Escher on Escher: Exploring the Infinite.* New York: Harry N. Abrams, Inc.

Evans, Patricia (1996). *The Verbally Abusive Relationship.* Holbrook, MA: Adams Media Corporation.

Feeney, Jr., Don J. (1996). The purposeful self, *Journal of Humanistic Psychology,* 36 (4), 94-115.

Frankl, V. (1963). *Man's Search for Meaning.* New York: Washington Square Press.

Friday, Nancy (1985). *Jealousy.* New York: Bantam Books.

Fromm, Erich (1956). *The Art of Loving.* New York: Bantam Books.

Gendlin, E. (1978). *Focusing.* New York: Everest House.

Hadley, Josie and Staudacher, Carol (1985). *Hypnosis for Change.* Oakland, CA: New Harbinger Pub.

Hay, Louise L. (1984). *You Can Heal Your Life.* Santa Monica, CA: Hay House, Inc.

Hendrix, Harville (1988). *Getting the Love You Want.* New York: Henry Holt and Co.

Hillman, James (1996). *The Soul's Code.* New York: Warner Books Edition.

James, Tad and Woodsmall, Wyatt (1988). *Time Line Therapy and the Basis of Personality.* Cupertino, CA: Meta Publications.

Jung, C. (1964). *Man and His Symbols.* New York: Bantam Doubleday.

Jung, C.G. (1971). Marriage as a Psychological Relationship, in Joseph Campbell (ed.), *The Portable Jung.* New York: The Viking Press.

Kasl, Charlotte Davis (1990). *Women, Sex and Addiction.* New York: Harper and Row.

Klaus, M. (1972). Maternal attachment: Impotence of the first post-partum days. *New England Journal of Medicine,* 286(9), 460-463.

Liebowitz, Michael (1983). *The Chemistry of Love.* Boston: Little, Brown and Company.

Lienhart, J. (1983). *Multiple personality and state dependent learning.* Doctoral dissertation, U.S. International University, San Diego.

Ludwig, Arnold M. (1966). Altered states of consciousness, *Archives of General Psychiatry,* 15, 225-234.

Luria, A. (1966). *Higher Cortical Functions in Man,* Translated by H. Teuber and K. Pribram. New York: Basic Books.

MacLean, P. (1973). *A Tribune Concept of the Brain and Behavior.* Toronto: University of Toronto Press.

Madanes, Cloe (1990). *Sex, Love and Violence.* New York: W.W. Norton and Co.

Maltz, Maxwell (1964). The Magic Power of Self Image Psychology. Englewood Cliffs, NJ: Prentice Hall, Inc.

Martin, Teresa Castro and Bumpass, Larry L., Recent trends in marital disruption, *Demography,* 26 (1989), 37-51.

May, Rollo (1969). *Love and Will.* New York: W.W. Norton and Co.

McClelland, David C. (1986). Some reflections on the two psychologies of love, *Journal of Personality,* 54:2.

Mellody, Pia, Miller, Andrea Wells, and Miller, J. Keith (1992). *Facing Love Addiction.* San Francisco: HarperCollins.

Moore, Thomas (1992). *Care of the Soul.* New York: HarperCollins.

Morris, Desmond (1997). *The Human Sexes.* New York: St. Martin's Press.

Ornstein, Robert (1997). *The Right Mind.* San Diego: Harcourt Brace.

Pearce, J. (1985). *Magical Child Matures,* 2nd ed. New York: Bantam Books.

Peele, Stanton (1987). *Love and Addiction.* New York: Penguin Books.

Piaget, J. and Inhelder, B. (1964). *The Early Growth of Logic in the Child.* Atlantic Highlands, NJ: Humanities Press.

Robertiello, Richard C. (1978). *Your Own True Love.* New York: Richard Marek Publishers, Inc.

Ross, Ernest L. and Cheek, David B. (1988). *Mind-Body Therapy.* New York: W.W. Norton and Co.

Rossi, E. (1980). Psychological shocks and creative moments in psychotherapy. In E. Rossi (ed.), *The Collected Papers of Milton H. Erickson on Hypnosis: IV. Innovative Hypnotherapy* (pp. 447-463). New York: Irvington. (Original publication 1973.)

Rossi, E. (1986). *The Psychobiology of Mind-Body Healing.* New York: W.W. Norton and Co.

Rossi, Ernest L. (1993). *The Psychobiology of Mind-Body Healing,* 2nd ed. New York: W.W. Norton and Co.

Schaeffer, Brenda (1997). *Is It Love or Is It Addiction.* Center City, MN: Hazelden Publishing Co.

Shakespeare, William (1996). *Romeo and Juliet.* New York: HarperCollins.

Singh, Dovendra (1993). *Psychology Today.* November/December, p. 8

Smith, M. and Jones, E. (1993). Neophobia and existential choice. *Journal of Humanistic Psychology,* 33(2), 90-107.

Stein, Murray (1998). *Transformation: Emergence of the Self.* College Station, TX: Texas A&M University Press.

Tart, Charles T. (1969). *Altered States of Consciousness.* New York: John Wiley and Sons, Inc.

Verny, T. and Kelly, S. (1981). *The Secret Life of the Unborn Child.* New York: Dell.

Welwood, John (1990). *Journey of the Heart*. New York: HarperCollins.
Werner, Emma (1992). *Overcoming the Odds: High Risk Children from Birth to Adulthood*. Ithaca, NY: Cornell University Press.

INDEX

About the Author

DON J. FEENEY, JR. is a clinical psychologist and Chief Executive Officer of Psychological Consulting Services.